# Foundations
# of
# Evangelical
# Theology

# Foundations
## of
# Evangelical
# Theology

## John Jefferson Davis

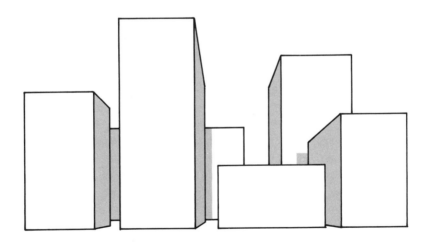

BAKER BOOK HOUSE
Grand Rapids, Michigan   49506

For Robin, Nathaniel, Elizabeth
and Susannah

# Contents

# Preface

This volume is intended to be a general introduction to the study of systematic theology. The topics usually treated in such introductions will be found here: theological method; revelation; reason; religious experience; scripture; ecclesiastical tradition; principles of biblical interpretation. An introductory chapter situates the evangelical theological tradition within the wider contexts of the Protestant Reformation, the intellectual and religious currents of the eighteenth and nineteenth centuries, and the particular influences of the American religious experience. This chapter expresses the conviction that every theology reflects a particular historical situation and should be appreciated in the light of that context.

This introduction to evangelical theology attempts to mirror the American experience rather than merely to respond to theological agendas established by the history of European theology. The attempt is also made to give prominence to the missionary context of theological reflection in the church. The ultimate aim of theological reflection is to assist in the church's task of bringing about the "obedience of faith ... among all the nations" (Rom. 1:5).

Evangelical theology is task-oriented reflection upon scripture in light of the practical needs of ministry and mission. Evangelical theology's task is to be the church's servant in the extension of the kingdom of God in the world and in the believer's heart.

A basic concern of the volume is to expound an evangelical

understanding of the basic nature of authority in theology and the church. The primacy of scripture in the evangelical understanding of authority is developed in relation to other complementary and competing sources of authority.

I wish to express my thanks to students whose insights and questions have contributed to the shaping of this book; to the trustees of Gordon-Conwell Theological Seminary, whose generous sabbatical policy facilitated the writing; and to Carrie Powell, who so competently typed the manuscript.

John Jefferson Davis
Hamilton, Massachusetts

# 1

# Between Fundamentalism and Modernity

For the last two centuries, wrote Paul Tillich in the first volume of his *Systematic Theology*, the perennial question for Protestant theology has been, "Can the Christian message be adapted to the modern mind without losing its essential and unique character?"[1] While most evangelicals today would agree that Tillich's theology was more successful in discerning the temper of the "modern mind" than it was in preserving the substance of the biblical tradition, the pertinence of his question nevertheless remains. In his own way Tillich was raising the question of the "contextualization" or, better yet, the *recontextualization* of the Christian tradition in light of the changing cultural situations in which it is received. For evangelical Protestants the question becomes, Can the evangelical tradition be adapted to the conditions of modern American life without losing its essential and unique character? Will a resurgent evangelicalism in America be able to sharpen its sense of self-identity and mission by retaining the best of its fundamentalist past while offering intellectually rigorous and creative solutions to the problems of the present?

It is essential for American evangelicalism to engage in serious theological reflection as it seeks answers to these questions. Sys-

1. Paul Tillich, *Systematic Theology*, vol. I, p. 7.

tematic theology, in its task of serving a particular ecclesial community in its mission and ministry, must be sensitive to the historical conditions that have shaped that community. It is appropriate, then, that a study of the foundations of evangelical theology should begin with an examination of the historic roots of the evangelical tradition and a consideration of how these conditions affect evangelical theology's agenda for the future.

## A Decade of Resurgence: 1970 – 1980

During the years from 1970 to 1980 evangelicalism became an increasingly visible presence in American life. The resurgence of evangelical religion in America was paralleled in other parts of the world by movements of revitalization in Judaism and Islam. Millions of believers around the world were rediscovering in their historic religious traditions resources for spiritual renewal and social stability in a world whose values and institutions seemed corroded by the acids of modernity. American evangelicals attained a new degree of social respectability, continued to grapple with unresolved conflicts from the fundamentalist era, and made significant strides in extending their evangelistic and social mission.

### "The year of the evangelical"

"The Bible Belt is ... bursting the bounds of geography and seems on the verge of becoming a national state of mind," commented *Time* magazine in 1977.[2] A year earlier pollster George Gallup, Jr., had announced to the American people that 1976 was the "year of the evangelical." American voters had elected a "born again" president, and Gallup's 1976 poll disclosed that 34 percent of the public claimed to have had a born again experience. Among Protestants, 48 percent identified themselves as "evangelicals." But, as Gallup pointed out, if evangelical religiosity seemed to be gaining, evidently evangelical morality was not, as political corruption, crime, tax evasion, and sexual promiscuity continued to plague American life.[3]

Nevertheless, 1976 and the decade as a whole manifested dramatic growth in evangelical activity. During that bicentennial year

2. *Time*, Dec. 26, 1977, p. 53.
3. In Richard Quebedeaux, *The Worldly Evangelicals*, p. 3.

seventeen thousand college students attended Inter-Varsity's Urbana missions conference, and many dedicated their lives to bringing the gospel to the farthest ends of the earth. The American Bible Society's *Good News* translation sold a million copies in its first month of publication, and Ken Taylor's *Living Bible* sold 2.2 million copies during the year.[4]

The 1970s were boom years for evangelical publishing houses and religious broadcasting groups. Popular books such as Hal Lindsey's *Late Great Planet Earth* and Charles Colson's *Born Again* became nationwide best-sellers. On a more scholarly level the evangelical resurgence was being chronicled and analyzed in such books as *The Evangelical Challenge* by Morris Inch, Donald Bloesch's *The Evangelical Renaissance*, Bernard Ramm's *The Evangelical Heritage*, Richard Quebedeaux's *The Young Evangelicals* and *The Worldly Evangelicals*, and *The Evangelicals* by David Wells and John Woodbridge.

By the end of the 1970s one new Christian television station was being established every month, and a number of prominent TV evangelists had organizational budgets that dwarfed those of the mainline denominations. Critics continued to question the spiritual depth of the evangelical surge, but there was little doubt that the movement had spawned a new growth industry for the print and electronic media.

### "Why conservative churches are growing"

The significance of these trends was not entirely lost on the leaders of the mainline denominations. In his 1972 study, *Why Conservative Churches Are Growing*, Dean M. Kelley brought to the attention of those leaders some facts of which they were already becoming painfully aware: mainline churches were suffering marked declines in membership, while the more theologically conservative groups were growing. It seemed somewhat paradoxical to Kelley that these conservative churches, "holding to seemingly outmoded theology and making strict demands on their members," had equaled or surpassed in their growth rates the growth in the population as a whole. During the first seven years of the 1970s the United Methodist Church lost 886,000 members,

4. John D. Woodbridge, Mark A. Noll, and Nathan O. Hatch, *The Gospel in America*, p. 11.

the United Presbyterian Church 526,000, and the Episcopal Church 476,000. By contrast, during the years 1965 – 1975 the Lutheran Church—Missouri Synod grew by 3 percent, the Church of the Nazarene by 8 percent, Southern Baptists by 18 percent, and the Assemblies of God by 37 percent.[5]

Kelley concluded that the conservative churches had been more successful than their liberal counterparts in providing their members with a sense of the meaning of life. Despite their allegedly "outmoded theology," the evangelical churches were engendering a sense of loyalty and commitment among their adherents that the more liberal churches were not able to match.[6]

### Some speak in other tongues

The charismatic or neo-pentecostal renewal emerged as an important current in the broader stream of American evangelicalism. Unlike the older Pentecostal and Holiness churches, which by force of circumstances became new denominations, the new charismatics have thus far been able to function as renewal agents within the older mainline structures. The neo-pentecostal experience began to emerge in the 1950s, received national publicity in 1960 in connection with the ministry of the Episcopal priest Dennis Bennett in Van Nuys, California, and thereafter became a significant presence in most of the major communions—Protestant, Roman Catholic, and Greek Orthodox.

As of 1974 the charismatic Full Gospel Business Men's Fellowship had some one thousand chapters in the United States, with new chapters being organized on the average of one every business day. The book *The Cross and the Switchblade* by Pentecostal preacher David Wilkerson sold millions of copies and was translated into twenty-three languages. Popular programs such as the "PTL Club" and the "700 Club" were beaming a distinctively charismatic ethos to their large television audiences.[7] A *Christianity Today* – Gallup Poll published in 1980 revealed that 19 percent of all American adults—more than 29 million—considered themselves Pentecostals or charismatics. Surprisingly, only one sixth of those who identified themselves as charismatics or Pentecostals

5. C. Peter Wagner, "Aiming at Church Growth in the Eighties," pp. 24–27.

6. Dean M. Kelley, *Why Conservative Churches Are Growing*, p. 101.

7. Robert H. Culpepper, *Evaluating the Charismatic Movement*, pp. 17–30.

reported speaking in tongues. And not all charismatics possessed evangelical convictions: only 59 percent held to a clearly evangelical view of salvation, and less than half believed in a personal devil.[8]

Reactions to the charismatic renewal have been as diverse as the movement itself. According to David duPlessis, a leading spokesman for the New Pentecostals, "God is doing something in our generation that has no equal anywhere in all the revivals in history." W. A. Criswell, a past president of the Southern Baptist Convention, could hardly disagree more. Glossolalia, for example, is hurtful and divisive, and only another instrument for "the tragic torture of the body of Christ."[9]

Reactions from leaders in the mainline churches have at times been surprisingly positive. According to Krister Stendahl, a former dean of Harvard Divinity School, "We need to have charismatics among us in the church if the church is to receive and express the fullness of the Christian life."[10]

The debate about the merits of the charismatic renewal is likely to continue, but as the 1970s drew to a close, it was increasingly apparent that the movement was a feature of American evangelicalism that was here to stay.

### The Battle for the Bible

The bicentennial year of 1976 was for many Americans an occasion for recalling such famous battles of the Revolutionary War as Bunker Hill. American evangelicals, however, were being caught up in battles of a different kind. Evangelical Christianity "is engaged in the greatest battle of its history," wrote Harold Lindsell that year in his controversial book *The Battle for the Bible*.[11] According to Lindsell, there were unmistakable signs of doctrinal erosion on the issue of the inerrancy of scripture in evangelical institutions such as the Southern Baptist Convention, Fuller Theological Seminary, North Park Theological Seminary of the Evangelical Covenant Church of America, the American Scientific Affiliation, and even the Evangelical Theological Society. Lindsell argued that the authority of scripture was the great "watershed"

8. Kenneth Kantzer, "The Charismatics Among Us," pp. 25 – 29.
9. Culpepper, *Evaluating the Charismatic Movement*, p. 13.
10. In Michael P. Hamilton, *The Charismatic Movement*, p. 57.
11. Harold Lindsell, *The Battle for the Bible*, p. 200.

issue for the twentieth-century church, as justification by faith was for the Reformation. Any denomination or school, he contended, that abandoned inerrancy would inevitably abandon other cardinal Christian doctrines.

*The Battle for the Bible* provoked an immediate storm of controversy within evangelical circles. Many agreed with Lindsell's contention that inerrancy was a vital issue for the church but were dissatisfied with his definition of the term. During the course of the ensuing debate it became evident that many of the issues represented a replaying of the events of the modernist controversy of an earlier generation. Was the doctrine explicitly taught by scripture, or was it only a theological inference from scripture? Did the concept of inerrancy include details of science and history, or was it limited to matters of faith and practice? Was inerrancy the historic view of the Christian church or a development of the seventeenth century or later? Could one consistently claim the designation "evangelical" while not holding to the strictest view of inerrancy? The issue's divisive potential became evident when evangelicals began taking opposite sides on each of the disputed questions.

In 1979 Jack Rogers and Donald McKim published a work which was widely perceived as a reply to Lindsell, *The Authority and Interpretation of the Bible.* According to Rogers and McKim, the view of inerrancy advocated recently by Lindsell and by A. A. Hodge and B. B. Warfield in the nineteenth century was stricter than scripture itself really warranted. Rogers and McKim were criticized by various evangelical leaders, including Francis Schaeffer, Carl F. H. Henry, John Gerstner, and Kenneth Kantzer, for advocating "limited" inerrancy, or inerrancy only in matters of faith and practice.

In October of 1978 the International Council on Biblical Inerrancy, a group of conservative scholars concerned to promote sound views of inerrancy in the American churches, issued the "Chicago Statement" on biblical inerrancy. The statement attempted to articulate a strong yet properly nuanced exposition of the issues, and was offered by the drafters in the hope that it would become a rallying point for diverse points of view.

In August of 1981, at a conference in Toronto called to discuss the authority of scripture, Jack Rogers claimed that many of his critics had misunderstood the thrust of *The Authority and Inter-*

*pretation of the Bible* and that he could support a strong view of biblical infallibility and inerrancy. It remains to be seen, however, whether this development indeed represented a genuine meeting of the minds on a volatile issue that seriously threatened the unity and momentum of evangelicalism in America.

### In the beginning

"The creationist assault against the concept of evolution ... is being pressed on a wide front and with increasing vigor," noted an editorial in the July, 1979, issue of *Scientific American*.[12] Many Americans believed that the issue of creation and evolution had been laid to rest after the trial of John T. Scopes in 1925 for teaching evolution in a Dayton, Tennessee, public school. The resurgent activity of "scientific creationists" during the 1970s, however, demonstrated that for many conservative Protestants in America the issue was far from settled. Scientific creationists were aggressively pressing textbook publishers, local school boards, and state legislatures for "equal time" in the interests of a "two-model" approach in teaching the origins of the world and the human race. During the 1920s opponents of evolution had sought to completely eliminate the doctrine from the public schools. Now pursuing a different strategy, creationists were not seeking to exclude evolution but were asking for "balanced treatment" of the two theories in textbooks and classroom discussions. The creationist point of view was to be presented not as a religious doctrine but as a scientific hypothesis supported by data from geology, paleontology, anthropology, biochemistry, astronomy, and other scientific disciplines.

As of April 1980, creationist legislation had been introduced in at least a dozen states, including Illinois, Florida, and South Carolina. During the following year such legislation was actually passed and signed into law in Arkansas and Louisiana, where it was promptly challenged in court by the American Civil Liberties Union, which charged that the new laws violated the First Amendment provisions of the separation of church and state.

Responsible for much of the creationist activity was the Institute for Creation Research, the research branch of Christian Heritage College in San Diego, operated by Pastor Tim LaHaye and the Scott

12. *Scientific American*, editorial, July, 1979, p. 72.

Memorial Baptist Church. ICR leaders Henry Morris and Duane Gish promoted the creationist cause throughout the country through their writings, radio and television appearances, and debates with evolutionists on college campuses.

The new creationists succeeded in sparking a new debate on science and scripture within the evangelical community. Some evangelical leaders felt that the views of Morris and others—that the earth was only ten to twelve thousand years old and that the fossil record was produced by the Noachic flood—were untenable on scientific grounds. Others felt that the scientific evidence for the ICR position was persuasive. If nothing else, it became evident that the new creationists had succeeded in bringing biblical theism out of the privacy of the sanctuary and the home Bible study and into the arena of public policy debate. The scientific establishment and the media community were taking note.

### New life in the ivory tower

In a *Christianity Today* interview Billy Graham was asked to look back over the last twenty-five years of the evangelical movement and comment on some of the movement's weaknesses. Graham pointed to the whole area of scholarship and the life of the mind: "We haven't challenged and developed the minds of our generation," he admitted. "Though there are many exceptions, generally we evangelicals have failed to present to the world great thinkers, theologians, artists, scientists, and so forth."[13]

Graham's sentiments echo those which Carl Henry had been voicing since the 1940s and 1950s. The problem with the older fundamentalism, out of which the new evangelicalism was born, was that it tended to ignore the doctrinal breadth of the historic creeds and "felt little obligation to exhibit Christianity as a comprehensive world and life view."[14] Henry's observations, made in 1957, pointed to a persistent weakness of a religious tradition that tended to value action and the feelings of the heart more than the life of the mind.

Signs of maturing evangelical scholarship began to appear in the 1970s. The first volume of Henry's *God, Revelation, and Authority* appeared in 1976 and was recognized as perhaps the

13. *Christianity Today*, July 17, 1981, p. 19.
14. Carl F. H. Henry, *Evangelical Responsibility in Contemporary Theology*, p. 33.

weightiest theological contribution by an American evangelical in decades. Two years earlier the publication of George Ladd's *A Theology of the New Testament* harvested a lifetime of scholarship by an evangelical whose work in biblical studies was recognized beyond his own conservative constituency. In 1978 Donald Bloesch, an evangelical theologian teaching at Dubuque Seminary in Iowa, published the first volume of *Essentials of Evangelical Theology*. Bloesch's work expounded the evangelical position in dialogue with Karl Barth, Roman Catholic theology, and other trends in current thought. The work of Henry and Bloesch marked the end of a long period of barrenness in systematic theology for American conservatives. If evangelical scholars were not yet taking the academic community by storm, they were at least increasingly earning the right to be heard with respect.

### Evangelical salt and light

Evangelicals made some advances in the area of social ministries during the 1970s. Evangelicals for Social Action was organized by Ron Sider and others in 1973 to promote social responsibility within the American evangelical community. The Lausanne Covenant of 1974, drafted at the International Congress on World Evangelization meeting in Lausanne, Switzerland, contained a strong statement on the necessity of working for peace, social justice, and reconciliation between classes and races. Publications such as *Sojourners, The Other Side, Radix,* and the *Reformed Journal* raised evangelical awareness on a broad range of social issues. In Mendenhall, Mississippi, John Perkins' Voice of Calvary Ministries was considered by many to be a model of community development and social ministry among the poor. The Christian Action Council, founded by Harold O. J. Brown of Trinity Evangelical Divinity School, quickly established itself as the leading Protestant pro-life organization in the country. World Vision's work in the areas of famine relief, education, and rural development was widely respected around the world. The Chalcedon Foundation of R. J. Rushdoony, through its ministry of research, publication, and seminars, actively promoted an aggressive vision of the lordship of Christ over all of life and the Christian reconstruction of society.

Such areas of progress notwithstanding, the impact made by evangelicals on society as a whole seemed rather negligible in

proportion to their growing numbers. This anomaly provoked
Charles Colson to remark, "Some 31 million Americans say they
are evangelicals, but it's a phony religious resurgence. We aren't
making a difference in the lives of the people around us."[15] Colson
had dispelled skepticism about the depth of his own conversion
experience by his commitment to ministering in American pris-
ons. Colson's Prison Fellowship now has a full-time staff of around
a hundred in thirty-five states, a budget of $3 million, and had a
goal of reaching ten thousand new inmates by the end of 1981.

Evangelical theologian Clark Pinnock also expressed some
doubts about the depth of evangelical social commitment. There
were disturbing signs that in a number of areas evangelicals were
accommodating to the culture rather than challenging it on the
basis of biblical truth. "I see a watering down of evangelical convictions," Pinnock observed in November of 1980, "which appears
also in social issues like feminism and homosexuality, where the
expectations of the circle we move in are very powerful, and make
us wish to have the scriptures agree with them."[16] Pinnock seemed
to be agreeing that the title of Richard Quebedeaux's 1978 book,
*The Worldly Evangelicals*, was not entirely off the mark.

### Thunder on the right

As the decade closed it was becoming apparent that the most
dynamic social influences in conservative Protestantism were em-
anating from the "new Christian right." Prominent television evangelists such as Jerry Falwell and Pat Robertson in Virginia and
James Robison in Fort Worth, Texas, were speaking out forcefully
on moral and political issues. Christian Right organizations such
as the Moral Majority, Christian Voice, and the National Federation
for Decency gathered large constituencies around such issues as
abortion, homosexuality, pornography, sex education, the Equal
Rights Amendment, declining family life, and IRS harassment of
Christian schools.

The Moral Majority, organized in June of 1979 by Baptist preacher
Jerry Falwell, by 1980 claimed 400,000 members nationally and
had political action committees in forty-eight states. The Moral
Majority and other Christian right organizations were thought to

---

15. *Newsweek*, Sept. 7, 1981, p. 41.
16. *Christianity Today*, Dec. 12, 1980, p. 64.

have had a significant role in shaping parts of the 1980 Republican platform and in influencing the November elections. Unlike the fundamentalists of previous generations, the Christian right leaders were willing to cooperate on selected issues with groups not sharing their particular religious convictions.

A national survey conducted by the Connecticut Mutual Life Insurance Company and published under the title *American Values in the 80s: The Impact of Belief* revealed some of the reasons for the Christian Right's visibility and influence. The researchers discovered that religious orientation rather than age, sex, education, or income was the most significant indicator of political involvement. The "intensely religious" were also the most likely to vote and to be involved in community action. "The increasing impact of religion on our social and political constitutions," the report states, "may be only the beginning of a trend that could change the face of America."

The report disclosed a significant gap between leaders in government, education, and media and the general public on moral issues. The gap was widest between the leaders and the "intensely religious." Many American leaders, the report concluded, seemed to be "out of touch with the current of faith which appears to be gathering strength among the public in this decade." Christian Right leaders were more effective than their establishment evangelical counterparts in sensing these new currents and frustrations, articulating them forcefully, and channeling them into tangible political results.

### Let the earth hear his voice

During the 1970s evangelicals continued to display their longstanding strengths in the areas of evangelism, church growth, and world missions. The 1974 Congress on World Evangelization in Lausanne involved 2,473 participants from 150 countries and 135 Protestant denominations. *Time* magazine called the gathering of evangelicals "a formidable forum, possibly the widest-ranging meeting of Christians ever held."[17] The delegates hammered out a statement that eliminated the dichotomy between evangelism and social ministry, maintained a high view of the authority of scripture, and called for vigorous outreach to the unevangelized.

---

17. In C. Rene Padilla, ed., *The New Face of Evangelicalism*, p. 9.

Billy Graham continued his successful worldwide ministry, reaching tens of thousands for Christ in his evangelistic crusades. There appeared to be no slackening in public demand for such forms of ministry. "We have more invitations from all over the world than we could take in two lifetimes," Graham said in a 1981 interview.[18]

The decade also witnessed the increasing prominence of the church growth movement in American ecclesiastical life. Founded in 1955 by Donald McGavran, a former Disciples of Christ missionary to India, the movement was promoted through McGavran's leadership as the founding dean of the Fuller School of World Mission and Institute of Church Growth. The ideas of the movement were propagated in publications such as McGavran's *The Bridges of God* (1955), the "magna charta" of the movement; *Understanding Church Growth* (1970), the basic text of the movement; *God's Ways to Keep a Church Going and Growing* (1973), by McGavran's associate Virgil Gerber; and *Our Kind of People* (1979), by C. Peter Wagner, one of McGavran's former students.

McGavran's application of sociological and anthropological tools to the study of church life and his advocacy of the "homogeneous unit principle"—the contention that churches grow best when they exhibit sociological homogeneity—have sparked considerable debate and controversy. Some evangelical leaders in England and Latin America have criticized the movement for its concessions to "American pragmatism." Others, such as missiologist J. Herbert Kane, consider the church growth movement "the most dynamic factor in the missionary enterprise of our day."[19] Debate will no doubt continue on the biblical underpinnings of church growth principles, but there seems little doubt that the movement will continue to make a vital contribution to the expansion of the church at home and abroad.

In the area of world mission Ralph Winter's concern to dramatize the needs of the "hidden peoples" was one of the crucial new developments of the decade. Winter's U.S. Center for World Missions, founded in 1977 in Pasadena, California, was designed to promote cross-cultural evangelism to reach the hidden peoples, "those estimated 16,750 'people groups' scattered throughout the

18. *Christianity Today*, July 17, 1981, p. 24.
19. J. Herbert Kane, " 'The White Man's Burden' Is Changing Colors," p. 63.

world among which there is no church present." Winter's research demonstrated that it was necessary for evangelical missions to understand the Great Commission in terms of ethnic and cultural groups rather than political nation-states, since many of these "people groups" were effectively hidden from sight behind national boundaries and were not being reached by the national churches or existing mission organizations. Winter claimed that the "hidden peoples" constituted over half the world's population. Reaching these groups with the gospel through cross-cultural mission "is surely both the most important and most neglected responsibility of the church," he argued.[20] The new awareness of the hidden peoples also challenges evangelical theologians to seek new ways of contextualizing the unchanging biblical message in terms of the diverse cultural and ethnic traditions of the groups that are yet to be reached.

## Evangelical Roots: From the Reformation to the 1960s

*Sola gratia, sola fide, sola scriptura*—by grace alone, by faith alone, by scripture alone; these watchwords of the Protestant Reformation have continued to be central for the theological identity of American evangelicalism. Sixteenth-century Reformers such as Martin Luther, John Calvin, Ulrich Zwingli in Zurich, John Knox in Scotland, and Thomas Cranmer in England labored to recover the essence of the gospel and the primacy of the Bible as the theological norms for the life of the church. Not works of merit but a gospel of grace; not forms and ceremonies but living faith in Christ and his word: such was the spiritually liberating message of the Protestant Reformation. The believer is not dependent on priestly mediators for an experience of divine grace but has immediate access to God through faith in the promises of the Word of God. While all parts of scripture may not be equally plain, the essential doctrines of salvation are understandable by all.

The Reformers' stress on the sovereignty of divine grace in the plan of salvation represented a rediscovery of the Pauline and Augustinian tradition in early Christianity. Luther, Calvin, and their associates were men who possessed impressive scholarly abilities. They displayed an appreciation of the creedal tradition of the early

20. *Christianity Today,* Dec. 12, 1980, p. 62.

church and a concern for the unity of the visible church that were frequently lacking in the fundamentalists of the twentieth century.

Though less well known, the so-called "left wing" of the Reformation made lasting contributions to the heritage of American evangelicalism. Evangelical Anabaptists such as Conrad Grebel and Felix Manz in Zurich questioned Zwingli's gradualist philosophy of reform and the ancient practice of infant baptism. These "Swiss Brethren," together with other Anabaptist groups such as the Hutterites and Mennonites, were theologically and sociologically distinct enough to be considered a separate stream in the larger Protestant Reformation. Their insistence on a sharp distinction between the church and the world, their understanding of the church as a pure and voluntary association of adult believers, and their doctrine of the separation of church and state have all left enduring marks on the evangelical tradition in this country.

During the century following the Reformation the theological insights of the Reformers were further refined and systematized. The theology of the Reformation found creedal expression in the Augsburg Confession (1530), the Formula of Concord (1577), the Second Helvetic Confession (1566), the Heidelberg Catechism (1563), and the Westminster Confession (1647). Orthodox theologians such as Wollebius (1586–1629), Cocceius (1603–69), Quenstedt (1617–88), and Turretin (1623–87) produced massive systematic theologies that rivaled in thoroughness and erudition the *summas* of the Middle Ages. The orthodox theologians of this period have often been criticized for petrifying the dynamic spirituality of the earlier Reformers and removing a proper sense of mystery from theology. A more sympathetic appraisal, however, will recognize in the work of these seventeenth-century men a passion to be biblical, an appreciation for the history of doctrine, and an insistence upon precision and coherence in theological expression which modern evangelical theology would do well to emulate.

### The great awakenings

The Reformation's emphasis on personally vital religion was reinforced by waves of spiritual awakening that rolled across America during the eighteenth and nineteenth centuries. The first stirrings of awakening are usually associated with the reforming efforts of Theodore Frelinghuysen, who labored among the Dutch Reformed Church of New Jersey in the 1720s. Through the preaching of Gilbert Tennent and others during the following decade the revival spread to Presbyterian and Congregational churches in the area. The preaching of Jonathan Edwards and George Whitefield brought the renewal in New England to its peak in the 1740s.

In England, John Wesley and his brother Charles led a profound revival which resulted in the founding of Methodism. In America Wesley's work was continued by Francis Asbury.

Toward the end of the eighteenth century and the beginning of the nineteenth, a second series of awakenings occurred in the United States. The revivals began with the Congregational churches of New England, spread to Presbyterian, Methodist, and Baptist churches, and then to the American churches generally. Timothy Dwight, president of Yale, preached a notable series of chapel sermons in 1802 that led one third of the students at Yale to profess conversion. James McGready and other itinerant evangelists brought a plain and forceful style of preaching to campmeetings in Kentucky and Tennessee; these preachers experienced remarkable success in these frontier settings. Charles Finney, one of the most prominent nineteenth-century evangelists, creatively adapted the spirit of the campmeeting to the needs of an urban environment. Finney's "new measures"—a direct form of personal address; towns mobilized in advance by visiting workers; special evangelistic meetings during weekday evenings—are still very much part of the practice of evangelists of the present day.

The spiritual revitalization produced by the Second Great Awakening led to an enormous burst of Protestant missionary activity. The cause of foreign missions prospered as never before, and the nineteenth century has been called with some reason the "Great Century of Missions." Historian Kenneth Scott Latourette, in his *History of the Expansion of Christianity*, observed that never before "had so many hundreds of thousands contributed voluntarily of their means to assist the spread of Christianity or any other religion." By the end of the nineteenth century Christianity had established itself as a truly global religion, with firm beachheads on every continent.

The First and Second Great Awakenings, which established evangelicalism as the dominant force in nineteenth-century American religion, at the same time produced theological tensions which are still very much in evidence in evangelical life. Can revivalism's insistence on personal religious experience be combined with intellectual rigor and an appreciation of culture and the life of the mind? How do parachurch organizations formed for evangelism and missions relate to the work of the established denominations? Both questions remain as very live issues on American evangelicalism's agenda for the future.

### The rise of biblical criticism

For the last three centuries modern biblical criticism has presented a massive challenge to the evangelical faith. The new forms of criticism presented a threat of the first order inasmuch as they questioned not merely external manifestations of the evangelical tradition but the very foundation upon which the tradition was based: the Bible itself. The shock waves loosed by critical scholars represented a "shaking of the foundations," and the tremors can still be felt in various parts of the evangelical landscape.

The first wave of criticism to reach America originated in the European Enlightenment of the seventeenth century. Richard Simon's *Critical History of the Old Testament* (1678), Thomas Hobbes's *Leviathan* (1661), and Spinoza's *Tractatus theologico-politicus* (1670) presented a rationalistic criticism that denied the miraculous element in scripture and asserted the existence of errors and contradictions in the text. This seventeenth-century criticism was an expression of a broader Enlightenment revolt against traditional ecclesiastical authority and an assertion of the supremacy of human reason over divine revelation.

These early efforts at biblical criticism were spread in a shallow form in America by Thomas Paine and Thomas Jefferson. Paine, the Revolutionary War patriot and author of *The Age of Reason*, dismissed the Old Testament as a collection of Israelite myths. Jefferson prepared his own version of the New Testament by removing all accounts of the miraculous. Such critical speculations did not, however, gain a significant foothold in the American churches during the eighteenth and early nineteenth centuries. The spiritual and political activities generated by the Great Awakenings and the Revolutionary War occupied the attention of the American people, and the speculations of the European critics seemed at that time to be only small clouds on the ecclesiastical horizon.

Although criticism was having little effect in the churches prior to the Civil War, the new methods were beginning to take root among New England intellectuals. After the Unitarians gained control of Harvard in 1805, a professorial chair at the nation's oldest university was endowed in 1810 for the promotion of "a critical knowledge of the Holy Scriptures." At Andover, Moses Stuart, a conservative biblical scholar, cautiously attempted to combine the new European approaches with his views of inspiration.

European critical studies continued to develop during the nineteenth century. David Friedrich Strauss's *Life of Jesus* (1835) portrayed the Gospels as mythical expressions of the faith of the early church. The Tübingen scholar F. C. Baur argued that only Romans, First and Second Corinthians, and Galatians were genuinely Pauline, and that Acts and John originated in the middle of the second century. Julius Wellhausen presented the documentary hypothesis in its classic form in *The Composition of the Hexateuch* (1877), and argued for an evolutionary reconstruction of the history of Israel in his *Prolegomena to the History of Israel* (1883).

The newer waves of European criticism began to batter American shores with full force after the Civil War. The ecclesiastical and intellectual struggles were typified by the debates between Charles A. Briggs and A. A. Hodge and B. B. Warfield in the pages of the *Presbyterian Review* during the 1880s. Briggs argued for the new critical positions, and Hodge and Warfield argued for "inerrancy in the autographs" in a famous article published in the April, 1881, issue. Briggs, who had earlier created considerable controversy with his *Biblical Study: Its Principles, Methods, and History* (1883), brought matters in the Presbyterian Church to a head with his inaugural lecture in 1891 as the new professor of biblical theology at Union Theological Seminary in New York. Briggs denied inerrancy, the Mosaic authorship of the Pentateuch, and the unity of Isaiah. In 1893 the General Assembly of the Presbyterian Church tried Briggs for heresy and suspended him from the ministry. He was subsequently received into the Episcopal Church, and Union Seminary severed its ties with the Presbyterians. The Briggs affair ended, but American evangelicalism's struggles with biblical criticism were far from over.

### Darwin comes to America

"Charles Darwin fired a shot heard round the theological world," wrote American historian Bert James Loewenberg.[21] The revolu-

---

21. Bert James Loewenberg, "Darwinism Comes to America," pp. 339 – 68.

tionary ideas presented in *The Origin of Species* (1859) and *The Descent of Man* (1871) were seen as serious threats to the biblical accounts of creation and the special place of mankind in the divine order of the universe. Darwin's ideas were popularized by John Fiske in the widely read books *The Destiny of Man* (1884), *The Idea of God as Affected by Modern Knowledge* (1885), and *Through Nature to God* (1899). Evolution was merely "God's way of doing things," argued Fiske.

Charles Hodge of Princeton, in his 1874 work *What Is Darwinism?* expressed the reservations of many conservatives. Darwinism was inherently atheistic, Hodge argued; natural selection obscured God's role in the design of the world. Not all conservatives took Hodge's position. To the conservative Scottish theologian James Orr evolution seemed "extremely probable and supported by a large body of evidence." The conservative Baptist theologian A. H. Strong wrote in 1907 that "a theistic evolution can recognize the whole process of man's creation as equally the work of nature and the work of God."[22] In 1911, B. B. Warfield, in a cautious comment, wrote that evolution, if very carefully guarded, might be a tenable theory of the "divine procedure in creating man."

Most Americans believed that the controversy over evolution was laid to rest after the Scopes trial of 1925, but the new wave of creationist activity which surfaced during the 1970s showed that issues of science and scripture were far from dead in conservative Protestantism.

### A changing social order

The nineteenth century brought sweeping social as well as intellectual change. The complexities of a rapidly emerging urban and industrial order challenged evangelical forms of ministry at the same time that Darwin and the higher critics were challenging the evangelical mind.

Cities were experiencing rapid population growth. In 1800 the population of New York had reached 60,000; by 1860 it had increased tenfold to 600,000. The U.S. population, which stood at 10 million in 1812, by the time of the Civil War had tripled to 31 million. Successive waves of European immigrants contributed to burgeoning population growth and were beginning to transform

22. A. H. Strong, *Systematic Theology*, p. 466.

the citadel of white Anglo-Saxon Protestantism into an ethnic and religious melting pot. Roman Catholicism and Judaism became more visible in American religious life.

The century witnessed an unparalled growth of new inventions and technology. In 1800 there had been seventy-seven patents on file; in 1850 there were a thousand. Rapidly expanding networks of railroad and telegraph lines broke down the provincialism of the old rural and small-town life. The railroads, which had only begun to operate in 1829, by 1860 had laid thirty thousand miles of track. The expansion of American industry brought new employment opportunities and a rising standard of living to countless thousands, as well as new forms of social conflict. Tensions between labor and management broke out into bloody conflicts in 1877, 1886, 1892, and 1894.

Though general levels of income rose dramatically during the century, not all groups shared equally in the new industrial prosperity. Blacks in the south, working-class immigrants in the northern ghettos, and farmers on western homesteads were frequently left out.

Evangelicals who had adapted the revival techniques of the frontier to urban conditions also attempted to adjust their ministries to the challenges of the new social order. The attempts were marked by some notable successes and equally notable failures. During this period evangelical churches largely failed to reach two groups in particular—black Americans and the urban working class. During the Reconstruction era many blacks discovered that while the Civil War had brought new freedom, there had been little change in the overall attitudes of many whites toward them. Meanwhile, as William Pannell has observed, for the most part the white evangelical church "moved up into the solid middle class and abandoned its heritage to those whose message was social reform without the gospel."[23] Even though they shared so many theological convictions, black churches and white evangelical churches experienced a parting of the ways that has continued to the present day.

Evangelical churches also experienced difficulty in reaching the immigrant workers in the cities. Differences of ethnic background and socio-economic status created barriers. Many evangelical

23. William Pannell, "The Religious Heritage of Blacks," p. 106.

leaders had little sympathy for the labor movement, and this contributed to the sense of estrangement between the two groups. Many members of the working class sought spiritual sustenance in the Roman Catholic Church or abandoned religious affiliations entirely.

It would be quite unfair, however, to conclude that evangelicals did not have notable achievements in the area of social ministry during the nineteenth century. The century's revivals produced a massive outpouring of benevolent activity. The church historian Philip Schaff remarked in 1854, "There are in America probably more awakened souls and more individual self-sacrifice for religious purposes, proportionately, than in any other country in the world." By 1831 the thirteen leading benevolent societies had gathered $2.8 million—an impressive figure when it is considered that only $3.58 million had been spent by government from the founding of the nation through 1828 for all internal improvements.

Nineteenth-century evangelicals saw no dichotomy between evangelism and social reform. Evangelist Edward Norris Kirk, preaching in Boston in 1842, reminded his listeners that when "men love their neighbors as themselves, the causes of poverty will be sought out, and the remedy applied as far as possible." Phoebe Palmer, an energetic Methodist laywoman and founder of the Five Points settlement house in New York, was one of many who were involved in evangelical ministries to the urban poor. Evangelicals were involved in establishing urban rescue missions, employment bureaus, orphanages, anti-slavery societies, medical dispensaries and clinics, fresh-air programs for children, and programs of holiday meals and disaster relief. The breadth of evangelical social concern during the century was such that even the secular press could not deny its impact. The *New York Observer* remarked in 1855, "Infidelity makes a great outcry about its philanthropy, but religion does the work."

Despite these evangelical efforts some American churchmen became convinced that structural and systemic changes were necessary to minister to the needs of the urban poor. Josiah Strong, a general secretary of the Evangelical Alliance, organized conferences in 1887, 1889, and 1893 to promote "social Christianity." Washington Gladden, an early leader in the social gospel movement, advocated the cause of the labor movement. The advocates of the "social gospel" were responding to a sense of social soli-

darity in America that had been weakened by frontier individualism, revivalism, and the impersonality of the new urbanized
social order. Society, these new voices were saying, must be seen
as more than an aggregate of competing individuals. The social
gospel movement, which emerged during the years 1865 – 80, began to flourish during the 1890s and reached theological maturity
in the work of its most prominent spokesman, Walter Rauschen-
busch, author of *Christianizing the Social Order* (1912) and *A Theology for the Social Gospel* (1917). Even though the movement
declined after the First World War, its heritage continues to challenge evangelicals to integrate the individual and corporate dimensions of social ministry.

### New conservative currents

During the course of the nineteenth century two conservative
trends emerged that have continued to influence the shape of
American evangelicalism: the holiness movement and dispensationalism. The holiness movement emerged from within the Methodist tradition as a result of a conviction that Wesley's teachings
concerning the second blessing and Christian perfection were no
longer being vigorously taught. The renewed emphasis on Wesleyan doctrines of sanctification were influential in the lives of
A. B. Simpson, founder of the Christian and Missionary Alliance,
and William and Catherine Booth, founders of the Salvation Army.
Holiness teachings were popularized in the widely read book by
Hannah Whitehall Smith, *The Christian's Secret of a Happy Life*
(1875). The Church of the Nazarene and the Church of God of
Anderson, Indiana, were formed as a result of controversies within
Methodism during the closing decades of the nineteenth century.

After the turn of the century a further development occurred
within the movement, shifting the focus of attention from the second blessing to the baptism of the Holy Spirit, understood in relation to speaking in tongues. In 1906 W. J. Seymour, a black minister
leading a revival at the Azusa Street Mission in Los Angeles, became convinced that "anyone who does not speak in tongues is
not baptized with the Spirit." The dramatic manifestations of glos-
salalia at the Azusa Street revival are often considered to mark the
beginning of the Pentecostal movement in the United States. The
movement led to the formation of a number of new Pentecostal
denominations, of which the Assemblies of God are the largest.

Pentecostal teaching was criticized both by conservative Calvinists such as Warfield, who argued that miraculous gifts had ceased with the apostles, and by some in the holiness churches who felt that the new teaching placed too much emphasis on the dramatic manifestations of the Spirit's gifts and not enough on continuing sanctification. In virtually all American churches, irrespective of denomination or theological tradition, the Pentecostal movement focused new attention on the reality of the Holy Spirit in the Christian's life and on the need for all believers to employ the Spirit's gifts for the work of ministry.

A second theological development that has continued to be a significant current within conservative Protestantism is associated with John Nelson Darby, an Englishman who was one of the leading promoters of the Plymouth Brethren movement. Darby's system of biblical interpretation, known as dispensationalism, was propagated through his own writings, lectures, and Bible study meetings and through conferences on biblical prophecy held in the United States during the 1880s. The system achieved wide circulation through the notes contained in the *Scofield Reference Bible* (1909). Dispensationalists held that there were seven distinct periods of biblical history, that unfulfilled Old Testament prophecies were to be literally fulfilled, that there were sharp distinctions between Israel and the church, and that the church was to be "raptured" out of the world prior to the great tribulation and the establishment of Christ's millennial reign on earth. The dispensationalist system became a strong influence especially in conservative Baptist and independent churches. These views, reflecting a pessimistic philosophy of history, tended to discourage social involvement and efforts to renew the larger denominations. More positively, the emergence of dispensationalism did produce renewed interest in eschatology and biblical hermeneutics in evangelical circles.

### The modernist-fundamentalist controversy

"What the liberal theologian has retained ... is not Christianity at all, but a religion which is so entirely different from Christianity as to belong in a distinct category," wrote J. Gresham Machen in *Christianity and Liberalism*.[24] According to Machen, who was not

---

24. J. Gresham Machen, *Christianity and Liberalism* (New York: Macmillan, 1923), pp. 6–7.

one to cloud the issues, modernists, in attempting to adapt Christianity to the "modern mind," had abandoned its historic substance. Modernists such as Harry Emerson Fosdick and Shailer Mathews were equally convinced that conservatives were simply closing their minds to the new discoveries of science and biblical criticism.

The controversy was strongest in five denominations: Northern Baptist, Northern Methodist, Presbyterian U.S.A., Disciples of Christ, and Protestant Episcopal. Reaching a peak during the 1920s, the often bitter ecclesiastical struggles left scars on the American churches that are still visible today.

During the latter part of the nineteenth century conservative Protestants responded to the pressures created by Darwinism and higher criticism through such widely attended conferences on biblical prophecy and interpretation as those at New York in 1877, Chicago in 1885, and Niagara Falls in 1895. At the Niagara Falls conference doctrines such as the inerrancy of scripture, the deity of Christ, the virgin birth, the substitutionary atonement, the bodily resurrection and second coming of Christ were set forth as fundamental articles of the faith.

During the years 1909–1915 Lyman and Milton Stewart, two wealthy evangelical laymen in Los Angeles, financed the publication and wide distribution of *The Fundamentals: A Testimony to the Truth*. This series of booklets by a broad range of conservative scholars and ministers responded to liberal challenges and, in the estimate of historian Mark Noll, offered "calm, well-reasoned, and well-balanced testimony to Christian truth." The publication of *The Fundamentals* marked a degree of cooperation among conservatives of various persuasions that was to largely disappear during the 1930s and 1940s.

During the 1920s the public's attention was focused on the controversy surrounding Harry Emerson Fosdick, the modernist Baptist minister who was then supplying the pulpit of the First Presbyterian Church in New York, and on the Scopes evolution trial in Dayton, Tennessee. The Fosdick affair was part of a larger struggle for control of the United Presbyterian Church and its institutions. Machen and other conservatives were alarmed by growing modernist influence in the Presbyterian seminaries and foreign missions program. When the conservatives lost control of Princeton Seminary, Machen, Robert Dick Wilson, and other con-

servative members of the faculty withdrew to form Westminster
Theological Seminary in 1929.

As the decade of the 1930s began, it was clear that the conservative drive to retain control of the major denominations had
failed. The Scopes trial, as reported by a partisan press, was widely
perceived as a victory for Clarence Darrow, evolution, and modern
thought. Many conservatives and fundamentalists withdrew from
their former communions to form independent churches or splin-
ter denominations.

It seems one of the paradoxes of American church history that
evangelicalism's great success during the nineteenth century may
have contributed to its downfall during the 1920s. The revival tradition, which greatly contributed to a numerical predominance
for conservatives, at the same time tended to emphasize personal
religious experience rather than rigorous theological reflection. As
a result, evangelicals were somewhat complacent and intellectually unprepared for the waves of new thought that were to batter
the churches after the Civil War.

### The new evangelicalism

"Fundamentalism . . . abdicated leadership and responsibility in
the societal realm," stated Harold John Ockenga, pastor of Boston's
historic Park Street Church, in a 1957 press release.[25] Ockenga,
who had been instrumental in the formation of the National Association of Evangelicals and who was later to become president
of Gordon-Conwell Theological Seminary, was a leading spokesman for the "new evangelicalism," a term he himself had coined
in 1947. Ockenga and other evangelical leaders such as Carl F. H.
Henry were calling on conservatives to recover the ecclesiastical
ground and theological breadth lost during the modernist controversy and to develop a form of evangelical Christianity that was
biblically sound, intellectually rigorous, and socially responsible.

The decade of the 1940s marked a number of significant advances for the new evangelicalism. In 1947 Henry, later to become
the editor of *Christianity Today*, in his *The Uneasy Conscience of
Modern Fundamentalism* issued a call for American conservatives
to combine social responsibility and biblical fidelity—a combination displayed by much of nineteenth-century evangelicalism but

25. In George W. Dollar, *A History of Fundamentalism in America* (Greenville, S.C.: Bob
Jones University, 1973), p. 204.

largely lost in a reaction to the theologically liberal social gospel. In a long stream of books and articles Henry urged evangelicals to add understanding to their faith and to engage in the serious theological scholarship that could draw the attention of a wider culture. The year 1947 also witnessed the founding of Fuller Theological Seminary, an institution envisioned as a place where precisely such a combination of evangelical faith and rigorous scholarship could be cultivated.

The closing years of the 1940s were significant ones for the renewal of evangelical scholarship. The publication of E. J. Carnell's *Introduction to Christian Apologetics* in 1948 established Carnell as one of evangelicalism's leading intellectual spokesmen. Carnell, who was later to become president of Fuller Theological Seminary, argued the case for conservative theology in *The Case for Orthodox Theology* (1959). The year 1949 saw the founding of the Evangelical Theological Society, a professional organization committed to the inerrancy of scripture and the promotion of evangelical scholarship.

During the 1950s Billy Graham emerged as the single most visible American evangelical. Thousands came to faith in Christ through his evangelistic crusades. Graham's policy of cooperating wherever possible with a broad spectrum of denominational leaders brought criticism from separatistic fundamentalists, who saw the new strategy as "cooperation with error." Graham was also the leading founder of *Christianity Today* in 1956, conceived as a rallying point for evangelicals in the English-speaking world.

Evangelicals continued to register gains on both intellectual and social fronts during the 1960s and 1970s (see pp. 23-24). The growing recognition of contributions made by evangelical scholars was signaled by the election of David A. Hubbard of Fuller as president of the American Association of Theological Schools in 1976, and by the election of Carl F. H. Henry as president of the American Theological Society in 1980. Evangelicals had not yet regained the intellectual predominance they enjoyed during the early decades of the nineteenth century, but they were no longer a segment of American theological life that could be safely ignored.

## Agenda for the Future

During the closing years of the twentieth century evangelical theology, poised between its fundamentalist past and the horizons of the modern world, will face challenges on many fronts. Three areas in particular promise to be foci of special theological concern: revelation and scripture, ecclesiology, and eschatology.

### Sources of the faith: revelation and scripture

During the 1980s and 1990s issues posed by the study of comparative religions are likely to move higher on the agenda of evangelical theology. A resurgent Islam, whose evangelistic efforts will be financed by a steady stream of petrodollars, will highlight the need for a Christian apologetic articulated in a global context. The proliferation of new communications technologies will continue to heighten the American Christian's awareness of the pluralism of world faiths and cultures. Can evangelical Christians recognize any truth value in the revelation claims of other faiths? Can the possibility of the salvation of those who have never had access to biblical revelation be entertained without compromising the finality of the work of Christ and the imperative of Christian missions? The need for continuing reflection in the area of an evangelical theology of world religions is apparent.

The question of world religions is closely related to the issue of revelation and culture. Carl F. H. Henry has predicted that one of the key intellectual issues for the 1980s "will concern especially the problem of hermeneutics, and centrally the question of revelation and culture."[26] Does the recognition that biblical revelation is contained in the thought forms of specific cultures endanger its claims for transcultural validity? How can one distinguish the transcultural norms from the culturally conditioned forms in which they are expressed? To what extent can social sciences such as cross-cultural anthropology and psychology be used in the interpretation of scripture without displacing the normative authority of biblical revelation? Such questions have been prominent in recent debates concerning feminism and homosexuality, but the issue of revelation and culture is hardly limited to these areas.

On the domestic front the question of revelation and culture has become a pressing issue in a political context. To what extent should Christians seek to have their biblical moral standards reflected in the civil law? What common ground exists between Christians and humanists in the areas of morality, law, and public

26. Carl F. H. Henry, "American Evangelicals in a Turning Time," p. 1062.

policy? Do Christian attempts to influence the law constitute a violation of First Amendment provisions concerning the separation of church and state? A broad range of moral issues—abortion, homosexuality, pornography, public education—require renewed evangelical reflection upon both the doctrine of general revelation and the history of the interpretation of American church-state relations.

The doctrine of scripture will continue to be near the center of evangelical theological reflection for the foreseeable future. For the last two hundred years the historical-critical study of the Bible has challenged the orthodox understanding of biblical authority, and the struggle is far from over. New issues continue to arise. To what extent can evangelical biblical scholars appropriate the results and methods of source, form, and redaction criticism without compromising the primacy of biblical authority? Continuing study of the relationship of revelation and history in the biblical texts is needed in this connection.

What terminologies are most adequate for expressing an evangelical understanding of biblical authority? Do terms such as "infallibility" and "inerrancy" continue to be serviceable, or are they in danger of "dying the death of a thousand qualifications"? The resolution of such questions, which are both theological and semantical in nature, is an urgent need in the interests of evangelical unity.

Issues of science and scripture continue to arise. Will neo-fundamentalist groups such as the Institute for Creation Research spark a renewed consideration of creation and evolution in evangelical circles? Will fresh progress be made in the difficult area of human origins, the fossil record, and the interpretation of Genesis 1 – 3? Do the results of modern anthropology conflict with traditional understandings of the fall and original sin? Issues of science and scripture, which have not been especially prominent in evangelical circles during recent decades, are likely to become the focus of renewed interest.

### The community of the faith: ecclesiology

Evangelicals need to give fresh attention to the doctrine of the church. Questions concerning the structure of the church, worship and liturgy, and the nature of mission will be prominent areas of theological reflection during the years ahead. The heritage of revivalism and the individualism of the American frontier have tended to obscure the corporate and historical dimensions of ecclesial understanding in the evangelical tradition. How do parachurch groups, so important in the evangelical experience, relate to biblical and historical understandings of the catholicity and unity of the church? What stance should evangelicals adopt in relation to proposals for church union promoted by mainline denominations? Is the methodology of the church growth movement soundly rooted in scripture, or has it been too heavily influenced by extrabiblical assumptions from the social sciences? Is the "homogeneous unit principle" consistent with the New Testament ideal of an inclusive church? These are some of the questions that are emerging in relation to the nature of the church and its structures.

Concern for church renewal has focused new attention on worship. A number of evangelical leaders are beginning to emphasize the value of liturgy and tradition in the life of the church. These leaders are urging a tradition that has historically emphasized the centrality of preaching to enrich its worship experience through a greater appreciation and use of the liturgical and sacramental resources of the historic church. The charismatic renewal, which has brought fresh spiritual vitality into many communions, needs to be integrated into established evangelical theologies of the ministry and gifts of the Holy Spirit.

In the area of missions, reaching the "hidden peoples" and mobilizing the churches for this task is of the highest priority. Evangelical theologians will be challenged to wrestle with the methodological issues raised by the necessity of recontextualizing traditional Western expressions of the faith in terms of cultures that are yet to be reached. In order to achieve greater Christian penetration of Islamic, Hindu, and Buddhist cultures, evangelical missionaries and theologians will need to develop new forms of interreligious and cross-cultural Christian apologetics.

### Consummation of the faith: eschatology

Eschatology, long a favorite interest of conservative Protestants, is likely to remain so during the decades ahead. Significant issues are calling for attention in the areas of both individual and general eschatology. The work of Elisabeth Kübler-Ross and Raymond Moody has focused new attention on death, dying, and claims for "life after life" that are contradictory to scriptural teaching. The infiltration of Eastern cults and sects into American society has helped to spread belief in reincarnation. Some evangelical scholars such as John W. Wenham have called for reconsideration of the traditional teaching of eternal conscious punishment of the lost.

In the area of general eschatology evangelicals need to move beyond preoccupation with details of the end time toward a comprehensive philosophy of history that is solidly rooted in scripture. Political turbulence in the Middle East will continue to challenge dispensational and covenant theologians alike to develop more comprehensive understandings of the place of Israel in the plan of God.

The years ahead may well witness a revival of postmillennialism in evangelical circles. This view, which was the dominant understanding among conservatives for much of the nineteenth century, expects Christianity to achieve a predominant position among the belief systems of the world prior to Christ's return. This predominance is to be achieved through the dramatic blessing by the Holy Spirit of the preaching of the gospel. A renewal of such a vision of the church's future, based not on some evolutionary optimism but on an aggressive confidence in the present sovereignty of the risen Lord, could infuse tremendous energy and hope into the urgent task of reaching the "hidden peoples" with the gospel of Jesus Christ.

## Bibliography

"Back to That Oldtime Religion," *Time*, Dec. 26, 1977, pp. 52—58.

Beaver, R. Pierce. "Missionary Motivation Through Three Centuries," in *Reinterpretation in American Church History*, ed. Jerald C. Brauer. Chicago: University of Chicago Press, 1968.

Brown, Jerry Wayne. *The Rise of Biblical Criticism in America, 1800–1870*. Middletown, Conn.: Wesleyan University Press, 1969.

*Connecticut Mutual Life Report on American Values in the '80s: The Impact of Belief*. New York: Research and Forecasts, Inc., 1981.

Culpepper, Robert H. *Evaluating the Charismatic Movement*. Valley Forge: Judson, 1977.

Dollar, George W. *A History of Fundamentalism in America*. Greenville, S.C.: Bob Jones University, 1973.

Gallup, George Jr., and Poling, David. *The Search for America's Faith.* Nashville: Abingdon, 1980.

Hamilton, Michael P., ed. *The Charismatic Movement.* Grand Rapids: Eerdmans, 1975.

Handy, Robert T. "Fundamentalism and Modernism in Perspective," *Religion in Life* 24 (1955):381—94.

Henry, Carl F. H. "American Evangelicals in a Turning Time," *Christian Century,* Nov. 5, 1980, pp. 1058—62.

————. *Evangelical Responsibility in Contemporary Theology.* Grand Rapids: Eerdmans, 1957.

Hutchison, William R. *The Modernist Impulse in American Protestantism.* Cambridge: Harvard University Press, 1976.

Kane, J. Herbert. " 'The White Man's Burden' Is Changing Colors," *Christianity Today,* July 17, 1981, pp. 62—64.

Kantzer, Kenneth. "The Charismatics Among Us," *Christianity Today,* Feb. 22, 1980, pp. 25 — 29.

Kelley, Dean M. *Why Conservative Churches Are Growing.* New York: Harper, 1972.

Latourette, Kenneth Scott. *A History of the Expansion of Christianity,* Vol. VII. New York: Harper, 1945.

Lindsell, Harold. *The Battle for the Bible.* Grand Rapids: Zondervan, 1976.

Loewenberg, Bert James. "Darwinism Comes to America," *Mississippi Valley Historical Review* 28 (1941):339—68.

Marsden, George M. "From Fundamentalism to Evangelicalism," in *The Evangelicals,* ed. David Wells and John Woodbridge. Nashville: Abingdon, 1975.

Marty, Martin E. *Righteous Empire.* New York: Dial Press, 1970.

Padilla, C. Rene, ed. *The New Face of Evangelicalism.* Downers Grove, Ill.: InterVarsity, 1976.

Pannell, William. "The Religious Heritage of Blacks," in *The Evangelicals,* ed. David Wells and John Woodbridge. Nashville: Abingdon, 1975.

Quebedeaux, Richard. *The Worldly Evangelicals.* San Francisco: Harper, 1978.

————. *The Young Evangelicals.* New York: Harper, 1974.

Ramm, Bernard. *The Christian View of Science and Scripture.* Grand Rapids: Eerdmans, 1954.

Strong, A. H. *Systematic Theology.* Philadelphia: American Baptist Publishing Society, 1907.

Tillich, Paul. *Systematic Theology,* Vol. I. Chicago: University of Chicago Press, 1951.

Wagner, C. Peter. "Aiming at Church Growth in the Eighties," *Christianity Today,* Nov. 21, 1980, pp. 24—27.

————— . "Recent Developments in Church Growth Understandings," *Review and Expositor* 77 (1980):507—20.

Webber, Robert E. *Common Roots: A Call to Evangelical Maturity.* Grand Rapids: Zondervan, 1978.

Webber, Robert E., and Bloesch, Donald, eds. *The Orthodox Evangelicals.* Nashville: Thomas Nelson, 1978.

Wenham, John W. *The Goodness of God.* Downers Grove, Ill.: Inter-Varsity, 1974.

Williams, J. Rodman. "A Profile of the Charismatic Movement," *Christianity Today,* Feb. 28, 1975, pp. 9—13.

Woodbridge, John D., Mark A. Noll; and Nathan O. Hatch, *The Gospel in America.* Grand Rapids: Zondervan, 1979.

# 2

## Nature and Method
## of Evangelical Theology

Having in the previous chapter outlined some of the more important historical influences that have shaped the evangelical tradition in the American context, we are now in a position to discuss more systematically questions of the nature and method of evangelical theology as a discipline.

### A Definition

Evangelical theology can be defined as *systematic reflection on scripture and tradition and the mission of the church in mutual relation, with scripture as the norm.* The various features of this definition will require some comment and explanation.

Theology is an attempt to think systematically about the foundations of the Christian faith and its contemporary applications. The goal is an understanding of biblical truth that is sound, coherent, and comprehensive. There are those who, being influenced by pragmatic or existentialist philosophies, are suspicious of all "systems." In all areas of life, however, whether it be medicine, law, ecology, or biblical truth, an integrated grasp of the subject matter in terms of its foundations and organic relations is essential for effective application of basic principles and the solution of novel problems.

Evangelical theology is a form of human reflection, the application of human consciousness to the data of biblical revelation and to earlier ecclesiastical understandings of those data. In this connection it is helpful to maintain a distinction between doctrine and theology.[1] *Doctrine* (cf. διδασκαλία, Eph. 4:14; διδαχῆ, Acts 2:42) refers to scriptural teachings on the foundations of the faith—e.g., the deity of Christ, his substitutionary atonement, bodily resurrection, second coming, and so forth.[2] *Theology* refers to the more developed ecclesiastical articulations, defenses, and applications of those doctrines—e.g., the Chalcedonian formulation concerning the two natures of Christ. In the latter case a term not found in scripture, *homoousios*, was used to preserve a biblical truth from heretical distortion. The biblical doctrine of man as the image of God (Gen. 1:26) provides the basis for a theological understanding of the sanctity of human life in relation to contemporary moral issues such as abortion, infanticide, euthanasia, and world hunger. The doctrine of justification by grace through faith alone provides a basis for a theological understanding of personal dignity and self-worth in Christian counseling. The distinction between doctrine and theology reminds us both of the normative priority of biblical doctrine over all later constructions and of the need to express biblical truth in fresh ways as new challenges arise in the course of the church's mission.

Evangelical theology is reflection on both scripture and tradition, with scripture as the norm. For evangelical theology scripture is both the primary source and the highest norm. However, the primacy of scripture does not exclude tradition as a secondary source and norm for theology. Evangelicals, who are prone at times to bypass two millennia of church history in order to focus on the primary sources, impoverish themselves by ignoring the Spirit's previous work in the church. A careful study of creeds, confessions, and other forms of Christian literature can deepen our understanding of scripture and prevent short-sighted theological efforts which merely "reinvent the wheel."

Evangelical theology is also reflection on the sources of the faith

---

1. David F. Wells, *The Search for Salvation*, pp. 39–40.

2. The doctrine/theology distinction can be seen within canonical scripture itself, of course—e.g., the kerygma as expressed in 1 Cor. 15:1–3 vs. the more developed theological constructions of John, Paul, and the other New Testament writers. As used in this work, however, "theology" refers to postcanonical ecclesiastical reflection.

and the mission of the church in mutual relation. Theology should never be a merely academic enterprise, but rather the search for biblical understanding in the context of the ministry and mission of the church. The point of theological reflection is to "let the earth hear His voice." Evangelical theology is properly "task theology," i.e., theology hammered out in response to the challenges posed by the Great Commission.

In discussing the nature of Pauline theology William L. Lane has argued that "Paul should be regarded as a 'task theologian,' that is, one who worked out his theological insights within the frame of reference provided by his task as an apostle to the Gentiles."[3] The Pauline practice provides a helpful paradigm for evangelical theology and is closely related to the issue of contextualization (pp. 60–72), which has become prominent in recent discussions of theological method.

## The Nature of Systematic Theology

### Historical alternatives

Over the course of church history various understandings of the nature of theology have emerged. In the early centuries of the church the predominant understanding, reflecting the influence of Augustine, was that of theology as *sapientia*, wisdom. Secular knowledge pertained to temporal things, while theology or wisdom pertained to eternal things, to God as man's highest good. Theological reflection was oriented to personal spirituality and sanctification, and often reflected the monastic context. The concern for personal spirituality as a focus of theology remained strong in the work of the Protestant Reformers, and is quite evident in the Puritan tradition. John Bunyan's *Pilgrim's Progress* is a classic expression of this emphasis. This note is also found in the *Form of Government of the Presbyterian Church in the U.S.A.* (1788), where it is stated that "truth is in order to godliness; and the great touchstone of truth [is] its tendency to promote holiness" (I, iv). The tradition of theology as *sapientia*, or biblical wisdom oriented to the spiritual life, was also emphasized in continental pietism, in Wesleyanism, and in Pentecostal and holiness churches in America.

3. William L. Lane, in Glenn W. Barker, William L. Lane, and J. Ramsey Michaels, *The New Testament Speaks*, p. 148.

During the Middle Ages the understanding of theology as *scientia* or "science" began to emerge. The question of theology's "scientific" status first became prominent with the rise of European universities in the thirteenth century. How was theology, as a discipline or organized body of knowledge, related to the other disciplines of the university curriculum? According to Aquinas, theology could be considered a "science" in the Aristotelian sense: "Sacred doctrine is a science because it proceeds from principles made known by the light of a higher science, namely the science of God and the blessed. Hence, just as music accepts on authority the principles taught by the arithmetician, so sacred science accepts the principles revealed by God" (*Summa Theologica* I.1.2).

This concept of theology as *scientia* or a comprehensive discipline based on first principles came to dominate the Middle Ages and is commonly known as scholasticism. While the older concern for personal spirituality was not ignored, the emphasis tended to shift toward the precise articulation and defense of doctrine. This scholastic influence was quite evident in seventeenth-century Protestant orthodoxy, and was continued in the conservative traditions of the Old Princeton and the Lutheran confessional theologies of nineteenth-century America.

In addition to *sapientia* and *scientia, orthopraxis* could be identified as a third model for understanding the nature of theology. From the beginning the church has realized more or less consistently that biblical truth is to be done (John 3:21; 1 John 1:6), and not merely contemplated.

More recently this focus on praxis has been emphasized in liberation theology. According to Gustavo Gutiérrez, theology is "a critical reflection on Christian praxis in the light of the Word."[4] James Cone asserts that Christian theology is a "theology of liberation." It is a "rational study of the being of God in the world in light of the existential situation of an oppressed community, relating the forces of liberation to the essence of the gospel."[5] Liberation theologies distort the gospel by substituting revolution for regeneration, but they do echo the world-transforming thrust of biblical truth.

This action orientation of liberation theology is reflected in a

4. Gustavo Gutiérrez, *A Theology of Liberation*, p. 13.
5. James Cone, *Black Theology of Liberation*, p. 17.

significantly different sense in the work of R. J. Rushdoony. According to Rushdoony, systematic theology "cannot simply be an exercise in thinking, and a systematization of biblical thought. It must be thinking for action in terms of knowing, obeying, and honoring God by fulfilling His mandate to us. . . . It is related to what happens in church, state, school, family, the arts and sciences, the vocations, and all things else."6 Systematic theology is a tool for extending God's dominion in the world; it is dominion-oriented. In his "Theses on Feuerbach," Karl Marx observed that "the philosophers have only interpreted the world, in various ways; the point, however, is to change it." In like fashion it could be said that the task of evangelical theology is not merely to interpret the world, but to transform it through the authority of the exalted Lord and his inspired Word.

A healthy evangelical theology, to properly equip the people of God for the work of ministry (Eph. 4:11–16), needs all three elements: *sapientia, scientia, orthopraxis.* A theology that loses touch with the dimensions of personal spirituality and Christian growth becomes sterile and academic. A theology that rejects the heritage of the great medieval and seventeenth-century scholastic systems will find itself in danger of losing the precision of thought and intellectual rigor that are essential to the theological task. A theology that loses sight of the dominion mandate (Gen. 1:28) and the Great Commission (Matt. 28:19–20) forgets that Christian knowledge is not an end in itself but an instrument for bringing about the "obedience of faith" (Rom. 1:5) among all the nations. Evangelical theology's proper context is the ministry and mission of the church, and its goal is to extend the reign of Jesus Christ to the uttermost parts of the earth.

## The nature of theological language

Any discussion of the nature of theology is closely related to the question of the nature of religious and theological language. In speaking about God and the invisible realities of faith, both the writers of scripture and theologians of the church have used models and analogies drawn from human experience. In divine revelation the infinite and invisible God has made himself known through the finite and visible forms of the created world and hu-

6. R. J. Rushdoony, *The Necessity for Systematic Theology,* p. 57.

man experience. The human relationship of a father and son becomes a model of the relationship between the first and second persons of the Trinity; a human household becomes a model for the church of God (1 Tim. 3:15); a general's victory in battle becomes a model for Christ's triumph over Satan at the cross (Col. 2:15); the redemption of a slave becomes a model for the Christian's redemption from sin (cf. 1 Cor. 6:20). Anselm's satisfaction theory of the atonement was modeled on the chivalric concepts of honor that pertained to the medieval social relations of lord and vassal. The vassal (man) had offended the lord's (God's) honor, but in this case only the God-Man, Jesus Christ, could offer as a man a satisfaction of infinite worth to a lord of infinite dignity.

Discussions in the philosophy of science can shed some useful light on the use of models in theology.[7] In these discussions distinctions are drawn between replica and analogue models. Replicas or scale models—e.g., a model of an airplane in a wind tunnel or an architect's scale model of a building—are smaller but "literal" and easily visualized models of the larger realities they depict. Analogue models, on the other hand, are not small "pictures" of the realities they represent but simulations of the structural relationships in question. When economists construct computer simulations of the American economy, or when a physicist for teaching purposes speaks of electricity as a fluid, analogue models are being employed. Real features of the realities in question are being modeled, but not in a literal, directly visualizable sense.

Religious language, since it speaks of spiritual realities that cannot be seen with the physical eyes (2 Cor. 4:18; Heb. 11:1), necessarily uses analogue rather than replica models. God is light (1 John 1:5) not in a literal physical sense, but in that light is an appropriate model for God's glory, purity, truth, and life-giving power. The Holy Spirit can be manifested in tongues of fire (Acts 2:3) because fire is an appropriate model for God's holiness, power, and judgment of sin.

Models are simply one aspect of the inherently analogical nature of religious language.[8] The use of analogy presupposes ele-

---

7. See Mary Hesse, "Models and Analogy in Science," and Max Black, *Models and Metaphors*; for a useful survey of models and religious language, see Norman L. Geisler, *Philosophy of Religion*.

8. For a discussion of analogy in religious language, see Geisler, *Philosophy*, pp. 268–89, and Battista Mondin, *The Principle of Analogy in Protestant and Catholic Theology*.

ments of both similarity and difference between the two entities being compared. The analogical nature of religious language is illustrated in biblical anthropomorphisms, metaphors, and similes. References to God's "right hand" do not imply that God has physical hands, but refer to the place of honor and authority. Jesus is the bread of life (John 6:35) not in a physical sense, but because communion with him is the source of eternal life. The kingdom of heaven is like a mustard seed (Matt. 13:3) because of its powers of remarkable growth. In each of these biblical illustrations elements of both similarity and difference are presupposed when aspects of human experience are employed to describe spiritual realities. Human language, when used of God and the spiritual realm, must be properly qualified in order to preserve the distinction between the Creator and the creature.

While biblical language is not univocal, i.e. unqualified, neither is it equivocal. While human language cannot transmit an exhaustive knowledge of an infinite God, it can become the vehicle of an adequate and genuine knowledge. Jesus Christ, the divine agent of creation (John 1:3; Col. 1:16), himself entered into the created order of human existence (John 1:14) as the mediator between God and man (1 Tim. 2:5), and revealed knowledge of God through the instrumentality of human speech. We can speak about God because God has first spoken to us about himself.

In other religious traditions human speech about the transcendent is equivocal. In the Buddhist tradition the concept of Nirvana is basically unthinkable and incomprehensible; the analogical link between human language and its ultimate referent is broken. A concept such as Nirvana is like the scaffolding around a house under construction which is abandoned when the job (enlightenment) is finished.[9]

There are important practical implications flowing from the analogical nature of religious and theological language. Analogy implies elements of difference as well as similarity; human language concerning God can never exhaust God's infinite reality or "put him in a box." Reflecting on the nature of models and analogies

9. "Ultimately, Nirvana is unthinkable and incomprehensible. It is only as a therapeutically valuable, though basically false concept that, during certain phases of our spiritual progress, can be of use to our thoughts and enter into the practice of contemplation" (Edward Conze, *Buddhism*, p. 112).

in religious discourse can remind us of the necessity of maintaining a proper humility in all our thinking and speaking of God.

To the extent that a model, analogy, or illustration reflects the circumstances of a particular culture, the missionary task may require fresh analogies to maintain effective communication of the biblical message. A number of African languages have no word for snow; consequently missionaries who translated the biblical phrase "white as snow" into these languages used an African simile, "white as egret feathers." The missionary task of the church links the discussion of analogies and models directly to the contextualization of the message itself.

## The Need for Systematic Theology

### Historical roots

In the early church systematic theological reflection arose in response to three pressing needs of ministry: the need to refute heresies that threatened the substance of faith itself; the need to catechize new converts in preparation for baptism and the Lord's Supper; and the need to preach and teach the Bible in a comprehensive manner. These needs are still very real in the church today.

The proliferation of cults in contemporary America heightens the need for ministers and lay people alike to have a systematic understanding of basic Christian doctrine. Cults such as the Jehovah's Witnesses appeal to scripture in support of their systems, and an uninformed Christian who has only a piecemeal knowledge of scripture can be defenseless against their arguments. An understanding of the fabric of Christian truth as a whole is needed to counter such mishandlings of the text of scripture. In the early church the "rules of faith," the prototypes of the Apostles' Creed and later systems of theology, provided the normative baselines for the proper interpretation of scripture in the face of heretical distortions. These rules of faith provided an understanding of the structure of the Christian faith as a systematic whole.

As was the case in the early church, so it is today. New converts need in-depth instruction in biblical truth in order not to be "blown about by every wind of doctrine" (Eph. 4:14). This is the catechetical function of theology.

It is indeed one of the ironies of modern religious life that so much biblical and theological illiteracy seems to abound in spite of the proliferation of Bible translations, commentaries, study aids, and radio and television preachers. In an interview for *Christianity Today,* Billy Graham was asked, "Does it bother you that so many evangelicals seem to be theologically illiterate?" The evangelist replied, "It bothers me terribly. . . . One of the great needs in America is Bible teaching in depth. Unless this happens, I fear we will see many distortions and errors creeping into evangelicalism in the future."

Ministers need to be thoroughly grounded in a systematic understanding of biblical truth in order to preach and teach with maximum effectiveness. The apostle Paul reminded Titus that leaders of the churches must be able to both give instruction in sound doctrine and refute those who contradicted it (Titus 1:9). Without a balanced grasp of Christian truth and its organic relations the minister will be less effective in dealing with false teaching. A systematic understanding of scripture can also function as a safeguard against an unbalanced teaching ministry, where the preacher constantly rides certain "hobby horses" rather than teaching the whole counsel of God.

### The American context

A number of elements in the American experience have militate against a proper appreciation of the role of systematic theology in the life of the church. The American historian Richard Hofstadter has called attention to the ways in which the nineteenth century revivals tended to reinforce anti-intellectual attitudes in the churches: "The Puritan ideal of the minister as an intellectual and educational leader was steadily weakened in the face of the evangelical ideal of the minister as a popular crusader and exhorter. In considerable measure the churches withdrew from intellectual encounters with the secular world, and gave up the idea that religion is part of the whole life of intellectual experience."[10] The warm feelings of the heart threatened to engulf the understanding of the head.

American church historian Sidney Mead has noted how revivalism's tendency to simplify all issues in the interests of results also tended to minimize the importance of deeper theological

10. Richard Hofstadter, *Anti-Intellectualism in American Life*, pp. 86–87.

reflection. "The over-simplification of issues, plus the primary emphasis on a personal religious experience, and on tangible numerical results," Mead observed, "left little room or encouragement for the traditional role of the church and its ministers in intellectual leadership."[11] After all, why bother with theological analysis when the numbers are looking good?

As we have already had occasion to note (pp. 27–28), the experiential emphasis in the evangelical tradition exacted its toll as the nineteenth century wore on. The conservative churches were largely unprepared for the new intellectual challenges posed by higher criticism and Darwinism, and by the 1930s the mainline denominations and major institutions of society had largely been lost to theological liberals and humanists.

The recent evangelical resurgence has continued in the same experiential vein. Several years ago Joseph Bayly, an astute observer of the evangelical landscape, noted that the "new blood that is replacing theology in the church's veins or arteries may be psychology or sociology, feelings or experience, relationships or revolution. But it is not theology, unless it be theology dangerously watered down."[12] Carl F. H. Henry has warned, "If the evangelical movement settles merely for popular appeals and does not sink its roots in theology, it will be in serious trouble in another generation."[13] Neither Bayly nor Henry is asking American evangelicals to abandon the experiential reality of their tradition; the point is to deepen that experience by grounding it in a solid understanding of its biblical roots. Experientialism without theological reflection has contributed to a loss of evangelical dominion. Loving God with both mind and heart is vital if evangelicalism is to be more than a private religious experience, and become once again a world-transforming power.

## The Legitimacy of a Systematic Theology

In light of the foregoing considerations, the need for an evangelical systematic theology in the life of the church seems quite evident. There are those, however, who have questioned the very

11. Sidney E. Mead, "Protestantism in America," p. 310.
12. Joseph Bayly, "Theology Needs Geritol," p. 81.
13. Carl F. H. Henry, in "Theology for the Tent Meeting," p. 82.

possibility and legitimacy of systematic theology as an enterprise. Three objectives in particular will be considered here: the so-called "Hellenization of the gospel" thesis; the matter of the unity of the canon; and the anti-creedal element in the American religious tradition expressed in the slogan "No creed but the Bible."

### The hellenization of the gospel

The idea that virtually all Christian theology since the apostolic age represents a corruption of the simple message of Jesus by the metaphysics of Greek philosophy has been a popular one since the eighteenth century. In his *Paraphrases and Notes on the Epistles of Paul* (1705 – 7) the English philosopher John Locke argued that the original Christian faith included only a simple belief in Jesus as Messiah. Joseph Priestley, an English Unitarian, argued in his *Corruptions of Christianity* (1782) that the original Unitarian faith had been corrupted by Greek philosophy. In his inaugural address in 1819 as the Dexter Professor of Sacred Literature at Harvard, Andrews Norton, a Unitarian biblical scholar, stated that biblical criticism could rediscover the "very striking evidence of the truth of our [Unitarian] religion" by removing the "accumulated rubbish" and "technical theology" that had concealed simple scriptural truth. The "accumulated rubbish" that Norton had in mind included such doctrines as the deity of Christ, affirmed in the Nicene Creed, the formula of Chalcedon, and later confessional documents.

This point of view was further developed by Edwin Hatch in *The Influence of Greek Ideas and Usages on the Christian Church* (1900). Hatch's thesis was adopted and given wide currency by Adolf Harnack in his influential studies on the history of dogma. According to Harnack, the gospel "entered into the world, not as a doctrine, but as a joyful message. ... It stripped off these forms with amazing rapidity, and united and amalgamated itself with Greek science."[14] Harnack believed that historical research into Christian origins would reveal not the supernatural Christ of Chalcedon but a very human Jesus of Nazareth, who preached the simple yet sublime gospel of the universal fatherhood of God, the brotherhood of man, and the ethical ideal of the Sermon on the Mount. Unfortunately for Harnack and his followers, such a merely

14. Adolf Harnack, *History of Dogma*, p. 272.

human Jesus is not to be found in the sources. As later New Testament scholarship was to demonstrate so convincingly, every stratum of the gospel tradition witnessed to a Jesus who acted with divine prerogatives, displayed miraculous powers, and was imbued with an eschatological outlook quite foreign to Unitarian and liberal constructions. Harnack proposed to rediscover the "real historical Jesus" of the Gospels, but in fact succeeded only in reading his own naturalistic assumptions into the texts.

The "Hellenization" process that Harnack considered such a tragedy was in fact an aspect of the contextualization of the gospel in the church's mission to the Greco-Roman world. Terms such as *homoousios* were borrowed from the Greek language in order to preserve the gospel substance from heretical distortion. The dogmas of the church were in fact a barrier to alien philosophical assumptions, like those of Arius, which were attempting to force the mystery of the person of Christ into the confines of Greek anthropological notions. Jaroslav Pelikan is quite correct in his judgment that "in the development of both the dogmas of the early church, the trinitarian and the christological, the chief place to look for hellenization is in the speculations and heresies against which the dogma of the creeds and councils was directed."[15] The fathers borrowed terminology from their culture to preserve the mystery of the person of Christ; the heretics allowed the philosophical assumptions to control the biblical revelation and consequently distorted its substance.

Closely related to the Hellenization debate is the thesis of Thorleif Boman and other biblical scholars that the Hebrew and Greek languages express quite different views of reality. According to Boman, Hebrew thought is dynamic, while Greek is static; Hebrews emphasized hearing, and the Greeks seeing; Hebrews thought concretely, and the Greeks abstractly. According to this point of view, since biblical thought, including the New Testament, is Hebraic, its message cannot be adequately treated in the form of a systematic theology, which presupposes a Greek mode of thought. According to Otto Betz, "It is not possible to grasp the Hebrew way of thought in the Bible with the systematic principle which came from the Greek mind and wove itself into Christian dogma."[16]

15. Jaroslav Pelikan, *The Emergence of the Catholic Tradition (100–600)*, p. 55.
16. Otto Betz, "Biblical Theology, History of," p. 436.

This thesis that "a language is an implicit metaphysics" has been sharply criticized by James Barr and Eugene Nida. According to Barr, in his important study *The Semantics of Biblical Language,* facile contrasts between Greek and Hebrew thought based on philological comparisons all too often reflect an outmoded view of language reflecting philosophical idealism, a view that took shape before the rise of modern scientific linguistics. Studies such as those of Boman approach philology too atomistically, overemphasizing individual words rather than seeing sentences and larger literary units as the basic carriers of meaning. These studies also display an inadequate appreciation of the importance of modern comparative linguistics and an inadequate use of historical linguistics in etymological studies.

Eugene Nida, the accomplished linguist and Bible translator, concurs in this general line of criticism. "The idea that the Hebrew people had a completely different view of time because they had a different verbal system does not stand up under investigation," he notes. "It would be just as unfounded to claim that the people of the English speaking world have lost interest in sex because the gender distinctions in nouns and adjectives have been largely eliminated. . . . Few peoples are so little interested in time as some of the tribes in Africa, many of whose languages have far more time distinctions than any Indo-European language has."[17]

The criticisms of Barr and Nida highlight the fallacies of inferring world views and national characteristics from the accidental features of grammar, syntax, and morphology. At the same time it can be recognized that biblical thought is indeed dynamic and immersed in history, and that theology needs to understand God's being and God's action in mutual relation.

### The unity of the canon

Another line of objection holds that systematic theology in the classical sense is impossible because there is no unified canon upon which it could be based. The German New Testament scholar Ernst Käsemann sees "irreconcilable theological contraditions" in the New Testament. The canon of the New Testament, in his view, "does not, as such, constitute the foundation of the unity of the

17. Eugene A. Nida, "The Implications of Contemporary Linguistics for Biblical Scholarship," p. 83.

church. On the contrary . . . it provides the basis for the multiplic-
ity of the confessions."[18] Given Käsemann's presuppositions, there
is no one systematic theology based on the New Testament but
many possible theologies, reflecting the particular "canon within
the canon" that one happens to choose.

Käsemann's approach reflects a long tradition of historical-
critical scholarship that has majored in ferreting out "contradictions" in the text where the believing church has historically seen
complementary points of view. Käsemann's approach has the serious demerit of imputing a good deal of stupidity and obtuseness
to the early church fathers, who evidently were incapable of recognizing the doctrinal contradictions that are so obvious to critical scholars. Since conformity to the orthodox rule of faith was
one criterion used by the early church, on Käsemann's presuppositions it seems difficult to account for the formation of the New
Testament canon at all. If the contradictions had been as real as
Käsemann thought, one would expect a canon much shorter than
our present twenty-seven books.

The atomizing, contradiction-seeking critical studies of the Bible
that have been so common during the last two centuries produced
serious losses of spiritual vitality in the churches influenced by
them. The excesses of critical scholarship brought about the inevitable reaction. The biblical theology movement, the development of redaction criticism, and the newer studies of the canon
by Brevard Childs and others have focused attention on the unifying themes of scripture. James Dunn, in *Unity and Diversity in the
New Testament*, has argued that the New Testament functions as
canon in marking out the limits of acceptable diversity within
Christianity. In spite of the diversity of outlook and practice within
early Christianity, the identity of the historical Jesus of Nazareth
with the exalted Lord, the object of faith and giver of salvation,
constitutes the unifying core of the New Testament. Other unifying
elements include a common faith with the same promises (for-
giveness, salvation, Spirit); a uniform monotheism; the Jewish
scriptures as a common basis of authority; a sense of the church
as the new Israel; baptism in the name of Jesus; participation in
the Lord's Supper; the experience of the Spirit as the mark of

18. Ernst Käsemann, *Essays on New Testament Themes*, p. 103.

belonging to Christ; love of neighbor as a touchstone of Christian conduct; expectation of the return of Christ.[19]

For the evangelical, the conviction of the fundamental doctrinal unity of the canon reflects faith in God's providential control of all history. The sovereign God who works all things according to the counsel of his will (Eph. 1:11) superintended the entire traditioning process that led to the formation of the canon. In their various ways all the writers of scripture pointed to Jesus Christ, who is the center and meaning of both testaments.

### "No creed but the Bible"

Barton Stone, founder of the "Disciples" or "Christian" movement, was a frontier revivalist who was ordained as a Presbyterian but who soon found Presbyterian doctrines and polity unsuitable. Stone considered all denominational structures suspect and vowed to acknowledge "no name but Christian and no creed but the Bible." In his effort to clean the slate of church history Stone concluded that eighteen centuries of creeds, confessions, and theologies should be "consigned to the rubbish heap of human invention on which Christ was crucified." Stone's "New Testament Christianity" had no use for the historic theology of the church.

The same anti-theological sentiments can be found in a later representative of the American revival tradition, Dwight L. Moody. "My theology! I didn't know I had any," Moody declared. "I wish you would tell me what my theology is."[20] Moody saw little or no value in the study of literature, drama, or the liberal arts; the Bible alone was enough for the Christian's education.

Quite a different point of view concerning the place of theology was expressed by J. Gresham Machen in *The Origins of Paul's Religion.* For Machen, the dichotomy between doctrine and the "practical" matters of life was a false one. Machen noted that the apostle Paul was not merely a "practical" Christian "... who regarded life as superior to doctrine, and practice as superior to principle. On the contrary, he overcame the principle of Jewish particularism in the only way in which it could be overcome; he overcame principle by principle. It was not Paul the practical mis-

19. James Dunn, *Unity and Diversity in the New Testament,* pp. 370–78.
20. In Hofstadter, *Anti-Intellectualism,* p. 108.

sionary, but Paul the theologian, who was the real apostle to the Gentiles."[21]

Evangelicals can honor the Bible as the primary source and norm for faith without denying the value of earlier creeds, confessions, and church theology. To turn our backs on the heritage of tradition shows a lack of humility and slights the Holy Spirit, whose teaching ministry to the church did not cease with the apostles.

### Systematics in relation to other seminary disciplines

Systematic theology, as a servant of the church in its mission, works in partnership with the other disciplines of the seminary curriculum. The disciplines of exegesis, Christian thought, and ministry share a common task of equipping the people of God for the work of ministry, in order to bring about the obedience of faith among the nations (Eph. 4:12; Rom. 1:5).

### Exegesis and biblical theology

Exegesis and biblical theology provide the curricular foundations in the evangelical seminary. Theological reflection and the practice of ministry are to be firmly grounded in the exegesis of Holy Scripture. Only scripture can authorize theological statements, and systematic theology must continually examine the adequacy of its exegetical foundations.

At the same time, evangelicals recognize the interdependence of the various disciplines. The exegete must pursue his or her task with awareness of the systematic implications of such work, with due regard to the history of interpretation in the church, and with awareness of the unifying center of biblical revelation, which is the gospel itself. Systematic theology can help the exegete to develop greater self-critical awareness of his own presuppositions, and the needs of ministry can remind the exegete that all biblical interpretation should be a servant to the church in mission.

"Biblical theology" emerged during the eighteenth century as a discipline distinct from dogmatics. The new discipline reflected the Reformation's *sola scriptura* emphasis and the new interest in the past generated by the Renaissance and the Enlightenment. During the nineteenth century biblical theology was developed in

---

21. J. Gresham Machen, *The Origins of Paul's Religion*, p. 17.

various ways by W. M. C. de Wette, W. Vatke, J. Wellhausen, F. C. Baur, and E. W. Hengstenberg. In this century its more prominent practitioners have included Oscar Cullmann, W. F. Albright, G. E. Wright, W. Eichrodt, and Gerhard von Rad.

In distinction from systematic theology, which is concerned with the biblical text primarily in terms of what it *means*, biblical theology's concern is primarily what it *meant*.[22] Biblical theology, as a descriptive and historical discipline, seeks to understand the text, book, or testament as it would have been understood by its original audience. It seeks to "distance" the text from the modern Western consciousness. Biblical theology heightens our consciousness of the original contextualization of the biblical message. The emphasis on "distancing" or "dewesternizing" the text is an essential moment in a larger hermeneutical process which seeks to recontextualize the text in various cultures in fulfillment of the missionary task.

### Christian thought

The various disciplines of Christian thought provide hermeneutical bridges between the historical investigations and the contemporary applications of the Word of God—linkage between what it meant and what it means. Church history traces the successive contextualizations of the gospel message in the life of the church across times and cultures. The study of church history provides case studies in Christian reflection and practice which can give the contemporary church "critical distance" in evaluating its own practice of ministry. Church history, together with the history of doctrine, provides an indispensable secondary source for systematic theology in its task of recontextualizing the sources of the faith in new cultural settings.

Ethics, apologetics, and philosophy of religion presuppose the foundational bases of exegesis and systematic theology. These disciplines link the integrative focus of systematic theology and the applicative focus of the disciplines of ministry.

If systematic theology is primarily concerned with "what we are to believe concerning God," Christian ethics is concerned with "what duties God requires of us." Ethics presupposes foundations in Christian dogma, and the proper orientation of dogmatics should always be to produce "the obedience of faith."

22. Krister Stendahl, "Biblical Theology, Contemporary," p. 419.

Apologetics and philosophy of religion are integrative disciplines in that they presuppose an understanding of biblical revelation as an ordered whole. They are applicative disciplines in that they promote the evangelistic and missionary task as the church encounters alien philosophies, ideologies, and religions. As is the case with systematic theology, the ultimate goal of the study of apologetics and philosophy of religion is a kingdom-extending one: to "take every thought captive to obey Christ" (2 Cor. 10:5).

### The work of ministry

If systematic theology is primarily reflection with a view toward application, ministry is primarily application in the light of ordered reflection. Systematic theology provides hermeneutical bridges between exegesis and ministry; ministry provides the essential goal and ecclesiastical context for theological reflection. If systematic theology needs exegesis to keep it firmly grounded in scriptural norms, it needs ministry to keep it oriented toward the imperatives of mission. Ministry likewise needs exegesis and systematics to avoid immersion in the tyranny of the present and the dangers of a shallow pragmatism.

In the ministry of the church—preaching, Christian education, pastoral counseling, administration, missions and evangelism—the meaning of the gospel is fleshed out in the life of God's people. The risen Christ, through the power and presence of his Word and Spirit, continues all that he began to do and teach (Acts 1:1), equipping the church for the work of ministry, bringing the people of God to wholeness and maturity. In the context of particular historical conditions, cultures, and ethnic groups the exalted Lord, working through his called and gifted servants, continues to implement his norms for faith, life, and work. The ultimate goal of ministry, like that of the other theological disciplines, is the extension of God's reign in the world, the progressive realization of the obedience of faith among all nations.

## Method in Systematic Theology: Contextualization

### A definition

Contextualization may be defined as *the articulation of the biblical message in terms of the language and thought forms of a par-*

*ticular culture or ethnic group.*[23] Since the task of evangelical theology is inextricably linked to the Great Commission, contextualization is an essential aspect of evangelical theology's systematic method. Contextualization is concerned with the translation of the biblical message as a whole from its Hebrew and Greek originals into the thought worlds of the peoples who are being reached in mission. Systematic theology's task is to provide hermeneutical linkage between the "what it meant" dimension established by biblical theology and the "what it means" dimension of ministry and mission. Contextualization is no academic matter, but an existential necessity for effective evangelism, Bible translation, church planting, Christian social action, and pastoral ministry. The word of the gospel is no mere external word, but a message whose destiny is to "become flesh" in the lives of people in every tongue and tribe and ethnic group (Rev. 7:9).

### The need for contextualization

As implied in the foregoing definition, the need for contextualization in theology arises as the church engages in mission. It is no accident that the earliest Christian theologies arose in a missionary context. Carl Braaten is certainly correct in stating that "the original matrix of Christian theology is the missionary church."[24] Jean Daniélou has noted how the theological treatises of early Christian apologists such as Justin Martyr, Athenagoras, and Tatian "were not simply legal arguments addressed to the emperor, but also elaborations of missionary themes."[25] The essential features of Christian missionary proclamation to the pagan world were being hammered out.

The concept of contextualization is equally pertinent to foreign and domestic mission. The need to plant indigenous churches among the 16,750 ethnic groups represented by "hidden peoples" constitutes an enormous challenge for evangelical theology and

23. Much of this material has been drawn from my article "Contextualization and the Nature of Theology," in John Jefferson Davis, ed., *The Necessity of Systematic Theology* (Grand Rapids: Baker, 1978), pp. 169—90.
24. Carl Braaten, *The Flaming Center: A Theology of the Christian Mission,* p. 13.
25. Jean Daniélou, *Gospel Message and Hellenistic Culture,* p. 13.

missionary work.[26] The nationalistic tides that have swept the nations of the Third and Fourth Worlds since the Second World War have made it imperative for any effective Christian mission to distinguish the gospel message from the trappings of Western culture. The apostle Paul recognized the need to distinguish the essence of the gospel from its original Jewish cultural matrix in order to penetrate the Greco-Roman world of the first century. Today evangelical missions face the challenge of distinguishing the gospel from the Euro-American cultural forms to which it has been so intimately related for the last several centuries. The recognition of the need for fresh contextualizations of the gospel is based not only on the requirements of mission, but also on the very catholicity of the gospel itself.

The need for serious attention to the issue of contextualization is also evident on the domestic front. Why is it that in spite of an apparent resurgence of evangelical religiosity in America, evangelicals have made little impact on the shaping of American education, mass media, literature, and culture generally? Part of the answer may be that evangelical piety has largely remained bottled up in its own ecclesiastical ghetto and has achieved little significant penetration of the commanding centers of American life. The vitality of private religious experience in and of itself makes little impact on the contours of public institutions. It is indeed true that "Christ is the answer," but American evangelicals need to be more adept in discerning the broader questions posed by the contemporary crises of our age. If theological liberals have been prone to compromise the biblical substance in deference to the "modern mind," evangelicals have preserved the biblical content but have all too often failed to penetrate the modern sensibility. Extending the dominion of the exalted Christ in American life requires new contextualizations of the timeless message in our own national life.

The process of contextualization is not merely related in a prag-

26. This is not to deny the fact that the great majority of Europe's 700 million people are not presently being confronted with an effective gospel witness. The focus on the "hidden peoples" here simply reflects the fact that in this latter case greater cultural distances are involved, and consequently the need for fresh contextualizations of the gospel seem more obvious. On the needs of Europe, see "Reaching the Unreached of Europe," in the Nov.-Dec., 1981, issue of *Europe Report*, published by Greater Europe Mission.

matic sense to the tasks of missionary communication; more generally, it arises from the nature of human understanding itself. All acts of human comprehension involve a "fusion of horizons" (see pp. 274–275)[27] when a message is transmitted from a sender to a receiver. The mental horizons of the sender and receiver fuse and interpenetrate when communication is successful. The elements of the sender's message are assimilated into the thought world of the receiver, and can both expand the receiver's mental horizons and alter his way of acting in the world.

This process is illustrated in ordinary acts of learning. A student being exposed for the first time to concepts such as the unconscious, the ego, the id, the will to power, and so on comprehends these terms when they have been assimilated to his preexisting conceptual framework and then are actually used in the interpretation of new experience. "Rote learning" does not constitute comprehension in the true sense, inasmuch as the concepts are not yet part of the user's operative conceptual framework. In rote learning there is a verbal awareness of certain concepts, but they remain external to the subject's conceptual horizons in terms of ongoing action in the world. A student in a mathematics course may be able to memorize certain formulas, but genuine comprehension has not occurred until the meaning of the formulas has been so assimilated that the student is able to apply them to the solution of novel problems. The act of comprehension, or "fusion of horizons," constitutes a process in which new concepts or new frameworks of meaning literally become extensions of our minds, as physical tools become extensions of our bodies when we use them.

Comprehending the gospel, like other acts of learning, involves such a fusion of horizons. The point of ministry and mission is not to produce rote learning or mere verbal assent to Christian formulas, but rather to bring about an assimilation and internalization of the message so as to effect a lasting alteration of the subject's horizon and his action in the world. The fusion of horizons that occurs in Christian conversion is more profound than that of simple acts of learning, in that the gospel not merely produces an alteration in a preexisting conceptual framework but itself forms the basis for an entirely new integrative focus for the

---

27. Hans-Georg Gadamer, *Truth and Method,* pp. 273, 337, 358.

subject's experience of the world. The gospel is assimilated to the subject's framework of meaning, reflecting the language and traditions of a particular culture, but those elements are then reoriented around the gospel as a new integrative center and world view. Christian conversion produces a new way of experiencing the world; the convert sees the world in a new way, because in Christ he is a new creation (2 Cor. 5:17). Growth in Christian discipleship involves a progressive fusion of horizons between the mind of Christ and the mind of the believer (cf. Rom. 12:2). Contextualization, then, is not just a tool for evangelists and missionaries; it is a reflection of the nature of human understanding in general and the act of comprehending the gospel in particular.

### Antecedents of contextualization

The more immediate antecedents of contextualization are to be found in the areas of missiology, Bible translation, and liberation theology. Missionaries and Bible translators, who have long been aware of the need for indigenous churches and forms of worship, recently have been extending their concerns to the need for indigenous theologies that are both biblically orthodox and "incarnated" in the receptor cultures. New developments in the areas of linguistics, communication theory, and cross-cultural anthropology provide potentially valuable tools for systematic theology from the side of missiology.[28]

Liberation theologians such as Gustavo Gutiérrez, James Cone, José Míguez-Bonino, and others have persistently stressed the importance of the particular social context in which the church's theology functions. There is a danger here that Christian theology can be reduced to a sociology of Marxist revolution, and the gospel to a human agenda for political change. Nevertheless, it need not be disputed that every theology is implicitly contextualized in some social matrix, and liberation theology is correct in calling for self-critical awareness of the functional relation between a theo-

28. For recent discussions in this vein see Eugene Nida, *Message and Mission: The Communication of the Christian Faith* (Pasadena: William Carey, 1960) and *Religion Across Cultures* (New York: Harper, 1968); Jacob A. Loewen, *Culture and Human Values: Christian Intervention in Anthropological Perspective* (Pasadena: William Carey, 1975); David J. Hesselgrave, *Communicating Christ Cross-Culturally* (Grand Rapids: Zondervan, 1978); Charles H. Kraft, *Christianity in Culture: A Study in Dynamic Biblical Theologizing in Cross-Cultural Perspective* (Maryknoll, N.Y.: Orbis, 1979).

logy and the surrounding social structures. The gospel exists to transform unjust social structures, not to legitimate them.

In the longer perspective, the interest in contextualization reflects the emergence of a strong historical consciousness in the eighteenth and nineteenth centuries. The rise of the historical-critical method and biblical theology heightened the awareness of the cultural distance between the world of the Bible and that of the modern interpreter. The historical study of scripture focused attention on the contextualization of the message at the "starting point of the hermeneutical trajectory."

The development of historical consciousness is also reflected in the emergence of the discipline known as the sociology of knowledge. Pioneers in this field such as Emile Durkheim, Karl Mannheim, Max Weber, and Max Scheler emphasized the influence of the social environment on the shaping of all human knowledge. The origins of the discipline reflect the insights of Karl Marx, but one can derive useful insights from this discipline without adhering to the socio-economic determinism of Marx. The sociology of knowledge can be a critical tool for self-examination in evangelical theology. The danger of an enculturated gospel that mirrors the culture rather than challenging it can be as real for conservative theologies as for modernistic ones.

Prior to the 1960s existentialist theologians such as Bultmann and Tillich were involved in their own form of contextualization. In this tradition of "hermeneutical theology," the overriding question was, in the words of Tillich, "Can the Christian message be adapted to the modern mind without losing its essential and unique character?"[29] Tillich proposed a "method of correlation" to link questions from the contemporary situation and answers from biblical revelation. The concept of correlating message and situation is certainly a sound one, as long as the biblical revelation rather than the cultural situation is the normative factor in the theological agenda.

Contextualization, then, is hardly a new phenomenon. All theologies have been implicitly contextualized in various social settings. The new elements in recent discussions have been self-conscious awareness of that fact and the emergence of this theme as an important item of theological method.

---

29. Paul Tillich, *Systematic Theology*, vol. I, p. 7.

The importance of these discussions has not been lost on evangelical scholars. In a presidential address to the Evangelical Theological Society, Stanley Gundry asked, "I wonder if we really recognize that all theology represents a contextualization, even our own theology? We speak of Latin American liberation theology, black theology, or feminist theology; but without the slightest second thought we will assume that our own theology is simply theology, undoubtedly in its purest form. Do we recognize that the versions of evangelical theology held to by most people in this room are in fact North American, white, and male and that they reflect and/or address those values and concerns?"[30]

Clark Pinnock, in an inaugural lecture at McMaster Divinity College in Hamilton, Ontario, urged evangelicals to adopt a "bipolar" method in preaching and theology. "We should strive to be faithful to historic Christian beliefs taught in scripture, and *at the same time* to be authentic and responsible to the contemporary hearers."[31] Both Gundry and Pinnock agree on the need for greater self-critical awareness among evangelicals and on the need for new contextualizations of the gospel that are both contemporary and biblically sound.

### Contrasts in method

In order to bring the characteristics of contextualization into sharper focus, it will be helpful to compare this approach with other understandings of the theological task. According to Charles Hodge, the great theologian of Old Princeton, the basic task of systematic theology is "the exhibition of the facts of Scripture in their proper order and relation, with the principles of general truths involved in the facts themselves, and which pervade and harmonize the whole."[32] For the sake of convenience this view might be characterized as a "concordance" model of systematic theology. The systematic task is primarily that of an orderly arrangement of biblical doctrines, together with an elucidation of their organic relationships. Systematics organizes the "facts" of the Bible, just as the natural sciences organize the facts of nature.

There is undeniably great merit in such a conception of theol-

---

30. Stanley N. Gundry, "Evangelical Theology: Where Should We Be Going?" p. 11.
31. Clark Pinnock, "An Evangelical Theology: Conservative and Contemporary," p. 23.
32. Charles Hodge, *Systematic Theology,* p. 19.

ogy. Hodge's model clearly assigns normative priority to the teachings of scripture, as any orthodox and evangelical theology must. The method also recognizes the nature of biblical revelation as an organic whole, rather than seeing it as a fortuitous collection of historical and religious texts. At the same time, the concordance model does not take adequate account of the social context of the theological task and the historicity of all theological reflection. The method tends to promote a repetition of traditional formulations of biblical doctrine, rather than appropriate recontextualizations of the doctrines in response to changing cultural and historical conditions. In practice, of course, Hodge and the Old Princeton theologians did interact with their own intellectual and theological milieus. The point is, however, that greater methodological self-awareness in the matter of theology's relationship to its social context becomes an urgent need if Christian faith is to be effectively communicated across cultures in fulfillment of the Great Commission.

A second contrast is provided by a "synthesis" model of theology. If the concordance model pays too little attention to the social context, synthesis theologies pay too much. In a desire for timeliness and "relevance," synthesis theologies compromise the substance of the gospel, and the culture becomes a theological norm rather than simply a point of contact. H. Richard Niebuhr has characterized this stance as the "Christ of culture" motif in the history of theology. The gospel of Jesus Christ is amalgamated with the highest insights and ideals of the culture. Examples of such synthesis theologies can be found in the Gnostic movement in the early church, in the nineteenth-century liberal theology of Schleiermacher and Harnack, in the early twentieth-century modernist theologies of Harry Emerson Fosdick and Shailer Mathews, in the existentialist theologies of Bultmann and Tillich, and more recently in the theologies of revolution, secularity, and the "death of God." By compromising the distinctiveness of the gospel, synthesis theologies in practice defeat the very aims they seek to achieve—i.e., influencing and persuading the secular culture. Synthesis theologies tend to be a temporary halfway house on the road to humanism, and in a generation or two disciples of these schools not uncommonly abandon the Christian label altogether.

The method of contextualization tries to steer a middle course between "acontextual" and "synthesis" theologies. The ideal is neither a "Christ above culture" nor a "Christ of culture," but rather "Christ transforming culture." A creatively contextualized evangelical theology actively engages in conversation with the culture, immerses itself in its thought forms, but steadfastly refuses to compromise the normativeness of the gospel in the face of alien and even hostile values. Evangelical theology seeks to understand humanistic culture not in order to gain its social approval, but in order to persuade, convert, and transform it. The culture may provide the point of contact, but the gospel itself must control the shape of the theological agenda. The method of contextualization could be termed a "transformational" model, inasmuch as themes and questions of the culture are employed as vehicles of communication, but are then given new content by being taken up into a biblical framework of meaning where the gospel itself is the integrative center.

### Biblical roots of contextualization

Contextualization is not a modern idea being imposed on the Bible from without but is reflected in the very fabric of biblical revelation itself. In both testaments divine revelation is expressed through the cognitive and social forms of particular cultures, as God deals progressively with his people in history. Charles Kraft suggests that the entire Bible can be seen as an inspired collection of "canonical case studies" in the contextualization of divine revelation. As God's revelation unfolds in history, various cultural forms provide the vehicle for the message, but the authority of the message and its abiding significance derive not from the culture, but from the sovereign God who is Lord of both revelation and culture.

In the Old Testament treaty forms of the second millennium B.C. in the ancient Near East, specifying the obligations of vassal states to the conquering king, are used to express Israel's obligations to Yahweh in the Mosaic covenant. Circumcision, a rite practiced elsewhere in the ancient Near East, is filled with new meaning and becomes the emblem of God's covenant with the patriarchs. As Old Testament revelation progressively unfolds, that revelation is mediated through the varying social circumstances that characterized the patriarchal period, the time of the judges, and the institution of the Davidic monarchy. God adapts both forms of worship and legal obligations to the needs of the succeeding periods. Worship becomes centralized in Jerusalem only with the accession of David as king. The relatively simple ethical obligations of the semi-nomadic patriarchal period pass over into the more complex legal codes necessary for the regulation of life in a settled agrarian and commercial society. God's own nature was not changing; God did, however, relate to his people in terms of their as-yet imperfect level of spiritual maturity and ethical practice. Old Testament revelation was a schoolmaster pointing to Christ (cf. Gal. 3:24), and the full meaning of the lessons could be absorbed only over a long period of time.

The center of New Testament revelation is Jesus Christ, the Word made flesh (John 1:1, 14). God, in the person of the Son, contextualized himself in human culture. The preexistent Son of God left his own heavenly "culture" to become a cross-cultural missionary, incarnating himself in the full reality of a first-century, Palestinian Jewish environment. The incarnation provides the paradigm for all legitimate forms of contextualization. The message is expressed through genuinely indigenous forms, but divine revelation, and not culture, controls the content of that message.

The New Testament writers contextualize the basic kerygma in various ways. Paul uses the forensic model of justification to explain the cross to his churches; John emphasizes the theme of eternal life. The Jewish milieu of earliest Christianity is quite evident in Matthew and James; Luke and Paul are especially interested in speaking to the Gentiles.

It was the special calling of Paul, the apostle to the Gentiles (Acts 9:15; Rom. 15:16) to bring the gospel of Jesus Christ from its original setting in Jewish culture into the Greco-Roman culture of the Hellenistic world. Paul insisted that Gentile converts, in order to be accepted as first-class Christians, were not to be compelled to live like Jews (Gal. 2:14). Paul, more clearly than the other apostles, was able to distinguish the transcultural essence of the gospel from its original Jewish forms. In the pursuit of his missionary calling Paul affirmed, "To the Jews I became as a Jew. . . . To those outside the law I became as one outside the law. . . . I have become all things to all men, that I might by all means save some" (1 Cor. 9:20–22). Paul did not alter the substance of the gospel; he did, however, adapt the outward form and expression of the gospel in order to communicate to his Gentile audience.

The need to continue biblical patterns of contextualization will be more and more evident as the task of Christian mission approaches a historic "third stage" of development. In the first stage the gospel took root within Jewish culture; in the second stage Christianity penetrated the Greco-Roman world. For the last nineteen centuries the Christian church has expressed its faith almost exclusively in terms drawn from Greco-Roman culture and its Euro-American derivatives. In the third stage of mission the numerical—and, quite possibly, spiritual—center of gravity of world Christianity will be shifting from its traditional Euro-American base to an Afro-Asian one. If present trends continue, for example, by the end of this century Africa will have more Christians than any other continent. The changing realities of church growth and world mission have inescapable implications for evangelical theology's task. At this "axial point" of world history it is once again vital to implement with biblical fidelity and Spirit-led creativity the type of contextualization practiced so successfully by the apostle Paul during the earliest years of cross-cultural mission.

### Risks and benefits

There is unquestionably an element of risk involved in any attempt to recontextualize the Christian message in a new cultural setting. As missiologist Arthur F. Glasser has warned, "Unless there is a disciplined effort put forth to listen to the voice of God in the whole of Scripture, distortion of truth and deviation from its central concerns will inevitably play havoc with what many herald as insightful contextualizing of theology and praxis."[33]

As is the case with other theological terms, "contextualization" can bear dramatically differing meanings, depending upon the presuppositions of the users. There is always the danger that, in the pursuit of communicable relevance, the substance of the gospel will be compromised through its amalgamation with non-Christian religious traditions or humanistic ideologies. But in spite of these potential hazards, recontextualizations must be attempted. Church history has shown that the gospel has in fact crossed many cultural boundaries without losing its essential substance. And Clark Pinnock, in a reference to the apologetic significance of the incarnation, noted that "Jesus Christ has

33. Arthur F. Glasser, "Help from an Unexpected Quarter or, the Old Testament and Contextualization," p. 409.

demonstrated that it is possible to penetrate culture without being assimilated by it."[34]

It should also be noted that more "traditional" understandings of missionary communication also have their risks. If a syncretizing "overcontextualization" of the message has its dangers, a traditionalistic "undercontextualization" of the message has dangers as well. The apostle Paul's Judaizing opponents, by too closely identifying the essence of the gospel with its original milieu of Jewish law and culture, not only were laying obstacles to the progress of mission, but were distorting the heart of the message itself. There is certainly a "heresy of innovation," but there can be a "heresy of tradition" as well. In the pursuit of its mission the church must be equally averse to compromising the gospel in the name of relevance and to fossilizing the message in any single cultural form.

A number of the benefits of contextualization have already been mentioned (pp. 61–63). A proper recontextualization of the gospel message can assist the church in achieving greater penetration of cultures both at home and abroad. The point of mission is not simply to "broadcast" the gospel, but to bring about the conversion and discipleship of individuals and the transformation of societies, the "obedience of faith among the nations." Insofar as effective communication is integral to achieving this goal, contextualization has a role to play. In the final analysis, of course, the sovereign power of the Spirit of God and the spiritual vitality of the church are more crucial than any methodology for the success of Christian missions. At the same time, methodological improvements should not be ignored.

The task of contextualization has implications for the way in which we hear the gospel as well as for the way we proclaim it to others. As R. H. S. Boyd has pointed out, if we really believe in one, holy, *catholic* church, then "the church in any land must be conscious of the rest of the world, of the *oikoumene*, for the Church of Christ is a fellowship which transcends space and time, and international cross-cultural contacts provide great enrichment."[35] Western Christians need to be willing to listen to and learn from the biblical insights of their Asian, African, and Latin American

34. Clark Pinnock, *Set Forth Your Case*, p. 138.
35. R. H. S. Boyd, *India and the Latin Captivity of the Church: The Cultural Context of the Gospel*, p. 139.

fellow believers. Wrestling with the issues posed by contextualization can make us more aware of the distinction between the essence of the gospel and our own culture, and consequently more sensitive to what the Spirit may be saying through the churches of the Third and Fourth Worlds.

## Bibliography

Baker, John Austin. "Postscript," in Jean Daniélou, *Gospel and Hellenistic Culture*. Philadelphia: Westminster, 1973.

Barker, Glenn W.; Lane, William L.; and Michaels, J. Ramsey. *The New Testament Speaks*. New York: Harper, 1969.

Barr, James. *The Semantics of Biblical Language*. London: Oxford University Press, 1961.

Bayly, Joseph. "Theology Needs Geritol," *Eternity*, Nov., 1977, p. 81.

Betz, Otto. "Biblical Theology, History of," *Interpreter's Dictionary of the Bible*. Nashville: Abingdon, 1962.

Black, Max. *Models and Metaphors*. Ithaca: Cornell University Press, 1962.

Boman, Thorleif. *Hebrew Thought Compared with Greek*. Philadelphia: Westminster, 1960.

Boyd, R. H. S. *India and the Latin Captivity of the Church: The Cultural Context of the Gospel*. London: Cambridge University Press, 1974.

Braaten, Carl. *The Flaming Center: A Theology of the Christian Mission*. Philadelphia: Fortress, 1977.

Brown, Jerry Wayne. *The Rise of Biblical Criticism in America, 1800–1870*. Middletown, Conn.: Wesleyan University Press, 1969.

Brunner, Emil. *The Christian Doctrine of God*. Philadelphia: Westminster, 1950.

Cone, James H. *Black Theology of Liberation*. New York: Harper and Row, 1970.

Conze, Edward. *Buddhism*. New York: Harper Torchbooks, 1959.

Daniélou, Jean. *Gospel Message and Hellenistic Culture*. Philadelphia: Westminster, 1973.

Dunn, James. *Unity and Diversity in the New Testament*. Philadelphia: Westminster, 1977.

Gadamer, Hans-Georg. *Truth and Method*. New York: Seabury, 1975.

Geisler, Norman L. *Philosophy of Religion*. Grand Rapids: Zondervan, 1974.

Glasser, Arthur F. "Help from an Unexpected Quarter or, the Old Testament and Contextualization," *Missiology* 7 (1979):403–9.

Graham, Billy. In "Candid Conversation with the Evangelist," *Christianity Today*, July 17, 1981, pp. 18 – 24.

Gundry, Stanley N. "Evangelical Theology: Where Should We Be Going?" *Journal of the Evangelical Theological Society* 22(1979):11.

Gutiérrez, Gustavo. *A Theology of Liberation.* Maryknoll, N.Y.: Orbis, 1973.

Harnack, Adolf. *History of Dogma.* 1885; rpt. New York: Dover, 1961.

Hatch, Edwin. *The Influence of Greek Ideas on Christianity.* 1890; rpt. New York: Harper, 1957.

Hengel, Martin. "Die Ursprünge der Christlichen Mission," *New Testament Studies* 18 (1971—72):18.

Henry, Carl F. H. In "Theology for the Tent Meeting," *Time,* Feb. 14, 1977, p. 82.

Hesse, Mary. "Models and Analogy in Science," *Encyclopedia of Philosophy.* New York: Macmillan, 1967.

Hodge, Charles. *Systematic Theology.* 1873; rpt. Grand Rapids: Eerdmans, 1960.

Hofstadter, Richard. *Anti-Intellectualism in American Life.* New York: Knopf, 1963.

Käsemann, Ernst. *Essays on New Testament Themes.* London: SCM, 1964.

Machen, J. Gresham. *The Origins of Paul's Religion.* New York: Macmillan, 1923.

Mead, Sidney E. "Protestantism in America," *Church History* 23 (1954):291 — 320.

Mondin, Battista. *The Principle of Analogy in Protestant and Catholic Theology.* The Hague: Martinus Nijhoff, 1968.

Nida, Eugene A. "The Implications of Contemporary Linguistics for Biblical Scholarship," *Journal of Biblical Literature* 91 (1972):73—89.

Pannenberg, Wolfhart. *Theology and the Philosophy of Science.* Philadelphia: Westminster, 1976.

Pelikan, Jaroslav. *The Emergence of the Catholic Tradition* (100—600). Chicago: University of Chicago Press, 1971.

Pinnock, Clark. "An Evangelical Theology: Conservative and Contemporary," *Christianity Today,* Jan. 5, 1979, p. 23.

————. *Set Forth Your Case.* Chicago: Moody, 1971.

Rushdoony, R. J. *The Necessity for Systematic Theology.* Vallecito, Calif.: Ross House, 1979.

Scharfstein, Ben-Ami, *et al. Philosophy East/Philosophy West.* New York: Oxford University Press, 1978.

Stendahl, Krister. "Biblical Theology, Contemporary," *Interpreter's Dictionary of the Bible.* Nashville: Abingdon, 1962.

Tillich, Paul. *Systematic Theology.* Chicago: University of Chicago Press, 1967.

Wells, David F. *The Search for Salvation.* Downers Grove, Ill.: Inter-Varsity, 1978.

Woodbridge, John D.; Noll, Mark A.; and Hatch, Nathan O. *The Gospel in America.* Grand Rapids: Zondervan, 1979.

# 3

## Divine Revelation

### Meaning and Existence of Revelation

"The royal dominion of God—this is the central point of his message—everything else turns on this, both his action and his speech."[1] This characterization by Emil Brunner of Jesus' proclamation rightly points to the kingdom of God as its crucial and unifying theme. In this chapter, as we explore the meaning, nature, and historical impact of divine revelation, the dominion motif will be a central concern. Divine revelation is the foundation of evangelical theology, and evangelical theology's task is not only to refine our understanding of God, but also to further the extension of God's reign in the world. As R. J. Rushdoony has noted, the Bible, as the normative deposit of God's revelation, "is a manual for dominion under God: it declares God's word and requirements, and it summons man to obey."[2] The ultimate goal of theological reflection is the goal of divine revelation itself: the realization of the "obedience of faith among all the nations."

### Meaning of revelation

Revelation could be defined as the "significant self-disclosure of God to man."[3] In his words and deeds God makes known his

1. Emil Brunner, *The Mediator*, p. 556.
2. R. J. Rushdoony, *The Necessity for Systematic Theology*, p. 57.
3. W. Mundle, "Revelation," p. 309.

name, his purposes, his ways, his will, his mysteries, his covenant, and his salvation in Jesus Christ.

The scriptures employ a variety of terms to express the concept of divine revelation. Among the more important are gālāh, "remove" or "uncover"; ἀποκαλύπτω and ἀποκάλυψις, "uncover, uncovering"; ἐπιφάνεια, "appearing"; δηλόω, "reveal, make clear, explain"; σημαίνω, "show, make known"; φανερόω, "manifest"; χρηματίζω, "reveal."

In the Bible revelation is a process initiated by God; it is a divine gift and bestowal, not a human insight or achievement. "What no eye has seen, nor ear heard, nor the heart of man conceived . . . God has revealed to us through the Spirit" (1 Cor. 2:9–10. Man is utterly dependent upon God for the knowledge of salvation and for knowledge of the ultimate meaning and destiny of human existence. Divine revelation is thus the criticism of all forms of human pretension to autonomy, pride, and self-aggrandizement, whether by an individual, an institution, or a nation. The Spirit-laden words of the prophets and apostles "have divine power to destroy strongholds . . . and every proud obstacle to the knowledge of God," and have the power to "take every thought captive to obey Christ" (2 Cor. 10:4–5).

In a broader sense revelation can be understood as involving an entire chain of events linking the original act-words of God, inspired reflection and inscripturation subsequent to them, the process of canonization, and acts of illumination by the Holy Spirit. All are actions of the sovereign God, who works all historical events according to his redemptive purposes (Eph. 1:11), and makes his will known through these word-acts preserved in scripture.

God reveals his nature and will in order to establish and extend his reign in the church and in the world. As Brunner has written, "God reveals himself because he wills to reign. The first aim of his speech is that he should rule. To believe, therefore, simply means to obey, . . . to yield to the attraction of his will, and to renounce utterly all attempt at resistance."[4]

In the Old Testament the God of Israel demonstrates his reality and lordship in history through his acts of judgment on Pharaoh's Egypt (Exod. 10:2) and by his victory at the Red Sea (Exod. 14:31).

4. Brunner, *The Mediator,* p. 550.

In his acts of judgment on an oppressive government and a system of false religion, Yahweh acts that Israel "may know that I am the Lord." In Egypt the Lord of Israel acted by "war, by a mighty hand and an outstretched arm" (Deut. 4:34), defeating his enemies, and gathering a covenant people for himself. Rahab the harlot recognizes the reality of Israel's God on the basis of his victorious conquests (Josh. 2:9—11). In the contest with the priests of Baal, Elijah is confident that Yahweh, the "God who answers by fire" (1 Kings 18:24), can make himself known as the true God in Israel (18:36). For Elijah, divine revelation comes not only as the "still, small voice," but also as the powerful act of God in space and time that triumphs over false religion in the conflicts of public history.

King Hezekiah prays for deliverance from Sennacharib, the Assyrian commander who is besieging Jerusalem and reviling the God of Israel as he has reviled the impotent gods of the conquered nations. "O Lord, our God," prays Hezekiah, "save us from his hand, that all the kingdoms of the earth may know that thou alone art the Lord" (Isa. 37:20). God rebuked the arrogance of Sennacharib by sending an angel of death that slew a hundred and eighty-five thousand in the Assyrian camp (37:36). God's reality was again demonstrated in the crisis of combat and the conflicts of history.

The prophet Ezekiel declares that the God of Israel is known in his judgments against the nations. His reality and power will be revealed in judgments against the Ammonites (25:7), against Moab (25:11), against Edom (25:14; 35:15), against the Philistines (25:17), against Tyre (26:6), against Egypt (29:17—21), and in the eschatological destruction of Gog (38:23). The refrain is constantly repeated: "Then they will know that I am the Lord." For Ezekiel, God's revelation is not known merely in private, pietistic experiences, but dramatically in the arena of world history, where God is bringing to ruin and destruction kingdoms and ideologies that defy his laws, his justice, and his truth.

The prophet Jeremiah is told that the divine word will judge kingdoms and nations. "See, I have set you this day over nations and over kingdoms, to pluck up and to break down, to destroy and to overthrow" (1:10). God's word is a fire, and a hammer which breaks the rock in pieces (23:29). If any nation will not be subject to that word—whether Judah or the Soviet Union or the United

States—"then I will utterly pluck it up and destroy it, says the Lord" (12:17).

As a man of inspired wisdom, Daniel is privileged to understand the mysteries of God. Daniel announces to the proud Nebuchadnezzar that he will experience temporary insanity and eat the grass of the field like a wild beast "till you know that the Most High rules the kingdom of men, and gives it to whom he will" (4:25). When human governments and institutions reject the revealed law-word of the sovereign God, society totters on the brink of insanity and barbarism.

In the New Testament age the arrival and victorious advance of the reign of God in the world continues to be a crucial theme, especially in the preaching of Jesus Christ himself. "The witness of the Baptist by word and deed (Matt. 3:2) and especially the initial preaching of Jesus (Mark 1:15) imply that God is now coming out of his previous concealment and that he will manifest his kingdom and usher in the promised time of salvation."[5] In the person, power, and preaching of Jesus the kingdom is arriving; the "kingdom of God is at hand." The divine revelation in Jesus is manifested and confirmed in his power over the agents of the kingdom of Satan. Jesus' exorcisms point to the inbreaking of God's Kingdom. "If it is by the finger of God that I cast out demons, then the kingdom of God has come upon you" (Luke 11:20). As Brunner has observed, in these powerful acts "he *commands* the demons. He is the victorious Divine Warrior; the demons are aware of this power when he confronts them; it is this which causes them to fear and tremble."[6]

The Jesus of history who revealed his divine authority and power in the destruction of the works of the devil (1 John 3:8) continues to do so as the ascended and exalted Lord of the church and world. Through the church he continues to wage war against the principalities and powers—whether lodged in governments, courts, educational systems, the mass media, or false religions—wherever God's laws, justice, and truth are being opposed. The apostle Paul prays that believers will have their eyes opened to a fuller revelation of the unsurpassable power of the risen Christ—a spiritual power available to the church in its mission in the

5. Albrecht Oepke, "ἀποκαλύπτω, ἀποκάλυψις," III, 580.
6. Brunner, *The Mediator*, p. 557.

conflicts of history (Eph. 1:15—23). The New Testament closes with
the unveiling of the magnificent vision of the exalted Christ, who
is Lord of lords and King of kings (Rev. 19:16), who rides forth in
the conflicts of history to judge and make war on his enemies.

The biblical word of revelation is not only a soul-saving word
but a world-shaking word as well. It is especially this latter aspect
that American evangelicalism, shaped by its pietistic and revivalistic heritage, needs to recover in our own day. The word of divine
revelation that conquers sin, death, and hell is also the word that
overcomes the world.

### Denials of the reality of revelation

Denials of the reality and meaningfulness of divine revelation
have been frequent and influential since the seventeenth century.
Naturalistic explanations of the universe and the meaning of human existence gained special prominence during the nineteenth
century through the influence of modern science and the philosophies of Darwin, Marx, and Freud.

A "positivistic" or purely naturalistic outlook on reality was articulated by the French philosopher Auguste Comte (1798—1857),
who identified three stages of human history. The first stage was
the theological (or "fictitious"), when man explained his experience of the world in terms of the gods. The second was the metaphysical (or "abstract") stage, when man began to develop
philosophic systems. The third stage, represented by Comte's own
outlook, was the scientific (or "positive") stage, where reality was
understood in terms of the categories of mathematics and the
natural sciences. There was, of course, no place for the supernatural or for divine revelation in this "enlightened" third stage of
human consciousness.

This positivistic outlook has been continued more recently in
the philosophy of A. J. Ayer, an advocate of the view known as
logical positivism. In his widely read *Language, Truth and Logic*,
Ayer expounded his "principle of verification": a sentence is meaningful if the proposition it expresses is either analytic or empirically verifiable.[7] The sentence "All liars distort the truth" is analytic,
or true by definition. The meaning of the predicate is contained

---

7. A. J. Ayer, *Language, Truth and Logic*, p. 5.

in the subject. On the other hand, a sentence such as "Water passes from the liquid to the gaseous state under the application of sufficient heat" is empirically verifiable. Its truth may be confirmed by laboratory experiment. All meaningful statements, argued Ayer, are subsumable under these two categories. Consequently, religious statements, being neither analytic nor empirically verifiable, are meaningless.[8] "All utterances about the nature of God are nonsensical," Ayer asserted.[9]

Critics were not slow to point out that Ayer's own principle of verification was neither analytic nor empirically verifiable. How then was its meaningfulness to be established? The principle then appeared in its true light—i.e., as a metaphysical statement of the sort that Ayer had intended to exclude. This principle of verification actually contained a *selective* metaphysical prejudice; the metaphysical assumptions of an Augustine or a Plato were screened out, but not Ayer's own naturalistic metaphysics. Like Kant before him, Ayer had defined "experience" (the "empirical") as naturalistic experience. Religious experience is not allowed to count as evidence, being ruled out by definition from the outset.

Ayer's strictures create more problems for liberal and neo-orthodox theologies than for classical evangelicalism, which roots its truth claims in the events and experiences of space, time, and history. The claim that the tomb of Jesus was empty on Easter morning is not merely a claim about private, subjective experience. The claim is made in relation to realities that were accessible to public investigation. If Christ is not risen from the dead (external historical event), faith (subjective reality) is worthless; "you are still in your sins" (1 Cor. 15:17). Evangelical theology, grounded in the bodily resurrection of Jesus Christ in space and time, accepts the risks of historical falsification, but in so doing avoids the charge of using theological language that is vacuous and equivocal.

By all accounts Charles Darwin must be reckoned as one of the prime shapers of the modern naturalistic sensibility. His *Origin of Species* (1859) and *The Descent of Man* (1871) offered explanations of the varieties of living forms and the origins of man that made

---

8. There are those, of course, who would argue that theological statements such as "God exists" or "God is benevolent" are analytic, but for the purposes of this discussion our main concern is with Ayer's contention concerning the empirical nonverifiability of religious language.

9. Ayer, *Language, Truth and Logic*, p. 115.

no appeal to supernatural factors or to the biblical story. While Darwin's work of 1859 presented no explicit frontal assault on the Christian convictions of the Victorian England in which he lived, the total impact of the *Origin of Species* was such as to promote religious skepticism in society at large and in Darwin himself. Reflecting on the impact of Darwinism from a later vantage point, the American philosopher William James could observe "a new sort of religion of Nature, which has entirely displaced Christianity from the thought of a large part of our generation." Some years after the publication of *Origin of Species* Darwin stated, "For myself, I do not believe that there ever has been any revelation."

Darwin's skepticism concerning revelation has been perpetuated among his followers. Julian Huxley, writing in *The Humanist Frame*, bases his humanistic faith squarely on an evolutionary understanding of reality. "In the evolutionary pattern of thought," according to Huxley, "there is no longer either need or room for the supernatural."[10] Like the earth itself, and man, the various religions evolved, but are destined "to disappear in competition with other truer and more embracing thought organizations."[11] With God out of the picture Huxley does not hesitate to draw the ethical consequences. Humanistic and evolutionary man "will have nothing to do with Absolutes, including absolute truth, absolute morality, absolute perfection and absolute authority."[12] Moral absolutes are the expression of the mistaken notions of a bygone age. Just how modern man is to summon the moral strength to resist Marxist-Leninism and other forms of totalitarianism that absolutize the state, Huxley does not tell us.

Along with Darwin, Karl Marx was another chief contributor to the anti-revelational ideologies of the modern era. According to Marx, "Man makes religion, religion does not make man. . . . Religion is only the illusory sun that revolves around man so long as he does not revolve around himself." For Marx, "man is the highest being for man"; religion is only the "opiate of the people" which must be abolished if oppressive social conditions are themselves to be abolished.[13]

Marx's animus against revealed religion has been perpetuated

10. Julian Huxley, ed., *The Humanist Frame*, p. 18.
11. Ibid., p. 19.
12. Ibid., p. 14.
13. Karl Marx, *On Religion*, pp. 35–36.

in later expressions of Marxist-Leninist doctrine. In the "Programme of the Communist International" (1928), a modern restatement of the *Communist Manifesto* of 1848, it is declared that "one of the most important tasks of the cultural revolution ... is the task of systematically and unswervingly combatting religion—the opium of the people." The proletarian state, while granting formal freedom of worship, "carries on anti-religious propaganda with all the means at its command and reconstructs the whole of its educational work on the basis of scientific materialism."[14] Marxist-Leninist dogma can allow no challenges to the totalitarian powers and pretensions embodied in the Marxist-Leninist state.

Together with Darwin and Marx, Sigmund Freud was a chief architect of the anti-theistic outlook of the modern age. His theories concerning the unconscious and the influence of infantile sexuality on human behavior have become part of the warp and woof of modern thought. Freud's theories offered a new way of interpreting not only psychological phenomena but human culture as a whole—a world view in direct competition with biblical theism. According to Freud, religious beliefs are expressions of wish fulfillment. They are "illusions, fulfillments of the oldest, strongest and most urgent wishes of mankind."[15] In its monotheistic forms religion replaces a fallible human father with an infallible divine one in order to protect the human psyche from the threatening forces of nature, fate, and human society itself. Revelation, then, is not a transcendent message from beyond human experience but the projection of man's own psychological needs and wishes on the screen of the infinite.

It is, of course, possible to criticize the various theories of Darwin, Marx, Freud, and other naturalistic thinkers on internal and theoretical grounds, and this has been done in various ways during the last century. At this juncture in history, however, it seems especially important to emphasize the practical evaluation of these anti-revelational theories and their practical refutation in the conflicts of public history.

Friedrich Engels proposed a pragmatic vindication of his own socialist theories: "The success of our actions proves the correspondence of our perception with the objective nature of the ob-

---

14. Emile Burns, *Handbook of Marxism*, pp. 1009–10.
15. Sigmund Freud, *The Future of an Illusion*, p. 30.

jects perceived."[16] In the long run, Engels believed, a true theory would be vindicated by its success in transforming the present world into a more just and humane society. False theories would be exposed as such by the dialectics of history.

Evangelical theology, based on the reality of the lordship of the risen Christ and a confidence in the progressive extension of the kingdom of God in history, does not shrink from a "trial by combat" with its ideological opponents. Evangelical theology is confident that divine revelation does provide the truest account of reality, and hence the basis for successful action in history.

Jesus said, "You will know them by their fruits" (Matt. 7:16). The long-term fruits of anti-revelational humanism have been bitter indeed in this century: the Stalinist murder of millions in the name of social justice, so chillingly chronicled in Solzhenitsyn's *Gulag Archipelago*; the murder of millions by the Marxist rulers of Cambodia; a million abortions a year in the United States; the widespread occurrence of mental illness and sexually transmitted diseases; rampant divorce; the breakdown of the family; declining achievement in public education; new surges of crime in the streets and acts of terrorism on the international front. The dialectics of history have not been kind to the pretensions of anti-revelational ideologies that promised heaven on earth without the God of heaven.

The evangelical community must, like Elijah of old, have the confidence that the truth of its claims can be vindicated in the struggles of history, that its God has the power "to answer by fire." Early Christians living in the Roman Empire did not shrink from the contest, and the church eventually saw the pagan gods of Rome relegated to the dustbin of history. So it must be today that evangelical Christianity must seek from God fresh spiritual power to vindicate the claims of Christ's kingdom in the struggles of law, public policy, education, and the economy. The kingdom of God consists not in talk, but in the demonstration of the Spirit and of power (1 Cor. 2:4; 4:20).

### Competing revelation claims

The advance of the kingdom of Christ in the world is opposed not only by those who deny the very existence and reality of divine

---

16. V. I. Lenin, *Materialism and Empirio-Criticism*, p. 137.

revelation, but also by those who make competing revelation claims. Why should the nations receive the Bible as the true revelation of God, rather than the Koran or the Bhagavad Gita? What about the claims of religious leaders such as Mary Baker Eddy and Joseph Smith and Sun Myung Moon, who claim to be the recipients of new revelations? The reality of competing revelation claims raises the issue of apologetics, which will be discussed further in relation to faith and reason (see pp. 130–141), but which calls for some preliminary consideration at this juncture.

The problem of conflicting revelation claims did not arise with the modern cults, or even in the early church. Already in the Old Testament the existence of false prophets threatened the faith and unity of the community of Israel. Micaiah contended with the false prophets gathered in the court of King Ahab of Israel (1 Kings 22). Jeremiah experienced frequent conflict with the false prophets of Judah who failed to warn the kingdom of God's impending judgment (2:26; 6:13–14; 14:13; 18:18; 23:9–22; 26:7–8; 27–29) and who themselves had become morally corrupt. Ezekiel spoke out against the false prophets who prophesied peace for Jerusalem in spite of its covenant breaking (13:16). Micah strongly criticized the false prophets who led the people astray and who were motivated by mercenary, man-pleasing desires (3:5).

The Old Testament gives several criteria for testing those who claim to be speaking for God. First of all, there is the question of the prophet's character and motivation. Are mercenary considerations prominent? Micah exposes the carnal motivation of those "who cry 'Peace' when they have something to eat, but declare war against him who puts nothing into their mouths" (3:5). These men-pleasing "prophets" tell the people what they want to hear— especially when they are being well paid. Unlike Amaziah, who is overly concerned with King Jeroboam's good opinion, Amos values his independence and the freedom to speak the prophetic word which that freedom brings (7:10–15).

In the second place, the fulfillment or nonfulfillment of the alleged prophecy is presented as a test. "When a prophet speaks in the name of the Lord, if the word does not come to pass or come true, that is a word which the Lord has not spoken; the prophet has spoken it presumptuously, you need not be afraid of him" (Deut. 18:22; cf. Jer. 28:9; Isa. 41:22–23; 42:9). The true God, unlike the false prophets and the idols of the nations, has the power to foretell the future because the future, like all history, is under his control.

This emphasis on historical fulfillment is important to retain in the face of the widespread tendency in critical scholarship to minimize or deny altogether the predictive element in prophecy. While the Old Testament prophets are largely concerned with speaking to their own times and circumstances in the light of the Great King's covenant demands, only a seriously distorted reading of the text can suppress the predictive element in it.

The matter of historical fulfillment is also important in relation to the common tendency in modern theology to attempt to insulate divine revelation from historical and empirical verification. Barth insists that there are no external tests for the Word of God; we can only grasp its truth from within the arch of the obedience of faith (*Church Dogmatics I*, 2, 535). There is no place for "rational" or "evidential" apologetics. In similar fashion Bultmann claims that the "word of preaching confronts us as the word of God. It is not for us to question its credentials."[17] Faith and unbelief are not arbitrary decisions, says Bultmann, because it is a matter of accepting or rejecting "that which alone can illuminate our understanding of ourselves."[18]

The Barthian and Bultmannian emphases reflect biblical revelation insofar as they point to faith as essential for a saving understanding of the gospel. It is true that without the illumination of the Holy Spirit man cannot comprehend the saving significance of divine revelation (1 Cor. 2:4 – 16; 2 Cor. 3:6 – 18; Eph. 2:18; Matt. 16:17). The Achilles' heel of this position, however, is that when the link between the revealed message and its historical and empirical moorings is severed, the basis for distinguishing true and spurious revelation claims is seriously eroded. Bultmann really has no good answer to the question, "Why believe the Bible rather than the Koran?"—especially in the face of the claim of a Muslim believer that the Koran "illuminates his self-understanding" in a definitive way. And are there not those who believe that the claims of Mary Baker Eddy or Joseph Smith have illuminated *their* self-understanding? An appeal to an almost exclusively subjective cri-

17. Rudolf Bultmann, *Existence and Faith*, p. 41.
18. Ibid., p. 42.

terion such as "self-understanding" is thoroughly inadequate as an answer to the claims of the new religious movements.

The dilemma of the neo-orthodox position at this point has been highlighted by Antony Flew in his well-known essay, "Theology and Falsification," in *New Essays in Philosophical Theology.* "Sophisticated religious people," notes Flew, "tend to refuse to allow . . . that anything conceivably could occur, which could count against their theological assertions and explanations."[19] In other words, modern theologians such as Barth and Bultmann attempt to shield their claims from all possibility of empirical falsification. The result, however, as Flew rightly points out, is that such theological language becomes vacuous and equivocal. Evangelical theology, on the other hand, makes claims that are in principle falsifiable. The claim that Jesus rose bodily from the dead implies that the tomb was really empty and that the body of Jesus is not to be found on this planet. By adopting an anti-supernaturalistic understanding of scientific law, neo-orthodox theologians have removed essential apologetic ground from beneath their feet.

There is yet a third criterion in the Old Testament for distinguishing true and false prophecy. With respect to the content of the message, the true prophet characteristically speaks in a way that is contrary to the "conventional wisdom." When the people are complacent and self-satisfied, the prophet warns of judgment; when they are enveloped in pessimism and despair, the prophet brings words of hope. The false prophet, on the other hand, cries "Peace" when judgment is needed (1 Kings 22; Mic. 3:5; Jer. 28), or judgment when consolation and hope is called for (cf. Jer. 29:11; Amos 9:11–12; Isa. 7:1–9). The true prophet tells the people what they *need* to hear; the false prophet what they *want* to hear.

The true prophet courageously challenges the moral consensus of the age. As Oepke has observed, the "true revelation of God hales corrupt and sinful nature mercilessly to judgment, and then leads on through judgment to grace and salvation."[20] This observation provides a timely warning to an externally prosperous American evangelicalism that finds it easier to speak of grace and salvation than to hale "corrupt and sinful nature mercilessly to judgment." Are success and social respectability blunting the cut-

---

19. Antony Flew and Alasdair MacIntyre, eds., *New Essays in Philosophical Theology,* p. 106.

20. Oepke, "ἀποκαλύπτω, ἀποκάλυψις," III, 576.

ting edge of evangelical preaching? Is there a danger that establishment evangelicalism could become a form of false prophecy?

In his pointedly titled study, *The Worldly Evangelicals*, Richard Quebedeaux has noted that "in the course of establishing their respectability in the eyes of the wider society, the evangelicals have become harder and harder to distinguish from other people."[21] He goes on to observe that some "evangelical women are taking advantage of abortion on demand. ... In 1976 there emerged a fellowship and information organization for practicing evangelical lesbians and gay men and their sympathizers."[22] While establishment evangelicals have spoken out against racism, poverty, and world hunger, the trumpet has sounded less clearly on issues that are not considered socially acceptable by the dominant secular humanist media—e.g., abortion, infanticide, homosexuality, fornication. Where the *Washington Post* and *New York Times* have not given their nod of approval, has establishment evangelicalism been prone to proclaim a lukewarm message, leaving any unpleasantness to fundamentalists and pre-Vatican II Roman Catholics? In order to avoid the danger of an enculturated form of false prophecy, the evangelical community as a whole would do well to ponder the sharp words of Dante: "The hottest places in hell are reserved for those who, in a time of great moral crisis, maintain their neutrality."

In the New Testament the struggle between true and false revelation continues. Miracles can attest the true revelation and have real evidential value (Matt. 11:4–6; 12:28; John 5:36; 20:31; Acts 2:43), but at the same time the church is warned about counterfeit miracles (Mark 13:22; 2 Thess. 2:9). Satan can appear as an angel of light (2 Cor. 11:14)—a timely warning in relation to the "Being of Light" reportedly encountered in so-called "life after life" experiences. And despite the claims of a Joseph Smith, angelic visitations are no assurances of true revelation (Gal. 1:8); claims which are inconsistent with the apostolic doctrines delivered once and for all to the saints (Jude 3) are to be rejected.

As in the Old Testament, the character of a prophet should be consistent with the message. "You will know them by their fruits" (Matt. 7:16). The message of the true servant of God produces

21. Richard Quebedeaux, *The Worldly Evangelicals*, p. 14.
22. Ibid., p. 117.

holiness and love in the lives of both bearer and receivers, rather than the destructive and deadly consequences of the teaching of a Jim Jones.

The true Spirit of God glorifies Jesus Christ (John 16:14) and not the pretensions of a human leader. The true Word of God produces a life of love (1 John 4:8) and obedience to the commands of Jesus Christ (John 14:21) and not the antinomianism of a situation ethic.

In the wider context of world religions the Christian faith makes unique claims. Alone among the world's great religions Christianity makes the claim that its founder, Jesus of Nazareth, a historically identifiable individual, was the very incarnation of God and overcame death by being resurrected in space and time. Unlike the revelation claims of many other religions those of Christianity are, at crucial points, open to empirical falsification. "If Christ has not been raised, your faith is worthless and you are still in your sins" (1 Cor. 15:17). The Christian faith affirms that the body of Jesus was not found in the tomb on Easter morning, because Jesus had truly and supernaturally been raised from the dead.

Because the evangelical faith is convinced that Christ is risen and is now enthroned with plenipotentiary authority at the Father's right hand, it expects a progressive verification of the truth of the Christian position in history. It believes that in the long run truth is stronger than error, and that the Word of Jesus Christ is stronger than the word of Mohammed, Buddha, Krishna, Marx, Lenin, or any other so-called prophet. The risen Christ is active even now as the Lord of history and of the kingdoms of this world, extending his kingdom on earth and exposing the claims of false religions. The evangelical faith is realistic about the opposition, suffering, and conflict to be encountered by the advancing church in its mission, but is not pessimistic about the fortunes of the gospel in history. A proper view of the plenipotentiary power of the exalted Christ (Eph. 1:16–23) banishes defeatist attitudes among the people of God and gives them courage for the ongoing struggles with their enemies. Evangelical theology is a theology of victory, because it is a theology based on the victory of the resurrected, exalted, and reigning Christ. It looks beyond the progressive verification of the Christian message in history to the eschatological verification of the message at the end of history, at the parousia. Then at the name of Jesus every knee will bow, "and every tongue confess that Jesus Christ is Lord" (Phil. 2:10–11).

Within history the Christian position may be dialectically contested in various ways, but at the end of history God himself in the resplendent glory of Jesus Christ will forever put an end to all dispute, and "God will be all in all."

## The Nature of Revelation

### Distinctions: general and special revelation

It has been customary in the history of theology to distinguish God's "general" and "special" revelation. Special revelation can be defined as that knowledge of God and his will which is given to a particular community. The revelation given to Israel and the early church and recorded in the scriptures of the Old and New Testaments constitutes the normative deposit of special revelation for evangelical theology. General revelation can be defined as that knowledge of God and his will which is given to mankind as a whole through nature, conscience, and history. In this section our focus will be on general revelation, since special revelation will receive detailed discussion in Chapter 6.

Both general and special revelation are integrally related to the royal dominion of God. General revelation, as God's "universal kingdom-word," presses the claims of God's moral authority on the consciences of all men. Special revelation, God's "particular kingdom-word," presses God's claims on the hearts of his chosen people, the church.

The Bible clearly teaches that there is an awareness of the Creator outside the boundaries of the covenant community. The psalmist declares, "The heavens are telling the glory of God; and the firmament proclaims his handiwork; ... their voice goes out through all the earth, and their words to the end of the world" (Ps. 19:1, 4). As the law reveals God's character to Israel (Ps. 19:7–13), so nature declares God's glory to the world (vv. 1–6).

In Psalm 47, a song of praise to the Almighty as the God of all the earth, it is written, "Clap your hands, all peoples! Shout unto God [Elohim] with loud songs of joy!" (v. 1). Here the Creator God recognized outside Israel by the peoples of the ancient Near East, and known as El, or by other cognate appellations, is identified with Elohim, the Israelite's nonspecific name for God. Later in the psalm (vv. 2, 9) Elohim is identified with the national God of Israel.

As the Jewish biblical scholar Cassuto has commented, "All nations, even those who know not Yahweh ... recognize at least 'Elohim, the universal conception of the Godhead."[23] The nations are invited to bring their dim awareness of God to full consciousness through a recognition of the God of Israel, who is a great king over all the earth (v. 2).

In the New Testament one of the most important texts for understanding God's universal kingdom-word is found in Rom. 1:19 ff. The Apostle Paul, surveying the decadent humanism and paganism of the Greco-Roman world, declares that "what can be known about God is plain to them, because God has shown it to them. Ever since the creation of the world his invisible nature, namely, his eternal power and deity, has been clearly perceived in the things that have been made. So they are without excuse" (vv. 19, 20). Given the revelation of God's existence, power, and righteousness through nature, an apostate human race has no excuse for its wanton rebellion against God's righteous standards for individuals and societal life. They cannot say, declares Paul, that "we didn't know any better." When mankind suppresses the light of creation (1:18) and the light of conscience (2:15), the law of God written upon the heart, the result is not a "neutral" society but a society progressively enveloped by false religions and philosophies, by immorality, and by social disorder and strife (1:18—32). The alternative to God's light, God's universal kingdom-word, is not neutrality but man's heart of darkness and a descent into anarchy and despair.

John Calvin, commenting on this Romans 1 passage, noted: "That there exists in the human mind, and indeed by natural instinct, some sense of deity (*divinitatis sensum*), we hold to be beyond dispute, since God himself, to prevent any man from pretending ignorance, has endued all men with some idea of his Godhead, the memory of which he constantly renews ... that all may be condemned by their own conscience when they neither worship him nor consecrate their lives to his service" (*Inst.* I.iii,1). Because of the inherent sense of deity in the human heart, individuals and societies are without excuse for their rebellion against God's kingly rule.

Inasmuch as questions of general revelation naturally arise in

---

23. U. Cassuto, *The Documentary Hypothesis*, p. 25.

a missionary context, it is not surprising to find several important references in the book of Acts. During the first missionary journey Paul tells the people of Lystra that the living God who made the heavens and the earth "did not leave himself without witness, for he did good and gave you from heaven rains and fruitful seasons, satisfying your hearts with food and gladness" (14:17). Through the orderly processes of nature and history—a reflection of God's faithfulness promised in the Noachic covenant (Gen. 8:21–22)— God was revealing himself as the benevolent heavenly Father whose goodness, like the rain, is given both to the just and the unjust (Matt. 5:45). Paul's appeal to general revelation was a reminder that man's life and its continuance is not found within himself but is the gracious provision of God.

In his speech at the Areopagus, Paul declares to the Athenian philosophers that the God of creation, dimly perceived by the Greek poets Epimenides and Aratus as the Creator and Sustainer of mankind (Acts 17:28), was now being fully revealed in the message of the crucified, risen, and returning Jesus. Paul's speech in Athens clearly indicates that while God's universal kingdom-word leaves mankind without excuse, only the special kingdom-word of the gospel can lead to a saving assurance of God's favor through the knowledge of Jesus Christ.

In this century the most publicized debate on the status of general revelation took place during the 1930s between Emil Brunner and Karl Barth. In his *Natural Theology* Brunner argued that the knowledge of God from nature was a presupposition for hearing the gospel, a "point of contact." In his reply to Brunner, *No!*, Barth denied that there was any valid natural knowledge of God in man; the gospel created its own point of contact. In the context of the German Christian movement of the 1930s, which was dangerously mixing an alien ideology of blood, race, and nation with the gospel, it is understandable that Barth reacted strongly to notions of general revelation or natural theology which, in his view, were threatening the integrity of the church. At the same time Brunner was correct in arguing that Barth's position did not do justice to biblical passages such as Psalm 19, Romans 1, Acts 14, and Acts 17. The entire debate is an interesting illustration of how theological issues can be so inextricably linked with the political and historical dynamics of the age. While Barth may not have done justice to the biblical witness concerning God's general revelation, he did see very clearly that God's special kingdom-word stands in judgment over all the kingdoms and institutions of this world, and that the church of Jesus Christ must ever be jealous of its own integrity, never surrendering itself to serve some alien ideology or culture. The church of Jesus Christ listens to one word, the word of the gospel, and bows only to one Lord, Jesus Christ, and to no other lords—not der Führer, not Marx, not Lenin, and not the American way of life or even the U.S. Supreme Court, where these are contrary to the kingdom-word of Christ.

More recently, the controversy in this country over the teaching of evolution and creation in the public schools has given the evangelical community fresh motivation to reconsider previous understandings of general revelation and natural theology. For centuries in Christian theology it had been the custom to argue from the design and order in nature to the existence of God as designer. The teleological argument for God's existence is found in Aquinas, and in Protestant circles was given classic formulation in William Paley's *Natural Theology* (1802). Paley argued that just as the existence of a watch implied a watchmaker, so design in the natural world implied the existence of God. This type of argument fell somewhat into disfavor due to the various criticisms of Hume and Kant, and especially with the influence of Darwin, whose theory of evolution replaced the divine Designer with "natural selection" and the "survival of the fittest."

In recent years, however, researches in molecular biology and biochemistry have lent renewed credibility to the design argument. An article in the January, 1955, issue of the *American Scientist* made the following admission: "From the probability standpoint, the ordering of the present environment into a single amino acid molecule would be utterly improbable in all the time and space available for the origin of terrestrial life." And yet in spite of such considerations, evolutionists have shown great zeal in their attempts to exclude any reference to creation in the public schools—thus manifesting the tendency of fallen man to suppress the truth of God's reality, spoken of by the apostle in Rom. 1:18. The psalmist knew that the "heavens are declaring the glory of God"; now, from the laboratories of the molecular biologists there can be seen fresh evidence of "God's footprints in creation." The creation-evolution struggle should alert the evangelical community to the need for clarifying and applying the claims of God's universal kingdom-word in various areas of contemporary social life, especially in relation to public policy and education (see p. 78).

### Revelation: act, image, word

Does divine revelation consist primarily in the acts of God, or in poetic images, or in inspired words? This question has been prominent in biblical and systematic theology for much of the twentieth century. The theme of revelation in history became a popular catchword in biblical theology, to a great extent in reaction to nineteenth-century liberalism's focus on religious feeling and ethical ideals as the vehicles of revelation.[24] This theme was also developed in reaction to classical evangelicalism's insistence on the Bible as an inspired deposit of verbal and propositional revelation.

In God Who Acts: Biblical Theology as Recital (1952), G. Ernest Wright argued that history and historical tradition were "the primary sphere in which God reveals himself,"[25] as opposed to words. According to Gerhard von Rad, in Old Testament Theology (1962—65), The Problem of the Hexateuch and Other Essays (1966), Genesis (1972), and Deuteronomy (1966), the Old Testament proclaimed the acts of Yahweh in history. It soon became apparent to critics that despite the biblical resonances of such approaches, there was a serious question of equivocation in theological language. If one is really ambivalent or skeptical about the relationship between "confessional" or "salvation" history (Heilsgeschichte) and "actual" history, what meaning is really being given to terms such as the "acts" of God? Did the waters of the Red Sea really part, or was such biblical language only a "confessional" way of speaking about some subjective religious experience? Perhaps all that actually happened at the Red Sea was that, for some strange reason, the people of Israel were given a new "self-understanding"? As Langdon Gilkey points out, unless one is willing to accept the biblical narratives more or less at face value, to speak of the "God who acts" is indeed an equivocal use of language.

In Salvation in History (1967), Oscar Cullmann attempted to avoid some of the difficulties of von Rad and Wright by affirming that

24. James Barr, "Revelation in History," p. 746.
25. G. Ernest Wright, God Who Acts: Biblical Theology as Recital, p. 55.

the eschatological acts of God are not so transcendent as to be hidden from public view. They become objective in history and consequently can become objects of faith.

Wolfhart Pannenberg has also written extensively on the theme of revelation in history in such works as *Jesus—God and Man* (1968), *Revelation in History* (1969), and *Basic Questions in Theology* (3 vols., 1970—73). According to Pannenberg, revelation is not so much a matter exclusively of the kerygmatic word, as Barth and Bultmann would have it, or of salvation history, as the biblical theology movement has suggested, but rather a matter of universal history. The course of world history is integrally tied to God's revelation because, in Pannenberg's estimation, it receives its unity from the goal established by the Creator who is Lord of history.

This latter emphasis represents a corrective to the ambivalence found in much of the biblical theology movement, which constituted something of an unstable halfway house between views of revelation stressing inward religious experience (e.g. Schleiermacher) and classical evangelicalism, which believes in a God who *really* can act supernaturally in space and time. At the same time, it would seem that Pannenberg, whose theology displays rationalistic tendencies, has not sufficiently stressed the role of the Holy Spirit in illuminating the meaning of divine activity in history for the believer. The cross and resurrection of Jesus Christ remain opaque to human consciousness until the Spirit of God illuminates the meaning of those historical events.

It must be said, however, that evangelical theology can appropriate the biblical theology movement's stress on the God who acts as a healthy corrective of imbalances in its own tradition. Much American evangelicalism, under the impact of pietism and revivalism, has lost sight of history as the arena of God's action. God encounters humankind not merely in the pew and in the small-group Bible study, but also in the struggles of politics, social conflict, and public policy formation, as the church wrestles with its humanistic and cultic opponents. But evangelical theology, when it is true to its own best traditions, believes in a "God who acts" more profoundly and less equivocally than does the biblical theology movement. It believes in an omnipotent Creator and Redeemer who is not the prisoner of the laws of nature, which he himself has ordained, but who is free to act in, with, or above those laws as he sees fit, in acts of ordinary or extraordinary providence. The God of evangelical theology is the God of the Bible, who acts in space and time to defeat his enemies and to extend his kingdom in the world.

R. J. Rushdoony has observed that Marxists believe in history, but not in God, while many Christians believe in God, but not in history; however, the essence of orthodoxy is to believe in both. The god of biblical theology who did not *really* act in biblical times is an idol; so is the god of pietistic conservatism, who supposedly has abandoned post-apostolic history to the devil. Evangelical theology believes in the God who acted in biblical times, and who continues to act through the resurrected and reigning Christ, who is active *now*, extending his kingdom. "Little children, keep yourselves from idols" (1 John 5:21).

While never as prominent as the proponents of biblical theology, there have been voices in twentieth-century theology that have stressed symbols and images, rather than events or words, as the primary vehicles of divine revelation. This emphasis has been developed in various ways by Austin Farrer in *The Glass of Vision* (1948), E. L. Mascall in *Words and Images* (1957) and *Theology and Images* (1963), and by Paul Tillich in his *Systematic Theology* and other writings. The stress here has been on the affective dimension of revelation. Biblical and religious symbols are not to be taken literalistically, but are mediums for an experience of the divine. While evangelical theology recognizes the experimental side of divine revelation and the analogical nature of religious language (pp. 47–50), it insists that biblical images and symbols are firmly rooted in the framework of history. It is especially the case in Tillich that an ahistorical thrust in the theory of religious symbolism opens the door to a dangerous dilution of the cognitive component of the biblical message.

The twentieth century has seen a long-running battle between neo-orthodoxy and classical evangelicalism over the "word" character of divine revelation. One of the preoccupations of the neo-orthodox tradition has been the persistent denial of the cognitive and informational dimension of revelation. According to Bultmann, "Revelation is an act of God, an occurrence, and not a communication of supernatural knowledge."[26] William Temple claimed that what "is offered to man's apprehension in any spe-

---

26. Bultmann, *Existence and Faith*,, p. 102.

cific revelation is not truth concerning God but the living God himself."[27] Gerhard Kittel believed that the New Testament writers never spoke "in order to communicate their own wisdom or any theological or philosophical ideas."[28] Emil Brunner was quite sure that divine revelation did not consist in "a book or a doctrine."[29] And so it went. It was quite clear that much of neo-orthodoxy had developed a strong allergic reaction to the notion of propositional revelation. In a reaction to one-sided emphases in dead orthodoxy, neo-orthodoxy went to another extreme and threw the baby out with the bathwater.

The persistent denials of the propositional component of revelation now appear in retrospect to be one-sided and just a bit silly, in the light of the biblical data (e.g. Luke 1:26; Matt. 2:22; Col. 1:26; 3:4; 4:4; Eph. 3:5; 6:19; 2 Cor. 2:14; 11:6, etc.) and the considerable literary productions of the neo-orthodox scholars themselves. If there is so little cognitive content in biblical revelation, what is there to talk about? Why all the voluminous commentaries and systems of theology? If God can be experienced, but not really known in an articulate way, then why not become mystics and leave all the scholarly apparatus to less enlightened souls?

The denials of the cognitive dimension of revelation have helped to disarm the church before its enemies and have contributed to the erosion of the substance of the faith. If the cognitive content of the faith cannot be clearly articulated, then neither can it be effectively preserved and defended. It is no accident that the "fathers" of the neo-orthodoxy of the 1930s, 1940s, and 1950s saw their theological "sons" sliding down the slippery slope toward the vagaries of the theologies of revolution, death-of-God theologies, theologies of play, secular theologies, and situation ethics during the 1960s and 1970s. With the cognitive controls removed theology becomes a ship without a rudder or a compass. As Carl F. H. Henry has observed, "Yahweh theology" degenerates into "yo-yo theology" when the cognitive norms of biblical revelation cease to function properly.

The enemies of Christianity are not so naïve as to believe that words, theories, and doctrines are not important for the effectiveness of a movement's action in the world. Lenin reminded some

27. William Temple, *Nature, Man and God*, p. 322.
28. In James Barr, *The Semantics of Biblical Language*, p. 208.
29. Brunner, *Revelation and Reason*, p. 8.

of his more pragmatic followers, "Without a revolutionary *theory* there can be no revolutionary *movement.*"[30] He also affirmed that there "can be no strong socialist party without a revolutionary theory which unites all socialists, from which the socialists draw their whole conviction, which they apply in their methods of fighting and working."[31] What is true for Marxism-Leninism as a world-transforming movement is also true for the church, the vanguard of the kingdom of the resurrected, reigning, and returning Christ. Acognitive theologies and anti-propositional theories of revelation cannot give decisive leadership to the people of God amid the conflicts of history. "If the trumpet gives uncertain sound, who will get ready for battle?" (1 Cor. 14:8).

Evangelical theology does not deny that God himself encounters his people through the word of preaching, or that the personal dimension of revelation is crucial. It does deny, however, any view of God's action which seems to imply that God is mute, or that revelation is an exercise in divine pantomime or dumbshow. The God who acts is also the God who speaks. The God who acts in history speaks intelligibly, interpreting for his people the significance both of his own revelatory acts and of their own historical situation. God's people need a heightened consciousness of the new revolutionary situation in order to fight victoriously on the basis of it, and that new consciousness is provided by the inspired, apostolic interpretation of God's special kingdom-word.

### The impact of revelation on society

The question of divine revelation has consequences that extend far beyond the bounds of the institutional church. The major institutions of Western civilization have been shaped in various ways under the impact of Judeo-Christian revelation. We now stand at a point in American history where the continuing and positive influence of that revelation can no longer be taken for granted. This influence is at many points being openly challenged or even repudiated. In this section we will explore the relationship, historical and contemporary, of divine revelation to three key institutions of American culture—law, science, and education.

---

30. Lenin, *Materialism and Empirio-Criticism,* p. 585.
31. Ibid., p. 572.

## Revelation, morality, and the law

Abortion, homosexuality, pornography, prayer in the public schools, creation v. evolution, "blue laws," casino gambling: some of the most controversial social and political issues of the 1980s have involved the complex interface between religion, morality, and the law. To what extent should Christians seek to have biblical standards of morality reflected in law and public policy, should opportunities for such influence arise? Do Christians—or other interest groups—have a right to "legislate morality" in a pluralistic society? Should Christians simply acquiesce in the contemporary moral decadence and attempt to preserve their own traditions in the privacy of the home and church? These are some of the troubling questions that arise when Christians seek to live out their faith in the context of a society that seems to be rapidly abandoning the deposit of divine revelation which has been so influential in the shaping of its institutions.

The influence of Judeo-Christian revelation has been a pervasive one in the history of American law and public policy. William Blackstone (1723–80), in his famous *Commentaries on the Laws of England*, stated that "upon these two foundations, the law of nature and the law of revelation, depend all human laws. That is to say, no human laws should be suffered to contradict these." In our terms, Blackstone was saying that general and special revelation should constitute the foundation of all law. Daniel Boorstin has noted that "in the first century of American independence, the *Commentaries* were not merely an approach to the study of law; for most lawyers they constituted all there was of the law."[32]

The influence of Blackstone was absorbed by Thomas Jefferson and by early generations of American lawyers who had a formative influence in the shaping of American traditions. In the Declaration of Independence, Jefferson wrote that the colonists were "appealing to the Supreme Judge of the world for the rectitude of [their] intentions . . . with firm reliance on the protection of Divine Providence." While Jefferson was no orthodox or evangelical believer, he did believe in the existence of a God who was the righteous Judge of individuals and nations, and he saw such a belief as foundational for a just society. In his charter for the University of Virginia he directed that proofs for God as the sovereign Lord

32. John W. Whitehead and John Conlan, "The Establishment of the Religion of Secular Humanism and Its First Amendment Implications," p. 25.

and Creator and Ruler of the world, and the moral requirements implied by this, be taught to all the students. Engraved on the walls of the Jefferson Memorial in Washington, D.C., are these words of our third president: "God who gave us life gave us liberty. Can the liberties of a nation be secure when we have removed a conviction that these liberties are the gift of God?" American educators and the justices of the U.S. Supreme Court today would do well to ponder Jefferson's reflections on the relationship of revelation and the law.

James Madison, the chief architect of the U.S. Constitution, studied Christian theology at Princeton with the Rev. John Witherspoon before becoming actively engaged in politics. Witherspoon, a Scottish Presbyterian, was the only clergyman to sign the Declaration of Independence. The Christian doctrine of original sin strengthened Madison's belief that it was unwise to concentrate power in the hands of government. The separation of powers in the U.S. Constitution reflects Madison's convictions concerning human nature, which in turn were influenced by his study of history and biblical revelation.

In another context Madison observed that "to suppose that any form of government will secure liberty or happiness without virtue in the people is a chimerical idea."[33] Madison knew that a free society, without governmental tyranny and oppression, presupposed a citizenry that, from moral and religious motivation, was capable of responsibility and self-restraint. If the citizens will not voluntarily restrain themselves, then in order to prevent anarchy and disorder they must inevitably be restrained by the coercive powers of the state. Madison believed that the motivation for voluntary self-restraint was to be found in the revealed teachings of the Christian religion.

The legitimate influence of Judeo-Christian revelation was long presupposed in American court decisions. In 1878 in *Reynolds v. United States*, the Supreme Court ruled against the Mormon practice of polygamy, on the grounds that polygamy was contrary to the Christian religion, the moral basis of American society. Since the 1960s, however, the Court has done an about-face, repudiating the historic influence of Christian teaching on the law. In Torcaso v. Watkins (1961), the Court struck down a Maryland statute requiring all Maryland public officials and employees to declare

---

33. Saul K. Padover, ed., *The Complete Madison*, pp. 48 – 49.

their belief in God. Secular humanism was recognized as a religion. In this key decision, the Court reversed a longstanding legal tradition and removed the theistic base from American government.

Given the decision in *Torcaso v. Watkins* (1961), the decision banning devotional Bible reading in the schools in *Abington v. Schempp* (1963) followed in due course. In a concurring opinion Justice William Brennan allowed that the words "under God" could be kept in the Pledge of Allegiance if not taken in the "Christian sense," i.e., in terms of their historical meaning.

In *Stone v. Graham* (1980) the Court struck down a Kentucky law requiring the posting of the Ten Commandments in public school classrooms. Such a practice could, according to the Court's opinion, have the undesirable effect of inducing "the schoolchildren to read, meditate upon, perhaps to venerate and obey the commandments." The justices seemed eager to rescue the schoolchildren of Kentucky from such a terrible fate. Jefferson, who once asked, "Can the liberties of a nation be secure when we have removed a conviction that these liberties are the gift of God?" would run the risk of having his charter for the University of Virginia declared unconstitutional, were it to be tested in today's courts. The alienation of today's Supreme Court from the spirit of the founding fathers, and from a large body of American Christians, is deep indeed.

The founders of the American constitutional and legal tradition realized that law needed a transcendent basis if it was not to degenerate into the tool of arbitrary despotism. In the words of Chief Justice John Marshall, the American system was to be "a government of laws and not of men." That ideal had a secure basis as long as law was understood to represent not merely the will of man but the expression of divine justice. The erosion and repudiation of the influence of revelation on the law has produced a sociological concept of law—i.e., law as the expression of the will of the dominant majority in society, apart from transcendent absolutes. Law then reflects the shifting opinions of the *Zeitgeist*, the "spirit of the age." The late Chief Justice Vinson, reflecting such a sociological view of law, could say, "Nothing is more certain in modern society than the principle that there are no absolutes."[34] The statement of former Chief Justice Hughes reflects the same

---

34. Rushdoony, *Messianic Character of American Education*, p. 323.

outlook: "We are under a Constitution but the Constitution is what the judges say it is."[35]

No society can in practice repudiate all absolutes; it merely replaces the absolutes of heaven with an absolute on earth: the power of the secular state. And such power can be cruel and arbitrary indeed. As R. J. Rushdoony has warned, "If law ceases to be the instrument of principled morality, of good against evil, it becomes an instrument then of power, and the end it serves is power. Accordingly, law is less and less today a protection of our persons and freedom from evil, and more and more the instrument of statist power."[36]

American evangelicals have, until rather recently, been largely unaware of the evolution in American law that has repudiated its Christian base. The result has been to reverse John Marshall's ideal and to produce "a government of men and not of laws." A society that repudiates the laws of the Great King will be subjected to the arbitrary and despotic laws of earthly kings. As the federal judiciary has continued to intrude ever more pervasively into the affairs of the family and of Christian schools, a growing number of Christians are becoming aware of the fundamental changes that have occurred in American law. That recognition is coming none too soon.

As we noted earlier, contemporary social issues such as abortion, homosexuality, and pornography raise the question of "legislating morality." In this confused but important area of public policy it is especially important for American evangelicals to clarify their understanding of the relationship of revelation, morality, and law, in order to be in a position for effective action.

Both history and common sense indicate that any society needs to enforce certain basic moral standards to maintain its own existence. As the British jurist Patrick Devlin has stated, "A recognized morality is as necessary to society as a recognized government. ... Society may use the law to preserve morality in the same way as it uses it to safeguard anything else that is essential to its existence."[37] Just as societies enact legal safeguards to protect the property and the physical safety of its citizens, so

35. Edward S. Corwin, *The Constitution and What It Means Today*, p. xiii.
36. Rushdoony, "Detente," p. 2.
37. Patrick Devlin, *The Enforcement of Morals*, pp. 10–11.

may it legally protect marriage, family, and moral values by prescribing certain forms of personal behavior.

The history of civilization shows that societies that make no attempt to regulate and discipline sexual behavior lose their cultural vigor and ability to withstand internal and external dangers. The idea that society should restrain certain forms of sexual expression is not a popular one in an individualistic American society that has been increasingly characterized by sexual permissiveness. Nevertheless, the record of history is clear in this matter. The sociologist Pitirim A. Sorokin, after a comparative study of a wide variety of civilizations spanning a period of several thousand years, concluded that "in the life processes of historical societies, the periods of their cultural and social growth have been almost uniformly marked by a very tempered sexual regime, while the periods of their decline have been stamped by sexual anarchy."[38] Sorokin goes on to observe that there "is no example of a community which has retained its high position on the cultural scale after less rigorous sexual customs have replaced more restricting ones."[39]

A society that fritters away its psycho-biological energies in sexual self-indulgence also tends to lose self-discipline and energy in other areas of culture. It is not accidental that American society, which since the 1960s has been characterized by a pronounced sexual permissiveness, during that same period has witnessed lagging economic productivity, declining student achievement in public education, a lowered level of military preparedness, a rising incidence of alcoholism, drug abuse, and violent crime, and high rates of divorce. Human behavior that is undisciplined in private inevitably has consequences that are visible in public, and which impact negatively on society as a whole.

Sorokin's conclusions concerning the crucial place of sexual discipline in a strong society are paralleled by J. D. Unwin's studies on the history of the institution of marriage in various cultures. Unwin, a British anthropologist, concluded that the "whole of human history does not contain a single instance of a group becoming civilized unless it has been absolutely monogamous, nor is there any example of a group retaining its culture after it has

---

38. Pitirim A. Sorokin, *The American Sex Revolution*, pp. 107–8.
39. Ibid., pp. 110–11.

adopted less rigorous customs."[40] Unwin's studies on marriage also imply the folly of any society's granting equal status to heterosexuality and homosexuality in its laws and customs. Strong marriages are crucial for a vigorous and enduring social order. "Marriage as a life-long association," notes Unwin, "has been an attendant circumstance of all human achievement, and its adoption has preceded all manifestations of social energy, whether that energy be reflected in conquest, in art and science, in the extension of the social vision, or in the substitution of monotheism for polytheism, and the exaltation of the conception of the one God."[41]

Viewed from a Christian standpoint, the historical research of Sorokin and Unwin can be seen as "tracing the footsteps of general revelation" in the history of civilizations. It confirms the truth of Rom. 2:15, which teaches that the law of God is written in the heart. Societies which conform to the basic moral principles constitutive for human nature prosper and prevail; those which ignore them embark on a path of self-destruction.

Christians are sometimes intimidated by cries against "legislating morality in a pluralistic society." Christian attorney John Whitehead has noted, however, that the pluralism many modern Christians hold "is only an excuse for evading the church's job. The Christian should make disciples of individuals, institutions, and cultures—not cower before alternative belief systems."[42] The fact of the matter is that *someone's* moral standards will be reflected in public policy, and Judeo-Christian standards have a far better track record in history than those of the secular humanists.

There is ample biblical evidence that God, who is the sovereign Lord of all the earth, holds all individuals and nations—not merely his special covenant people—accountable to basic moral principles. All human beings, whether they acknowledge the fact or not, are created in God's image (Gen. 1:26–27) and consequently have a basic sense of right and wrong (Rom. 1:18–32; 2:14–15), distorted though it may be through sin. God sent his judgment upon the generation of Noah (Gen. 6 – 8) and upon Sodom and Gomorrah (Gen. 18), and these peoples, guilty of violence, immorality, and injustice, could not plead ignorance as an excuse, claiming they had not been given special revelation like the Jews. The

---

40. J. D. Unwin, "Monogamy as a Condition of Social Energy," p. 663.
41. Ibid.
42. John W. Whitehead, "The Secularizing of America," p. 21.

prophets of Israel teach that God's righteous standards apply not only to the covenant people, but in a general way to the Gentile nations as well (Isa. 13; Jer. 25:12–38; Amos 1:3–2:3; Nah. 1–3; Zeph. 2:8–15). Any nation which persistently disregards the basic requirements of God's moral law does so at its own peril.

The New Testament also teaches that there is a basic moral awareness in mankind that is not limited to the church. C. H. Dodd has pointed out that the parables of Jesus presuppose that relationships such as those of parent and child, master and servant, king and subject, friend and friend, "disclose upon examination certain basic laws or maxims which are the mirror of the Creator's pattern for human life."[43] Even evil men have an awareness that fathers should provide good things for their children (Luke 11:13).

In the epistles key passages such as Rom. 1:18–32 and 2:14–15 have already been noted. In 1 Cor. 5:1 Paul writes, "It is actually reported that there is immorality among you, and of a kind that is not found even among pagans." Paul's rebuke to the Corinthians presupposes that even pagans have an awareness that incest is wrong.

In 1 Peter 2:12 ("Maintain good conduct among the Gentiles, so that in case they speak against you as wrongdoers, they may see your good deeds and glorify God") and 1 Peter 3:16 ("Keep your conscience clear, so that, when you are abused, those who revile your good behavior in Christ may be put to shame"), some moral consciousness common to both Christian and pagan is assumed. "The implication," writes Dodd, "is that there is in pagans a capacity for sound moral judgment, a *communis sensus* which will lead them to recognize as good that which the revealed Law of God declares to be good."[44] That awareness may be distorted and suppressed, but it is there nonetheless by virtue of man's creation in the image of God.

In recent years the First Amendment provisions concerning the separation of church and state have been misconstrued in such a way as to intimidate many Christians from bringing their moral principles to bear on matters of public policy. The relevant clauses of the amendment, which actually does not contain the phrase "separation of church and state," read, "Congress shall make no

43. C. H. Dodd, *New Testament Studies*, p. 136.
44. Ibid., p. 133.

law respecting an establishment of religion, or prohibiting the free exercise thereof." The First Amendment, ratified in 1791, was not intended to restrict the right of Christians to influence public policy, but was rather intended to restrict the power of the federal government to interfere in the affairs of the church. The founding fathers were anxious to maintain the freedom and independence of the churches, and thus wished to prohibit Congress from establishing one denomination as the official state church, as was the case in England and other European nations. The Establishment Clause applied only at the federal level; there were statewide established churches in Connecticut until 1818 and in Massachusetts until 1832.

The force of the Establishment Clause was hardly to discourage Christian influence on American laws and institutions; such influence rather was presupposed by the drafters of the amendment. The First Congress did not expect the amendment to conflict with the Northwest Ordinance of 1787, reenacted in 1789, which set aside federal lands for schools, many of which were controlled by religious organizations. The ordinance stated that "religion, morality, and knowledge being necessary to good government and the happiness of mankind, schools and the means of learning shall forever be encouraged." Biblical morals were understood to be the foundation of good government and a free society rather than its enemy, as contemporary secular humanists seem to suggest.

In the context of contemporary political debates it is important for Christians to realize that the contention that the mere influence of religious ideas on American law constitutes an "establishment of religion" is a falsification and distortion of the original meaning of the First Amendment. Christians should loudly and persistently protest any distortion of the rules of fair play in American life that would discriminate against the values of Jesus Christ and discriminate in favor of the values of Freud, Marx, Darwin, or Hugh Hefner. Even in the *Abington v. Schempp* Bible-reading case Justice Clark noted that the government "may not establish a 'religion of secularism' in the sense of affirmatively opposing or showing hostility to religion, thus preferring those who believe in no religion over those who do believe." Constant vigilance is needed on the part of Christians to ensure that this is true in practice.

A more aggressive posture by Christians in the area of public-policy formation does not mean that Christians should seek the enactment of *all* biblical precepts. As a general rule of thumb, where scripture indicates that the unbeliever has moral awareness through general revelation (cf. Rom. 1:18–32), then legislation in that area can be appropriate. Restricting pornography, homosexual behavior, and the killing of unborn children can be argued on general revelational or natural law grounds; compelling church attendance or Christian baptism cannot.[45]

In the drafting of legislation on a particular moral issue, the degree of community support is an essential factor to be considered. As the Talmudic tractate *Baba Batra* observed, "One may not enact an ordinance which the majority of the community cannot observe." Political action to achieve specific legislative goals must go hand in hand with evangelistic and educational ministries that attempt to produce in society a moral consciousness that will be supportive of higher ideals in the law. Premature enactment of laws with little community support may, in the long run, retard the causes they seek to promote.

### Judeo-Christian revelation and the origins of science

Science and technology are among the dominant institutions of Western civilization. Few people today are aware of the fact that the origins of modern science are rooted in assumptions drawn from Judeo-Christian revelation. In the twentieth century it has become increasingly clear that the impact of science and technology on human life is deeply influenced by the values of the society in which they function. Thus not only in its historical origins, but also in its contemporary applications for good or for evil, the practice of science has important connections with Judeo-Christian revelation.

The eminent philosopher and mathematician Alfred North Whitehead, in his study *Science and the Modern World*, pointed out how the Christian belief in a rational God and a good creation laid the intellectual basis for modern science—a basis lacking in ancient India or China. The Christian theologians of the Middle Ages insisted on the wisdom and rationality of the Creator, "conceived as with the personal energy of Jehovah and with the rationality of a Greek philosopher."[46] The faith in the very possibility of science, which was "generated antecedently to the development

45. Questions concerning the penal sanctions of Old Testament civil laws, as understood by the "theonomy" movement in American Reformed circles, will be discussed in relation to hermeneutics in Chapter 8.

46. Alfred North Whitehead, *Science and the Modern World*, p. 18.

of modern scientific theory, is an unconscious derivative from medieval theology."[47]

Stanley L. Jaki, a noted historian of science, supports Whitehead's thesis. In *The Road of Science and the Ways to God*, Jaki likewise affirms that a rational belief in the existence of a Creator played a crucial role in the rise of science and all its advances. "Science found its only viable birth with a cultural matrix permeated by a firm conviction about the mind's ability to find in the realm of things and persons a pointer to their Creator."[48]

Statements of great seventeenth-century pioneers of science reveal the Christian presuppositions of their work. In letters of 1613 and 1615 Galileo wrote that God's mind contained all the natural laws; consequently he believed that the occasional glimpses of these laws which the scientist gained were revelations of God. "From the Divine Word, the Sacred Scriptures and Nature did both alike proceed," he wrote; "nor does God less admirably discover himself to us in Nature's action than in the scripture's sacred dictions."[49]

This outlook was shared by Isaac Newton. At the end of the second edition of his *Principia*, first published in 1687, the great British scientist stated that this "most beautiful system of the sun, planets, and comets, could only proceed from the counsel and dominion of an intelligent and powerful Being." For Newton and the seventeenth-century founders of modern science, the power and wisdom of the God of the Bible were the intellectual presuppositions for the very possibility of science. Galileo and Newton agreed with the apostle Paul that the power and wisdom of God were clearly displayed in the things that had been made (Rom. 1:20).

During the eighteenth and nineteenth centuries, under the impact of Enlightenment rationalism and positivism, science became increasingly secularized, though many scientists remained believers where personal faith was concerned. The notable French mathematician and physicist Laplace (1749–1827) expressed the growing spirit of secularity in official science. When asked by Napoleon why his system of celestial mechanics contained no references to God, Laplace is reported to have said, "Sir, I have no need of that hypothesis." In the work of Charles Darwin, God's

47. Ibid., p. 19.
48. Stanley L. Jaki, *The Road of Science and the Ways to God*, p. vii.
49. In F. J. Rutherford *et al.*, *The Project Physics Course*, p. 76.

creative work in nature was replaced by an impersonal process of natural selection, and in the world view of Marx and Engels science was understood in terms of a purely materialistic view of reality.

It comes as no great surprise to discover that a scientific method largely secularized in the eighteenth and nineteenth centuries could find itself flirting with the occult in the twentieth. In a letter to the editor of the *Boston Globe* of Feb. 8, 1978, Kenneth W. Walton, then an instructor in psycho-biology at the Harvard Medical School and a long-time practitioner of Transcendental Meditation, wrote that "I can vouch that the human abilities to levitate and to become invisible are as real as the radio and the airplane."

Dr. Elisabeth Kübler-Ross, the well-known psychologist and researcher on death and dying, has evidently been involved in spiritism. According to the April, 1977, issue of the *Spiritual Counterfeits Project Journal*, Dr. Kübler-Ross, when speaking to an audience in September of 1976, declared that "last night I was visited by Salem, my spirit guide, and two of his companions, Anka and Willie. They were with us until three o'clock in the morning. We talked, laughed, and sang together. They spoke and touched me with the most incredible love and tenderness imaginable. This was the highlight of my life."

Scripture warns that no human activity, science included, is religiously neutral. If the practice of science is not influenced by the Spirit of God, then it, like other human enterprises, can find itself seduced by alien spirits.

As noted earlier, the impact of science and technology on human life will be shaped by the values of the society in which they function. A society permeated by biblical theism can find in science a great source of material abundance and human freedom. A society which rejects that theistic base and replaces it with the idolatrous claims of the secular state can find science to be an instrument of tyranny, oppression, and destruction—as both Orwell's *1984* in fiction and Marxist-Leninist societies in fact demonstrate. Christians, called to be the salt of the earth and the light of the world, are to shape and permeate their society with biblical values, so as to maintain the possibility of a humane and life-affirming science, one dedicated to the service of the Creator-King rather than to the oppression and destruction of his creatures.

## Biblical revelation and American education

It is not widely known today that the idea of popular education originated with the Protestant Reformation. The Reformation had placed the Bible at the center of the church's life, and Luther and Calvin wanted all believers to be able to read the Bible for themselves.

This concept of education for the purpose of biblical literacy is found in the Massachusetts School Code of 1647, the first public school law in the English colonies: "It being one chief project of the old deluder, Satan, to keep men from the knowledge of the Scriptures...." Hence the need for schools. Each township of at least fifty households was required to pay a schoolmaster to teach their children. The law of 1647 established no centralized state board of education or compulsory attendance laws; education was still recognized to be the primary prerogative and responsibility of parents.

Harvard College, America's oldest institution of higher learning, was established because the Bay colonists were concerned to maintain an educated ministry. Harvard's curriculum was originally established with the Bible at its center. A pamphlet titled "New England's First Fruits" (1643), the oldest extant document relating to the original purposes of the institution, clearly states a Christian philosophy of education: "Let every student be plainly instructed and earnestly pressed to consider well, the main end of his life and studies is to know God and Jesus Christ which is eternal life, John 17:3, and therefore to lay Christ in the bottom, as the only foundation of all sound knowledge and learning."[50] From the Bible as the foundation of all knowledge in 1643 to student-sponsored showings of *Deep Throat* on campus in 1981— the changes have been dramatic indeed for Harvard.

It is indeed one of the great tragedies of American history that schools originally established to promote biblical literacy are now, by force of law, among the most efficient institutions in American society for promoting ignorance of biblical truth. Classrooms originally envisioned as vehicles for enhancing the child's commitment to biblical revelation are now, by Supreme Court decree, repressing awareness of those religious and moral values.

50. Rosalie K. Slater, *Teaching and Learning America's Christian History*, p. vii.

This fateful evolution in the character of American schools did not happen by accident. Samuel Blumenfeld, in his recent study *Is Public Education Necessary?* based on careful research in primary historical sources, has convincingly shown how compulsory, government-controlled education was the brainchild of a Unitarian elite in New England. After taking control of Harvard in 1805, this Unitarian elite agitated successfully to introduce into the United States the Prussian model of compulsory, government-controlled schools. Horace Mann, the so-called "father of public education," was a zealous lobbyist for this Unitarian clique.

It is important for evangelicals to realize that from the beginning the movement to establish government-controlled schools was a religious struggle. The Unitarians rejected orthodox biblical doctrines such as the deity of Christ, the penal, substitutionary atonement, and original sin. Rejecting the biblical doctrine of original sin, they believed in the perfectibility of human nature and saw government schools as a revolutionary tool for molding the rising generation and remaking society.

As R. J. Rushdoony has pointed out in *The Messianic Character of American Education*, the government-school crusaders pursued their goals with religious zeal and had grandiose and utopian hopes for their enterprise. Francis Wayland Parker (1837–1902), praised by humanist John Dewey as the "father of progressive education," expressed his boundless faith in statist education: "I await the regeneration of the world from the teaching of the common schools of America." What had heretofore been understood as the work of the Holy Spirit the "progressive" educators were now to accomplish.

Parker's faith was shared by Emma Marwedel, a pioneer in the kindergarten movement. "I believe in the power of the kindergarten to reform the world," she confidently stated. With the old-fashioned doctrine of original sin out of the way, there seemed to be no limits on what the new educational methods could accomplish.

Many conservative Christians in the nineteenth century were willing to support the Unitarian scheme, despite its suspect theological associations, for two reasons. First of all, they believed they could control the system; second, they believed that such government schools, reflecting Protestant values, would be an effective instrument for socializing the growing number of Roman Catholic immigrants. History has demonstrated that this decision, based more on pragmatism than principle, was a foolish one.

Not all conservatives were willing to jump on the government-school bandwagon. In 1887 A. A. Hodge, the conservative Presbyterian theologian, wrote, "I am sure as I am of Christ's reign that a comprehensive and centralized system of national education, separated from religion . . . will prove the most appalling enginery for the propagation of anti-Christian and atheistic unbelief, and of anti-social, nihilistic ethics, individual, social and political, which this sin-rent world has ever seen."[51] The history of American education has proved that Hodge was a better prophet than the "progressive" educators.

Hodge saw more clearly than many of his fellow nineteenth-century Christians that no area of human life, education included, is religiously neutral, and that in the long run basic principles have a way of working out their own inner logic, despite the best intentions of their proponents. A system of government schools originating in theological liberalism evolved over the succeeding decades into one propagating secular humanism.

In the latter part of the twentieth century the consequences of driving divine revelation from the classroom are so evident that even the humanistic educational establishment admits that American education faces a crisis. According to Roy P. Fairfield, editor of *Humanistic Frontiers in American Education*, "American education is in crisis. It faces disaster at all levels. Something must be done quickly if we are to rescue humans from continuing damage."[52] There is no recognition here, of course, that humanism's principles and values might be at the root of the problem. Evidently the crisis can be managed with more money, more programs, more sex education, better retirement benefits for teachers, a more efficient federal Department of Education, more government-funded studies, etc.

But what exactly is the crisis that Fairfield and other humanists are willing to acknowledge? The dimensions of that crisis are by now quite familiar to most American parents. "Today," says Blumenfeld, "most of the young adults who emerge from the process read poorly, write miserably, have stunted vocabularies, cannot do

51. Rushdoony, *The Messianic Character of American Education*, p. 335.
52. Roy P. Fairfield, ed., *Humanistic Frontiers in American Education*, p. 9.

arithmetic well, know little geography and less history, and know virtually nothing about the economic system in which they live."[53]

A government-sponsored survey by the National Assessment of Educational Progress study group found that in science, writing, social studies, and mathematics the achievement of U.S. seventeen-year-olds dropped regularly during the decade 1970—1980. Another national survey, conducted by Opinion Research Corporation of Princeton, N.J., found that 21 percent of the adults surveyed could not read a want ad, a job application form, a label on a medicine bottle, or a safety sign at their place of work.

The humanistic faith in the essential goodness and perfectibility of human nature was facing some rather rough sledding during the 1970s, as violence in the classrooms continued to mount. In 1979, 110,000 teachers reported being attacked by students, an increase of 57 percent over 1977—78. It may be recalled that in *Stone v. Graham* the Supreme Court was anxious to protect schoolchildren from the influence of the Ten Commandments, striking down a Kentucky law mandating their posting in school classrooms. Had the justices spent a bit more time in some of our nation's urban schools, perhaps their perception of the value of moral and religious restraints might have been different.

With the influence of divine revelation screened out by force of law, classroom teaching inevitably takes place within a relativistic and permissive moral framework. Dr. Lester A. Kirkendall, a leading American sexologist, writing in a discussion guide prepared for SIECUS (Sex Information and Education Council of the United States), states that the purpose of sex education "is not primarily to control and suppress sex expression, as in the past, but to indicate the immense possibilities for human fulfillment that human sexuality offers."[54] What is the solution when these "immense possibilities for human fulfillment" produce epidemics of sexually transmitted diseases, pregnancies out of wedlock, and teenage abortions? More humanistic sex education, obviously.

Christian parents should recognize clearly their obligation to provide a truly *Christian* education for their children. Parents are commanded to surround their children with the continuous and pervasive influence of biblical truth (Deut. 6:6—9). Evangelicals,

53. Samuel Blumenfeld, *Is Public Education Necessary?* p. 7.
54. Fairfield, *Humanistic Frontiers*, p. 54.

who confess the primacy of divine revelation in their theology, must apply this conviction in their social ethics and philosophy of education. The establishment of new Christian schools and the improvement of existing ones, so that biblical revelation is again at the center of the entire learning process, is one of the most vital aspects of Christian discipleship (cf. Matt. 28:19—20, the Great Commission) and mission that American evangelicals are called to fulfill in this century. Divine revelation is the word of the Great King, and that word, at the foundation of the educational process, is a crucial instrument for the extension of Christ's kingdom in American society and the world.

## Bibliography

Ayer, A. J. *Language, Truth and Logic*. New York: Dover, 1952.

Barr, James. "Revelation in History," *Interpreter's Dictionary of the Bible, Supplementary Volume*. Nashville: Abingdon, 1976.

————. *The Semantics of Biblical Language*. London: Oxford University Press, 1961.

Bartsch, H. W., ed. *Kerygma and Myth*. New York: Harper Torchbooks, 1961.

Blumenfeld, Samuel. *Is Public Education Necessary?* Old Greenwich, Conn.: Devin-Adair, 1981.

Brunner, Emil. *The Mediator*. Philadelphia: Westminster, 1947.

————. *Revelation and Reason*. Philadelphia: Westminster, 1946.

Bultmann, Rudolf. *Existence and Faith*. New York: Meridian Books, 1960.

Burns, Emile. *Handbook of Marxism*. London: Victor Gollancz, 1936.

Calvin, John. *Institutes of the Christian Religion*, tr. Ford Lewis Battles. Philadelphia: Westminster, 1960.

Cassuto, U. *The Documentary Hypothesis*. Jerusalem: Magnes Press, 1961.

Corwin, Edward S. *The Constitution and What It Means Today*. 14th ed. Princeton: Princeton University Press, 1978.

Devlin, Patrick. *The Enforcement of Morals*. London: Oxford University Press, 1968.

Dodd, C. H. *New Testament Studies*. Manchester: University of Manchester Press, 1953.

Fairfield, Roy P., ed. *Humanistic Frontiers in American Education*. Englewood Cliffs, N.J.: Prentice-Hall, 1971.

Flew, Antony, and MacIntyre, Alasdair, eds., *New Essays in Philosophical Theology*. New York: Macmillan, 1955.

Freud, Sigmund. *The Future of an Illusion.* 1928; rpt. New York: Norton, 1961.

Gilkey, Langdon. "Cosmology, Ontology, and the Travail of Biblical Language," *Journal of Religion* 41 (1961):194–205.

Henry, Carl F. H. *God, Revelation, and Authority,* Vol. II. Waco, Tex.: Word, 1976.

Huxley, Julian, ed. *The Humanist Frame.* New York: Harper, 1961.

Jaki, Stanley L. *The Road of Science and the Ways to God.* Chicago: University of Chicago Press, 1978.

Kennedy, D. James. "God's Purpose for His Church," *Presbyterian Journal,* Sept. 2, 1981, pp. 7–9.

Lenin, V. I. *Materialism and Empirio-Criticism.* New York: International Publishers, 1927.

Marx, Karl. *On Religion,* ed. Saul K. Padover. New York: McGraw-Hill, 1974.

McDonald, H. D. *Theories of Revelation.* Grand Rapids: Baker, 1963.

Moule, C. F. D. "Revelation," *Interpreter's Dictionary of the Bible.* Nashville: Abingdon, 1962.

Mundle, W. "Revelation." *New International Dictionary of New Testament Theology.* Grand Rapids: Zondervan, 1978.

Oepke, Albrecht. "ἀποκαλύπτω, ἀποκάλυψις," *Theological Dictionary of the New Testament,* ed. G. Kittel, tr. G. Bromiley. Grand Rapids: Eerdmans, 1965. III, 563–92.

Padover, Saul K., ed. *The Complete Madison.* New York: Harper, 1953.

Quebedeaux, Richard. *The Worldly Evangelicals.* San Francisco: Harper, 1978.

Rogers, Jack, and McKim, Donald K. *The Authority and Interpretation of the Bible.* San Francisco: Harper, 1979.

Rushdoony, R. J. "Detente," *Chalcedon Report,* Dec., 1981, pp. 1–2.

————. *The Messianic Character of American Education.* Nutley, N.J.: Craig Press, 1968.

————. *The Necessity for Systematic Theology.* Vallecito, Calif.: Ross House, 1979.

Rutherford, F. J., et al. *The Project Physics Course.* New York: Holt, Rinehart, Winton, 1970.

Schlorff, Samuel P. "Theological and Apologetical Dimensions of Muslim Evangelization," *Westminister Theological Journal* 42 (1980):335–66.

Slater, Rosalie K. *Teaching and Learning America's Christian History.* San Francisco: Foundation for American Christian Education, 1965.

Sorokin, Pitirim A. *The American Sex Revolution.* Boston: P. Sargent, 1956.

Temple, William. *Nature, Man and God.* 1934; rpt. New York: St. Martin's Press, 1964.

Unwin, J. D. "Monogamy as a Condition of Social Energy," *Hibbert Journal* 25 (1927):663–77.

Whitehead, Alfred North. *Science and the Modern World.* New York: Macmillan, 1925.

Whitehead, John W. "The Secularizing of America," *Moody Monthly,* July/Aug., 1981, pp. 18–21.

Whitehead, John W., and Conlan, John. "The Establishment of the Religion of Secular Humanism and Its First Amendment Implications," *Texas Tech Law Review* 10:21 (1978):1–66.

Wright, G. Ernest, *God Who Acts: Biblical Theology as Recital.* Chicago: Henry Regnery, 1952.

# 4

## Reason:
## A Kingdom-extending Tool

### The Need for Reason

"We destroy arguments and every proud obstacle to the knowledge of God, and take every thought captive to obey Christ," wrote the apostle Paul to the Corinthians (2 Cor. 10:5). Paul understood clearly that the task of extending the kingdom of God involved a battle for the human mind—a spiritual warfare against human philosophies and ideologies that denied the truth of the gospel or its relevance to all of life. Human reason, a good gift of the creator God, is to be a servant to the church in its mission of subduing the earth (Gen. 1:28) and discipling the nations (Matt. 28:19–20) to the glory of God.

American evangelicals in this century have not adequately appreciated the importance of rational analysis and intellectual rigor for effectively penetrating the culture for Christ. According to Carl F. H. Henry, all too few evangelical leaders have manifested "a call to intellectually powerful analysis of the cultural crisis and the task it implies for vital evangelical impact."[1] Billy Graham has admitted that "evangelicals have not tried to capture the intellectual initiative as much as we should. We haven't challenged and de-

1. Carl F. H. Henry, "Evangelicals: Out of the Closet but Going Nowhere?" p. 22.
2. Billy Graham, in "Candid Conversation with the Evangelist," p. 19.

veloped the minds of our generation."[2] The evangelical tradition, focusing largely on personal religious experience, has not been effective in challenging the reigning ideologies entrenched in the institutions that command the heights of American culture.

The anti-intellectual tendencies which have diminished the cultural impact of evangelicalism are in part rooted in the revivalism of the nineteenth century. The methodology of revivalism promoted an emphasis on religious feeling, personal experience, and immediate decision, rather than careful intellectual analysis of the broader dimensions of culture and institutional life. The horizons of the evangelical mind tended to shrink from the wide vision of God's sovereignty over all of life to the more narrow confines of the impact of grace on the individual heart. During this period, as historian Richard Hofstadter has noted, to a considerable extent "the churches withdrew from intellectual encounters with the secular world, gave up the idea that religion is a part of the whole life of intellectual experience, and often abandoned the field of rational studies on the assumption that they were the natural province of science alone."[3] The evangelical failure to appreciate adequately the place of the life of the mind in the work of the kingdom thus unwittingly contributed to the secularization of American life that is so prominent in the closing decades of the twentieth century.

In this chapter, as we examine the role of reason in systematic theology, we will first see some examples in the history of theology and culture where its place has been exaggerated. We will then look at various historical influences that have tended to minimize the place of human reason. And finally we will examine, in the light of scripture, reason's proper servant role in the extension of the kingdom of God.

## The "Apotheosis" of Reason

### In theology

For the last several centuries, as Tillich noted, the primary question preoccupying Protestant theology has been whether or not the Christian faith could be successfully accommodated to the modern mind without abandoning that faith's essential substance.

3. Richard Hofstadter, *Anti-Intellectualism in American Life*, pp. 86–87.

The world view of modern science has been so persuasive that many have felt that a thoroughgoing reconstruction of the Christian faith was in order. Since the time of the Enlightenment rationalistic and deistic trends in theology have seen human reason rather than divine revelation as the norm of religious belief.

Immanuel Kant's *Religion Within the Limits of Reason Alone* (1793) was symptomatic of such rationalistic trends. According to Kant, miracles were superfluous to true religion; the essence of religion consisted in the heart disposition to fulfill human duties as divine commands. Kant's rationalistic approach reduced Christianity from a supernatural religion of redemption to a rather naturalistic code of morality.

In colonial America a small minority of thinkers were influenced by the deistic philosophies of Europe. Ethan Allen, the hero of Fort Ticonderoga in 1775, was also the author of *Reason the Only Oracle of Man*. A deistic standpoint was also expressed in Elihu Palmer's *Principles of Nature*. Thomas Paine's *Age of Reason* was the most widely read deistic work in America. According to Paine, deism "honors reason as the choicest gift of God to man ... and rejects, as the fabulous inventions of men, all books pretending to be revelation." Paine's deism left no place at all for miracles or special revelation.

The ideas of Allen, Palmer, and Paine are illustrations in American history of an exaggerated view of the role of human reason, but these ideas did not make a great impact on colonial America. The Great Awakening earlier in the century had dramatized the vitality of supernatural, biblical Christianity, and most Americans during the eighteenth century rejected the deists' ideas as extreme expressions of unbelief.

It was only during the latter part of the nineteenth century and the earlier part of the twentieth that rationalism significantly penetrated American theology and denominational life. Prior to the Civil War the awakenings and revivals had produced a high level of resistance to rationalistic influences in American Christianity. After the Civil War the influence of biblical criticism, Darwinism, science and techology, and the social changes produced by industrialization and urbanization shook the beliefs of many in the churches. The conflict between the historic and the revisionist conceptions of the Christian faith and biblical authority were focused in the modernist-fundamentalist controversies of the 1920s.

In some respects the modernists continued the anti-supernaturalist emphases of the earlier deists, but with the added weight of nineteenth-century higher criticism and great faith in the power and authority of modern science. In his widely read book *The Modern Use of the Bible* modernist leader Harry Emerson Fosdick observed that for "modern" Christians miracles are considered to be "indissolubly associated with ancient ignorance and as vanishing when intelligence arrives."[4] Modernists, said Fosdick, proclaimed their "freedom from bondage to the mental formulas of the past."[5] Such "mental formulas" included the verbal inspiration of the Bible, the virgin birth, the deity of Christ, the substitutionary atonement, the bodily resurrection, and the visible return of Christ at the end of the age.

Such rationalistic concessions to the modern mind abandoned the substance of the faith and, not surprisingly, led to a loss of spiritual vitality in the churches. Even the modernists at times seemed to be aware of the intellectual deficiencies of their anti-creedal, anti-dogmatic position. Shailer Mathews, in *The Faith of Modernism*, admitted that "if the temptation of the dogmatic mind is toward inflexible formula, that of the Modernist is toward indifference to formula."[6] Ironically modernism, which was rationalistic at many points in its anti-creedalism and aversion to theological precision, shared the anti-intellectual tendencies of many of its fundamentalist opponents. It too showed itself to be a stepchild of the experiential tradition of the American revival system.

The modernist apologetic program of reconstructing the Christian faith along lines presumably more suitable to the modern mind proved to be a failure. Modernism in the end was acceptable neither to consistently orthodox Christians nor to consistent humanists. The modernists failed to see clearly that the "offense" to the modern mind was not merely this or that doctrine, but biblical theism as such. Was God or man the highest reality and lord of history? No compromise was possible.

The humanist leader John Dewey saw the weakness of the modernist approach. "Christianity seems to the modern mind to be more rational than some of the earlier doctrines that have been

4. Harry Emerson Fosdick, *The Modern Use of the Bible*, p. 157.
5. Ibid., p. 183.
6. Shailer Mathews, *The Faith of Modernism*, p. 172.

reacted against," he wrote. "Such is not the case in fact. The theological philosophers of the Middle Ages had no greater difficulty in giving rational form to all the doctrines of the Roman church than has the liberal theologian of today in formulating and justifying the doctrines he entertains."[7] In other words, Dewey's "modern mind" had not been satisfied by modernist reconstructions; nothing less than the repudiation of the existence and moral authority of the personal, transcendent, and sovereign God of the Bible would suffice. More clearly than the modernists, Dewey saw where the real battle lines in later twentieth-century culture would be drawn: between a militant and consistent biblical supernaturalism and a militant and consistent secular humanism. Halfhearted compromises were destined to fall by the wayside.

### In culture

The virtual apotheosis of human reason in some areas of culture since the time of the Englightment of the eighteenth century is reflected in expressions of faith in science as the key to truth and human liberation. According to Sigmund Freud, religious beliefs were "illusions, fulfillments of the oldest, strongest and most urgent wishes of mankind."[8] Freud's world view was based on a scientific rationalism that had no place for the supernatural. "Our god *logos* is perhaps not a very almighty one, and he may be able to fulfill only a small part of what his predecessors have promised," Freud admitted. "No, our science is no illusion. But an illusion it would be to suppose that what science cannot give us we can get elsewhere."[9] Given Freud's atheistic understanding of human nature, his faith in scientific method as the key to therapy is really not surprising. What is surprising is the persistent faith in Freud's naturalistic doctrines despite the lack of convincing evidence that his methods are statistically effective.

In our own day B. F. Skinner's behavioristic psychology is an influential expression of scientific rationalism in America. Like Freud, Skinner is committed to an atheistic and materialistic view of human nature. "Man," he says, "is much more than a dog, but like a dog he is within range of a scientific analysis."[10] Since man

7. John Dewey, *A Common Faith*, p. 34.
8. Sigmund Freud, *The Future of an Illusion*, p. 30.
9. Ibid., pp. 54—56.
10. B. F. Skinner, *Beyond Freedom and Dignity*, pp. 200—201.

does not possess a transcendent spiritual nature as the image of God, Skinner believes man can be manipulated and molded in the interests of a scientific utopia projected by the scientific elite. "A scientific view of man offers exciting possibilities," he thinks. "We have not yet seen what man can make of man."[11] Those who take seriously the biblical doctrine of original sin, and remember the long history of man's abuse of concentrated power, will not be eager for Skinner and his fellow travelers to proceed with the experiment.

There are pervasive signs in modern culture of skepticism concerning the merits of a scientific rationalism like that of Freud or Skinner. Science practiced within the framework of a purely materialistic and mechanistic world view leaves no place for the higher moral and spiritual aspirations of mankind. As chemist and philosopher Michael Polanyi has observed, such a reductionistic science does not "recognize the existence of any ultimate irreducible entities above the level of elementary particles or their wave functions. Thus all life, all human beings, and all works of man—including Shakespeare's sonnets and Kant's *Critique of Pure Reason*— are ultimately to be represented in terms of their ultimate particles."[12] Such a materialistic and naturalistic science stifles the human spirit and denies the independence and reality of its highest ideals.

Ironically at this juncture of history, science, which began as a program of liberation from ignorance, prejudice, and superstition, is itself in danger of becoming obscurantist. As early as 1929 Alfred North Whitehead pointed to the dangers of a science which, by claiming to be a universal explanation of all reality, actually suppressed vital dimensions of human experience. "The obscurantists of any generation are in the main constituted by the greater part of the practitioners of the dominant methodology," he observed. "Today scientific methods are dominant, and scientists are the obscurantists."[13] No doubt Whitehead had in mind attempts to reduce religion, morality, conscience, and even human consciousness itself to "nothing but" the impersonal interactions of physical particles. Recent attempts to suppress the hypothesis of

11. Ibid., p. 215.
12. Michael Polanyi, "History and Hope," p. 190.
13. Alfred North Whitehead, *The Function of Reason*, p. 44.

divine creation in relation to the origin of living forms also come to mind.

Faith in science as a global framework of truth and meaning has also been expressed in America by the movement that has come to be known as "secular humanism." According to John Dewey, one of the leading philosophers of the movement, "there is but one method for ascertaining fact and truth—that conveyed by the word 'scientific' in its most general and generous sense."[14] There was no room, of course, in Dewey's scheme for unique truths of divine revelation; there was no God to reveal them.

In England, Bertrand Russell, the atheistic philospher and mathematician, expressed great faith in the powers of human reason to reform the world. "Thus rational doubt alone," he wrote in 1941, "if it could be generated, would suffice to induce the Millennium."[15] A little philosophic skepticism, he thought, would be sufficient to temper the dogmatisms of Roman Catholic clerics and Bolshevik revolutionaries.

A fundamental flaw in liberal, humanistic creeds like those of Dewey and Russell was pointed out by Dorothy Sayers during the Second World War: the liberal humanitarian leaders of the West, represented a "cut flower" form of idealism that attempted to retain the fruits of Christian values without the roots of living faith and doctrinal commitment. "We on our side," she wrote, "have been trying for several centuries to uphold a particular standard of ethical values which derives from Christian dogma, while gradually dispensing with the very dogma which is the sole rational foundation for those values. The rulers of Germany have seen quite clearly that dogma and ethics are inextricably bound together. Having renounced the dogma, they have renounced the ethics as well—and from their point of view they are perfectly right."[16]

Sayers' remarks concerning Nazism in an earlier generation apply even more forcibly to an aggressive Marxism-Leninism threatening the West today. A halfhearted and inconsistent humanism, weakened by hedonism and sexual indulgence, will be no match for a more consistent and ruthless humanism. Why, after all, should a humanist, believing in no God, no life after death, no absolute standards of right and wrong, resist tyranny to the death rather

14. Dewey, *A Common Faith*, p. 33.
15. Bertrand Russell, *Let the People Think*, p. 27.
16. Dorothy Sayers, "Creed or Chaos," pp. 15–16.

than appease it? The inconsistent and halfhearted humanism of the West, with its misplaced faith in science and human reason, simply is incapable of summoning the spiritual resources necessary to stem Marxist aggression from without or the degradations of sexual anarchy within. The spiritual bankruptcy of the humanist faith is becoming more and more apparent in the closing decades of the twentieth century.

The misplaced faith in human reason has had tragic political consequences during the last several centuries. During the French Revolution, the French mathematician and rationalistic philosopher Condorcet stated, "We have witnessed the development of a new doctrine which is to deliver the final blow to the already tottering structure of prejudice." What was this new doctrine by which the goddess Reason would deliver mankind? "It is the idea of the limitless perfectibility of the human species."[17] Evidently the Reign of Terror, which was under way at the time of Condorcet's writing and which eventually killed some seventeen thousand French citizens, did nothing to shake the philosopher's confidence in the perfectibility of human nature.

The Enlightenment's faith in the ability of human reason and scientific materialism to produce a utopian society was taken up by Marxism-Leninism. According to the official "Programme of the Communist International" (1928), which still expresses the philosophy of international communism, "Communist society will abolish the class divisions of society. ... It will abolish all forms of exploitation of man by man. ... For the first time in its history, mankind will take its own fate into its own hands." The new socialist society will "bury for ever all mysticism, religion, prejudice and superstition, and will give a powerful impetus to the development of all-conquering scientific knowledge."[18]

Even after the atrocities of Stalin's concentration camps, the revelations of the Gulag, the genocide of millions in Cambodia by the Pol Pot regime, and the invasion of Afghanistan, there are those, chiefly in Western universities and media centers, who are still enamored with the messianic claims of Marxism. To the imprisoned members of Solidarity, however, crushed by the oppression of Poland's Marxist leaders, the promise that communism would

17. Francis Schaeffer, *How Should We Then Live?* p. 121.
18. Emile Burns, *Handbook of Marxism*, pp. 985–87.

"abolish all forms of exploitation of man by man" must seem like a bitter and cruel joke indeed.

## Escape from Reason

### Historical examples

If there have been many examples in history of exaggerated confidence in reason, there have also been many examples in culture and church of an escape from reason. Especially during the last several centuries there have been forces steadily working in the church and culture that have tended to minimize the importance of the rational dimensions of human life and faith. The consequence of these irrationalistic trends has been, as we shall see, to reduce the effectiveness of the church in its mission to extend the kingdom of God in the world.

One influence that has been noted earlier stems from the awakenings and revivals that were so influential in shaping the character of American churches in the nineteenth century. The revival system as it was developed in the last century brought fresh spiritual vitality to churches throughout the nation, but often at the cost of emphasizing the experiential dimensions of the faith to the detriment of its intellectual substance. Church historian Edwin Gaustad has observed that the "discrediting of 'human learning,' characteristic of only a minority during the [eighteenth century] Awakening, later became typical of a majority of Protestantism."[19]

The experiential and pragmatic thrust of the revival system was reflected in much of the preaching of that period. "A pragmatic America and a frenetic frontier," observed Gaustad, "asked of the sermon only that it work."[20]

Similar observations have been made by historian Richard Hofstadter in his valuable study *Anti-Intellectualism in American Life.* The revivalists, he observes, "were not the first to disparage the virtues of the mind, but they quickened anti-intellectualism; and they gave to American anti-intellectualism its first brief moment of militant success."[21] Such tendencies were to come into full

---

19. Edwin S. Gaustad, *The Great Awakening in New England*, p. 139.
20. Ibid.
21. Hofstadter, *Anti-Intellectualism*, p. 74.

bloom during the modernist-fundamentalist controversies of the 1920s.

The impact of the revival system was to reduce the respect for learning that had been especially characteristic of New England Puritanism during the seventeenth and eighteenth centuries. T. J. Wertonbaker, in his study of New England Puritanism, noted that while "the New England leaders tried desperately to close the doors of their Zion to heresy, they threw them wide open to philosophy and science. They accepted knowledge as an ally and had no fear of it as an enemy, since scientific truth could not clash with revealed truth." The New England ministers eagerly read the new scientific works of Newton, Kepler, and Boyle, and sought to use them to buttress the biblical faith.[22] The split between piety and scholarship that was later to plague the evangelical tradition had not yet occurred.

It would not be accurate to conclude, however, that the anti-intellectual influences of the awakenings and revivals were universal. John Wesley, whose work was criticized by some of his contemporaries for its "enthusiasm" and emotionalism, made a special point of replying to the charge. "It is a fundamental principle with us," he stated, "that to renounce reason is to renounce religion; that religion and reason go hand in hand, and that all irrational religion is false religion." Wesley's affirmation is well worth pondering in regard to evangelical interest in charismatic and "relational" styles of Christian experience.

The anti-intellectual currents deriving from revivalism have been augmented by various trends outside the church. The impact of Charles Darwin's *Origin of Species* and *The Descent of Man* was to promote an image of man which focused on his biological rather than rational characteristics. Man was the "naked ape" rather than a divinely created being "a little lower than the angels." Philosophically, the effect of Darwinism was to reinforce the pragmatic temper of American life. In a Darwinian framework the question was not whether ideas and beliefs were true in any absolute sense, but whether or not they promoted the survival of the race.

The philosophy of Friedrich Nietzsche represented in many respects a strong reaction against the stress on human reason

---

22. T. J. Wertonbaker, *The Puritan Oligarchy: The Founding of American Civilization*, pp. 252, 264.

characteristic of European philosophy during the seventeenth and eighteenth centuries. In *Beyond Good and Evil* (1886) Nietzsche contended that moral progress derives from men of action who trust will and instinct over reason. The traditional Christian values of established society were invented by the weak to control the strong; such values must be "transvalued." Nietzsche's antinomian and iconoclastic amoralism bore bitter fruit in Germany during the 1930s. Its echoes can still be heard in the punk rock of the present generation.

The vastly influential work of Sigmund Freud, which reflected a fundamental commitment to scientific rationalism, in other respects promoted the irrational elements of modern life. Human behavior, Freud contended, was far less rational than commonly believed. By stressing the unconscious roots of human behavior in instinct and sexual drives, Freud deemphasized the role of rational reflection. Thinking in many cases was little more than "rationalization." Freud's views reflected and reinforced a dualism which has become pervasive in the twentieth century, namely a dualism between the determinsm of science and the antinomian "freedom" of human sexual drives.

More recently Theodore Roszak has described the irrationalism of the youth counter culture of the 1960s in *The Making of a Counter Culture*. The "flower generation" staged a neo-romantic revolt against science, technology, and reason in favor of feeling, sexuality, drugs, rock music, fantasy, and Eastern mysticism. The new heaven of peace, love, and freedom failed to materialize as expected, but the arational experientialism of those years lingers on in a younger generation of Americans.

The pendulum of social and spiritual change seems to be poised for a swing in the opposite direction. Pitirim A. Sorokin has noted how arational, sensate cultures eventually tend to elicit a reaction. "Ideational [faith-oriented] culture and law come usually after the disintegration of over-ripe Sensate culture and man, with appetites let loose, with hedonism, skepticism, and sensualism rampant, with the human personality deeply demoralized and disorderly."[23] America in the closing decades of the twentieth century would certainly be characterized as an "over-ripe Sensate" culture. Evan-

---

23. Pitirim A. Sorokin, *Social and Cultural Dynamics*, vol. I, p. 621.

gelicals should be prepared to seize the spiritual opportunities that the coming reaction is sure to bring.

The tendency to escape from reason into the world of religion is not limited to evangelical revivalism. At the other end of the theological spectrum the thought of Rudolf Bultmann represents an important twentieth-century example of the tendency to denigrate reason's proper role in the Christian life. One finds in Bultmann's theology a virtually complete dichotomy between faith and reason. Faith, he says, "must not aspire to an objective basis in dogma or in history on pain of losing its character of faith."[24] Bultmann thinks that for faith to seek an objective and historical basis, subject to the normal means of rational and scientific verification, is to fall into a new form of "works righteousness."

It is impossible, however, to separate the act of faith and the object of faith in the manner proposed by Bultmann. As H. P. Owen has observed, " 'Believing in' is impossible without some measure of 'believing that.' "[25] In similar fashion Pannenberg has noted the essential connection that must be maintained between faith and its rational basis. "The essence of faith," he states, "must come to harm precisely if in the long run rational conviction about its basis fails to appear."[26]

Bultmann's separation of Christian faith from its rational and historical basis is untenable in light of the New Testament itself. The apostle Paul, in speaking of the bodily resurrection of Jesus as a genuine historical event, states unambiguously that "if Christ has not been raised, your faith is worthless; you are still in your sins" (1 Cor. 15:17). No matter how sincere the faith, salvation is not an actuality for the Corinthians if the body of Jesus is still in the tomb. For the apostle, saving faith is very definitely tied to a historical fact. The facticity of the resurrection is a necessary precondition of an authentic Christian experience of redemption.

Any theology which, like Bultmann's, severs the link between inward faith and its rational, historical foundation leaves the believer defenseless in the face of claims by competing religious movements. On Bultmann's grounds there is no adequate way of distinguishing "faith" in Jesus from "faith" in Krishna or Mary Baker Eddy. Why Jesus rather than Buddha or Mohammed? Re-

24. Rudolf Bultmann, *Faith and Understanding*, vol. I, p. 15.
25. Charles W. Kegley, ed., *The Theology of Rudolf Bultmann*, p. 47.
26. Wolfhart Pannenberg, *Basic Questions in Theology*, vol. II, p. 28.

jecting the role of reason and history in authentic faith leaves the believer without the tools for distinguishing true revelational claims from spurious ones.

A final anti-intellectual trend that needs to be considered relates to the question of cultural relativism. With the rise of comparative anthropology as a distinct discipline, many people in the West have become more aware of the diversity of customs and values that exists among the world's various cultural and ethnic groups. It is sometimes suggested that even analytical thinking and Aristotelian logic is a Western invention. The French scholar Levy-Brühl, for example, has contended that primitive man was "prelogical" in his thought and inclined toward the mystical and magical rather than the logical and analytic perception of the world. Careful field observations have not supported Levy-Brühl's speculations. As Bronislaw Malinowski has noted, summarizing a wide range of observations, "every primitive community is in possession of a considerable store of knowledge, based on experience and fashioned by reason."[27] The law of cause and effect and the principle of noncontradiction are applied by "primitive" societies in agriculture, weather observation, navigation, warfare, and other aspects of social life. As common sense would indicate, any group that consistently ignored the law of cause and effect and the principle of noncontradiction would doom itself to speedy extinction.

One also occasionally hears the contention that while Western thinking is logical, Eastern thought is essentially mystical. This simplistic generalization does not stand up under careful examination. Analytical and mystical modes of awareness are found in both East and West. Aristotelian logic was certainly developed in the West, but its basic structures are found in cultures around the world.

Dan Daor, in the context of a careful historical study of modes of argument in Indian and Western philosophy, concludes that "Indian philosphical reasoning is as careful and logical as that of the West. There are certainly differences in emphasis and style, but not in intrinsic logicality."[28] Daor notes that the *reductio ad absurdum* type of argument is common to Indian, Chinese, and

27. Bronislaw Malinowski, *Magic, Science, and Religion,* p. 26.
28. Dan Daor, "Modes of Argument," p. 163.

European philosophy. He specifically notes that "the Chinese intuitively used the same modes of inference used by the Greek and Indian philosophers."[29]

These results are in accordance with what one might expect given the biblical doctrine of human creation in the image of God. An essential aspect of that divine image is man's rationality and power of analytic thought. The proposition that "2+2=4" is as valid in New Delhi as it is in New York or Moscow. Careless generalizations about the cultural relativity of basic human logic are simply not supported by careful cross-cultural studies in the history of philosophy.

Any theological tradition or ecclesiastical communion that denigrates the proper role of human reason in the Christian's life and the church's mission thereby contributes to its own cultural impotence. Human reason, subject to the authority of scripture and the illumination of the Holy Spirit, is an essential instrument in the fulfillment of the cultural mandate (Gen. 1:26–28) to subdue the earth to the glory of God. Spirit-guided reason must analyze the great issues of the day and, in the light of scripture, propose more cogent solutions than the humanists can offer. To the extent that American evangelicalism has not properly valued the life of the mind it has conceded major areas of the culture to the control of unbelief. To the extent that American evangelicalism corrects this deficiency it will be more effective in extending the kingship of Jesus Christ throughout American culture.

## Reason's Servant Role

### Biblical perspectives

For evangelical theology human reason is neither an autonomous master nor a useless appendage, but a servant of the resurrected and reigning Christ in the work of the extension of his kingdom. According to the biblical story human reason, like man himself, is the good creation of God, now subject to the power and bondage of sin, and yet renewable through the work of Christ and the Holy Spirit. This biblical perspective calls for further attention before considering the more particular issues of the role of reason in systematic theology.

29. Ibid., p. 181.

Various terms are used in scripture to refer to the faculty of human reason. In the New Testament we find νοῦς, mind, intellect, understanding, reason; νοέω, perceive, understand, gain insight; διάνοια, understanding, mind, thought; σύνεσις, faculty of comprehension, insight, understanding.

In the Old Testament there is no distinctive word for reason or mind as such. The seat of thinking is the heart (lēb; lēbāb; cf. Prov. 16:23; Isa. 6:10).

In scripture reason is not an autonomous and value-free element of human nature. The understanding of moral and spiritual truth is integrally related to the state of the will and the disposition of the heart toward God. "If any man's will is to do his [God's] will," Jesus said, "he shall know whether the teaching is from God or whether I am speaking on my own authority" (John 7:17). A rebellious will, indisposed to obey God, refuses to hear the self-evidencing witness of the voice of God.

The same point is made in a different way by the apostle Paul in Rom. 1:18, where he speaks of those who, in spite of the clear revelation of God's righteous character through the creation, "suppress the truth in unrighteousness" (τὴν ἀλήθειαν ἐν ἀδικίᾳ κατεχόντων). Rebellious man attempts to cover up the evidence of general revelation which threatens his personal autonomy and self-centered lifestyle.

Both texts (John 7:17; Rom. 1:18) clearly demonstrate that in the biblical world view human reason in its actual use, especially in matters moral and spiritual, reflects man's basic spiritual orientation—as either the servant of God or the rebel against God. No neutral standpoint is possible.

The scripture clearly teaches that all things created by God are good in and of themselves (Gen. 1:31) and are to be received with thanksgiving (1 Tim. 4:4). This creational goodness encompasses man's nature in general and his powers of reason in particular. The image and likeness of God in which man was created (Gen. 1:26–27) includes, though it is not limited to, man's rational powers. Man's rational and linguistic endowments set him apart from the lower creation and allow him to exercise dominion over it on God's behalf. Without the intellectual ability to discover and apply the laws of God's creation, man could not be successful in fulfilling the cultural mandate (Gen. 1:26, 28).

In Gen. 2:19 Adam is given a prophetic as well as a kingly role in the naming of the animals. The power of bestowing a name implies both proper authority over that which is named and insight concerning its created nature. Adam's naming of the animals can be seen as an illustration of the prophetic task of the covenant people in interpreting all aspects of human experience in terms of divine revelation and the commandments of God. This prophetic dimension of the cultural mandate would be impossible, of course, without the God-given endowment of reason and understanding. And as the Old Testament scholar Ludwig Koehler has pointed out, in biblical thought insight is not an independent achievement of man; all true knowledge comes from God.[30]

In the fourth chapter of Genesis the further outworkings of the cultural mandate are described. Even in a fallen world, due to the common grace of God, those outside the covenant line are able to develop the potentialities implanted in the creation. Human culture develops through the discoveries of agriculture, animal husbandry, music, metallurgy, and city building. In the hands of apostate man the exercise of the cultural mandate results in the self-glorification of man (e.g. the Tower of Babel), rather than the priestly offering of the fruits of man's labor to the covenant God. Nevertheless, the people of God are not to abandon the realm of culture to unbelievers, but through the godly use of reason and the application of God's law and the empowerment of the Spirit reclaim those spheres of culture for the rightful sovereignty of God the Father and Jesus Christ.

If the Bible teaches clearly that reason was originally created as a good gift of God, it teaches with equal clarity that in the present state of existence human reason is marred and damaged by sin. Man suppresses the clear truth of God in unrighteousness (Rom. 1:18). In matters moral and spiritual his thinking is futile and his mind senseless and darkened (Rom. 1:21). The unregenerated human mind is hostile to God and is constitutionally incapable of submitting itself to God's law (Rom. 8:7). Apart from the illuminating power of the Holy Spirit, the wisdom of God and the word of the cross are only foolishness to those who hear it (1 Cor. 2:14). Satan, the "god of this world," blinds the minds of unbelievers to prevent them from seeing the light of the gospel in Jesus Christ (2 Cor. 4:4). The unbelieving Jews do not even understand the true

30. Ludwig Koehler, *Old Testament Theology*, pp. 99 – 126.

meaning of the Old Testament, since a veil lies over their minds; only in Christ is the veil removed (2 Cor. 3:14—16). Prior to conversion the mind of man is darkened to spiritual truth, alienated from the life of God, because of the sinful hardness of heart (Eph. 4:17—18). The world does not comprehend the motives, values, and goals of the believer, because it did not comprehend those of Christ himself (cf. 1 John 3:1).

This biblical truth concerning the noetic effects of sin does not teach that the unbeliever cannot be a good accountant or farmer, but that in moral and spiritual matters there is a fundamental difference of perception between the believer and the unbeliever. And this fundamental qualitative difference, produced by regeneration, is basic for an evangelical theology.

For systematics, the natural blindness of unregenerate human reason to saving truth means that reason is not to be the final judge of divine revelation. Divine revelation has an inner coherence and rationality that must be understood on their own terms. Divinely revealed doctrines such as the Trinity, the deity of Christ, the virgin birth, and the final resurrection of believers transcend the powers of natural reason but do not contradict it.

The doctrine of the noetic effects of sin does not mean that reason has no place whatever in testing competing revelation claims. The New Testament clearly teaches that regenerate reason, in submission to the authority of the apostolic teaching, is to "test the spirits to see whether they are of God" (1 John 4:1). Such statements imply the legitimacy of a coherence test of truth—i.e., checking the consistency of new doctrinal claims with the teachings already known to be true. The apostle Paul states unequivocally that any revelation claim that is inconsistent with the apostolic gospel already known is to be rejected, even if it is preached by an angel from heaven (Gal. 1:8). It should be noted that in these instances (1 John 4:1; Gal. 1:8) regenerate reason is not functioning as an autonomous theological norm; rather, as the servant of apostolic doctrine it tests new claims by that received standard. Unregenerate reason has no right to judge the truth of the gospel. Spiritual truth is understood only by those who have received the Spirit of God (1 Cor. 2:14).

The biblical teaching concerning the noetic effects of sin has clear implications for Christian ethics. The scriptures, and not the social sciences or public opinion polls, are the norm of Christian morals. Psychological and sociological research which interprets human behavior through the categories of unregenerate human reason must not be allowed to usurp the normative authority of biblical revelation. Sociological studies can discover empirical truths about how persons actually behave in a fallen world and with a fallen human nature; they must not, however, be allowed to set the standards of how people *ought* to act. The discovery that $x$ percent of the American adult population engages in homosexual activity is a descriptive and not a prescriptive statement. The descriptive findings of the social sciences may confirm at many points the truth of revelation, but the normative interpretation of human experience must always proceed from a biblical starting point. The sociological facts are not self-interpreting but must be seen within a philosophical framework in which biblical revelation provides the controlling assumptions.

The doctrine of the noetic effects of sin is crucial for Christian scholarship generally. All of life is to be interpreted not through the categories of fallen human reason, but on the basis of a world view controlled by divine revelation. The presuppositional differences deriving respectively from systems of thought determined by regenerate and unregenerate reason are more obvious in the clearly value-laden disciplines such as philosophy, ethics, psychology, sociology, and political science, which have to do with the study of human nature. But in principle these distinctions apply to all the academic disciplines. Consequently, the Christian educator will seek curricula that view *all* aspects of human experience in the light of God's word. The true meaning of human life and thought is seen only through the spectacles of scripture. The facts of human experience call for interpretation in terms of a framework controlled by biblical revelation. This renewal and reformation of Christian scholarship is necessitated by the mandate to exercise godly dominion in all the earth (Gen. 1:26–28), to disciple the nations according to the laws of Christ (Matt. 28:19–20), and to have the Christian mind continually transformed by the truth of Jesus Christ (Rom. 12:1–2). The extension of God's kingdom in the world requires full recognition of the fact of the noetic effects of sin, and then the overcoming of those effects through the transforming power of the resurrected and reigning Christ's word and Spirit.

At the level of popular culture the fact of the darkening of the human mind accounts for the pervasive misunderstanding and misrepresentation of biblical religion. It is no accident that biblical Christianity is generally distorted on network television and by the mainstream secular media. A fallen human mind, which is suppressing the truth in unrighteousness (Rom. 1:18), may not consciously intend to misrepresent the truth of the gospel; it is only natural, however, that it actually does so. This is another vitally important cultural example of the biblical truth that the unregenerate mind does not comprehend spiritual realities (1 Cor. 2:14). But this does not excuse the unbeliever's behavior. When unbelievers distort or demean the Christian message, God will hold them morally accountable for those distortions. God is not mocked (Gal. 6:7). It is incumbent upon Christians in our day to interpret their own experience and belief systems to the general public on biblical grounds, and to seize new media opportunities presented by satellite, cable, and low-power television broadcasting technology. These new technologies, when placed at the service of a biblical world view and sense of evangelical mission, can be powerful tools for the extension of the kingdom and for winning the battle for the minds of this generation.

The teaching of the noetic effects of sin is not the Bible's last word on the role of reason in the Christian life. Through the regenerating work of the Holy Spirit the mind darkened by sin is to be progressively renewed in the image of the Creator (Eph. 4:23–24; Col. 3:10). The believer's mind is to be continuously transformed by the truth of Christ (Rom. 12:1–2), so that we have the mind of Christ (1 Cor. 2:16). In this life we see through a glass darkly (1 Cor. 13:12), and the effects of sin on the understanding will not be totally removed prior to the consummation of all things; yet substantial progress is both possible and necessary.

For the believer renewed by God's word and Spirit the real antithesis is not between faith and reason, but between regenerate and unregenerate reason or, alternatively, between a *faithful* and a *faithless* use of reason. The real question is, which kingdom does reason serve—man or God's? The believer has been delivered from the kingdom of darkness to the kingdom of God's beloved Son (Col. 1:13).

For evangelical theology faith is not merely intellectual assent to theological propositions, although saving faith does involve propositions (1 Cor. 15:17). The devil is a monotheist, but that belief in and of itself does not constitute saving faith (James 2:19). Neither is faith mere blind credulity, a "faith in faith" or belief in some unknown God or higher power. Rather, authentic biblical faith is a disposition of the human subject to trust and believe in God in response to evident truth (cf. Rom. 1:18–20; John 5:36; 10:25; 14:11). Faith does not mean believing in God despite a lack of evidence, but the willingness to see the evidence for what it really is (John 7:17), and consequently to acknowledge God and to be subject to his authority in all areas of life. Biblical faith is a way of seeing, a "second sight" by means of which we perceive the unseen but very real spiritual realities through the creation and the preached word of God (cf. 2 Cor. 4:18; Rom. 1:18–20; Ps. 19:1). As such, faith is a most reasonable response in the face of God's evident truth.

### In systematic theology

In systematic theology reason performs three essential functions. It helps demonstrate the coherence and organic relationships of the various elements of biblical truth; it defends biblical revelation from skeptical attack; and it helps apply biblical revelation to contemporary social and ethical problems.

A coherent and integrated grasp of the various facets of biblical revelation is needed to maintain a balanced and effective understanding of the Christian life and the church's mission. Just as the proper relationship and tuning of the various parts of an automobile engine are important for maximum power and efficiency, so the proper grasp and "tuning" of the truths of scripture as an integrated whole are important in the life of the church.

The biblical doctrine of creation, for example, has important implications for a balanced view of salvation, the mission of the church, and eschatology. Because God's original creation—including the human body—was good, it is natural that Jesus' saving ministry on earth was also manifested in acts of physical healing. It is quite appropriate that the church's mission be understood in terms of ministry to the whole person, involving bodily needs, although conversion is the top priority. Biblical eschatology teaches the doctrine of the resurrection of the body, not merely the immortality of the soul.

Throughout the centuries reason has performed an apologetic function in the defense of the faith from skeptical attack. At the same time, there always have been some Christians who seemed to believe that rational defenses of the faith were either unnecessary or illegitimate. Celsus, a second century opponent of the church, was reported to have complained about the Christians that "some will not give or hear reason about their faith, but stick to 'Ask no question, but believe' and 'Thy faith shall save thee' and 'The wisdom in the world is a bad thing and the foolishness a good.' "[31]

The early Christian father Tertullian once asked, "What has Athens to do with Jerusalem? What concord is there between the Academy and the Church? Knowing Jesus Christ we need no speculative inquiry, and possessing the gospel no further research" (De praescriptione 7). Tertullian, in spite of such rhetorical flourishes, did not actually abandon rational investigation and historical inquiry. He argued that the historical evidence pointed to the antiquity of the apostolic teaching of the church and to the novelty of the heretics' doctrine.

Luther could say, "Reason is the devil's prostitute and can do nothing but blaspheme and defile everything God speaks and does." This could easily be misunderstood unless it is realized that Luther was speaking of unregenerate reason. In another context he wrote, "Before faith and the knowledge of God reason is darkness in divine matters, but through faith it is turned into a light in the believer and serves piety as an excellent instrument."[32]

In the New Testament it is evident that a rational defense of the faith can be appropriate. The apostle Peter writes, "Always be prepared to make a defense [ἀπολογία] to any one who calls you to account for the hope that is in you" (1 Peter 3:15). The distinctive values and way of life manifested by the Christian in a pagan culture provide opportunities to explain and defend that way of life in personal conversations.

The missionary preaching of the apostle Paul in Damascus, Athens, Thessalonica, Corinth, and Ephesus contained a strong apologetic element. Luke uses the terms συμβιβάζω ("prove"), διαλέγομαι ("argue, discuss"), and πείθω ("convince, persuade") to describe Paul's preaching to Jews and Greeks, especially in the synagogues (Acts 9:22; 17:2; 18:4; 18:19; 19:8–9; 24:25). Paul sought

31. A. D. Nock, Conversion, p. 205.
32. Ewald Plass, comp., What Luther Says, vol. 3, pp. 1165–66.

to persuade and convince his listeners of the truth of the gospel and to overcome their objections.

After surveying the relationship of faith and reason in the Pauline epistles, Günther Bornkamm concludes that "Paul assigns a highly important role to human reason and rationality in the Christian's understanding of himself and in all the spheres of his life."[33] Similarly, Dieter Kemmler, in a study of Paul's preaching as illustrated in the Thessalonian epistles and in Acts 17, concludes that "Paul in his preaching was concerned to anchor the gospel in the νοῦς [mind] of the Thessalonians. This can also be regarded as characteristic of Paul's teaching in general."[34] While there is no doubt that the great apostle to the Gentiles had many profound mystical and charismatic experiences, there is also no doubt that he was deeply concerned about the rational explication and defense of the gospel.

There is general agreement in evangelical circles that there is a legitimate place for apologetics in the life of the church, but there is no unanimity concerning the best methodology for such an enterprise. The two main schools in American evangelicalism are known as "evidentialism" and "presuppositionalism." Proponents of both schools share a commitment to the infallibility of scripture and the fundamentals of the faith, but differ in philosophical judgments concerning the proper starting point for apologetics and on the question of how much common ground the believer and unbeliever share in religious discussions.

The evidential point of view is represented in such works as John Warwick Montgomery's *History and Christianity* and *Faith Founded on Fact* and Clark Pinnock's *Reason Enough*. Evidentialists argue that the believer and the unbeliever have common ground in the laws of logic and the evidences of history. According to this school an impartial consideration of the evidences of reason, nature, and history leads to the very probable conclusion that God exists, that Christ rose from the dead, and that Christianity is true. The evidential approach can claim a long and distinguished pedigree in the history of the church, and seems immediately applicable in personal conversations with inquirers.

The presuppositional approach has been advocated forcefully

---

33. Günther Bornkamm, "Faith and Reason in Paul's Epistles," p. 97.
34. Dieter/Werner Kemmler, *Faith and Human Reason*, p. 206.

by Cornelius Van Til in *The Defense of the Faith* and *A Christian Theory of Knowledge*. This point of view is represented in somewhat different form by Gordon Clark in *Religion, Reason, and Revelation*.

According to Van Til the existence of the triune God of the Bible and the inerrancy of scripture are the indispensable presuppositions of the meaning and truth of any fact whatsoever. "Facts" and "evidences," argues Van Til, are only properly understood when seen within a framework or world view controlled by scriptural assumptions. The biblical world view discloses the resurrection not as a "freak of nature," but as the revelation of Christ's deity and the authentication of all his claims.

Van Til has often been criticized for minimizing the role of historical evidence in establishing the Christian case. Why not, for example, accept the Koran rather than the Bible as one's presuppositional base? This line of criticism is not entirely fair, since Van Til does recognize the important role of evidence in distinguishing various revelation claims. He has, however, quite correctly insisted that the evidence is seen for what it truly is only in the light of scripture.

There is no question that the New Testament appeals to historical evidences in its own confirmation (John 5:36; 10:25; 14:11; Luke 24:38–39; Acts 1:3). At the same time, the equally clear scriptural teaching concerning the noetic effects of sin makes it impossible to grant the unbeliever equal standing in the evaluation of spiritual truth. Apologetic conversations will of course appeal to reason and evidence, but the believer will constantly seek to present and interpret the data within a framework controlled by biblical revelation. It is precisely this insistence on the cruciality of a biblical world view for the proper interpretation of all human experience that many have seen as the key advantage of the presuppositional approach.

One key area of Christian apologetics, the theistic proofs, has been receiving renewed attention in recent years. Since the time of Hume and Kant in the eighteenth century many Protestant theologians have seen little value in the traditional proofs for the existence of God. There are signs that this common opinion is being reevaluated. Norman L. Geisler, in *Philosophy of Religion*, presents a detailed argument for the validity of the cosmological proof. Richard Swinburne, in his important recent work, *The Ex-*

*istence of God*, has shown the weakness of many of the criticisms made by Hume and Kant. Swinburne argues that the various proofs have a cumulative impact and, taken together, constitute good inductive arguments for the existence of God. Efforts like those of Geisler and Swinburne demonstrate the rational strength of Christian theism in the face of its philosophical critics. Such renewal of confidence in the rational strength of theism is important for extending the dominion and influence of biblical thinking in the world of intellect and culture.[35]

A third major function of reason in evangelical theology consists in the application of scriptural truth to contemporary social and ethical problems.[36] The unchanging truths of scripture need fresh application in various times and cultures as the church pursues its mission of bringing all nations to the "obedience of faith" (Rom. 1:5).

This inferential role of reason is recognized in the Westminster Confession's statement on scripture: "The whole counsel of God, concerning all things necessary for his own glory, man's salvation, faith, and life, is either expressly set down in scripture, or by good and necessary consequences may be deduced from scripture" (I.vi). These "good and necessary consequences" link biblical text and contemporary context.

Today there is an urgent need for evangelical theology to demonstrate the implications of biblical truth for the institutions of American culture that show such manifest signs of weakness and decline. The biblical doctrine of the creation of all human beings in the image and likeness of God is the divine criticism of all attempts to legitimize abortion, infanticide, or euthanasia. The doctrine of original sin points to the dangers of concentrated state power and underscores the wisdom of a philosophy of limited government. As James Madison, himself a former student of the Rev. John Witherspoon, wrote, "The accumulation of all powers ... in the same hands may justly be pronounced the very definition of tyranny."[37] The state is not to usurp the proper role of

---

35. On the weaknesses of Kant's religious epistemology, see John Jefferson Davis, "Kant and the Problem of Religious Knowledge," in *Perspectives on Evangelical Theology*, ed. Kenneth S. Kantzer and Stanley N. Gundry (Grand Rapids: Baker, 1979).

36. Another major function of reason, the interpretation of scripture, will be considered later in connection with hermeneutics (Chapter 8).

37. Saul K. Padover, ed., *The Complete Madison*, p. 348.

church, family, economy, or school, but to function within its own divinely appointed limits.

In these and other ways reason, as the servant of divine revelation, is to assist in the extension of the reign of Christ in all areas of life. The point is not merely to interpret the world in the light of biblical categories, but to transform it. Reason, as a "candle in the hands of the Lord," has an important role to play in the fulfillment of the dominion covenant to subdue the nations in the name and authority of the resurrected and reigning Christ, who is Lord of all.

## Bibliography

Berger, Raoul. *Government by Judiciary.* Cambridge: Harvard University Press, 1977.

Bornkamm, Günther. "Faith and Reason in Paul's Epistles," *New Testament Studies* 4 (1957—58):93—100.

Bultmann, Rudolf. *Faith and Understanding,* Vol. I. London: SCM, 1969.

Burns, Emile. *Handbook of Marxism.* London: Victor Gollancz, 1936.

Clark, Gordon. *Religion, Reason, and Revelation.* Philadelphia: Presbyterian and Reformed, 1961.

Daor, Dan. "Modes of Argument," in Ben-Ami Scharfstein, *et al., Philosophy East/Philosophy West.* New York: Oxford University Press, 1978, pp. 162—95.

Davis, John Jefferson. "Kant and the Problem of Religious Knowledge," in *Perspectives on Evangelical Theology,* ed. Kenneth S. Kantzer and Stanley Gundry. Grand Rapids: Baker, 1979.

Dewey, John. *A Common Faith.* New Haven, Conn.: Yale University Press, 1934.

Fosdick, Harry Emerson. *The Modern Use of the Bible.* New York: Macmillan, 1924.

Freud, Sigmund. *The Future of an Illusion.* 1927; rpt. New York: Norton, 1961.

Gaustad, Edwin S. *The Great Awakening in New England.* New York: Harper, 1957.

Geisler, Norman L. *Philosophy of Religion.* Grand Rapids: Zondervan, 1974.

Graham, Billy. In "Candid Conversation with the Evangelist," *Christianity Today,* July 17, 1981, pp. 18—24.

Harder, G. "Reason," *New International Dictionary of New Testament Theology.* Grand Rapids: Zondervan, 1978.

Henry, Carl F. H. "Evangelicals: Out of the Closet but Going Nowhere?" *Christianity Today,* Jan. 4, 1980, pp. 16—22.

Hofstadter, Richard. *Anti-Intellectualism in American Life.* New York: Knopf, 1963.

Kegley, Charles W., ed. *The Theology of Rudolf Bultmann.* London: SCM, 1966.

Kemmler, Dieter Werner. *Faith and Human Reason: A Study of Paul's Method of Preaching as Illustrated by 1–2 Thessalonians and Acts 17:2–4.* Leiden: E. J. Brill, 1975.

Koehler, Ludwig. *Old Testament Theology.* Trans. A. S. Todd. Philadelphia: Westminster, 1957.

Leith, John H., ed. *Creeds of the Churches.* Richmond: John Knox, 1973.

Malinowski, Bronislaw. *Magic, Science, and Religion.* Garden City, N.Y.: Doubleday, 1954.

Mathews, Shailer. *The Faith of Modernism.* New York: Macmillan, 1924.

Montgomery, John Warwick. *Faith Founded on Fact.* Nashville: Thomas Nelson, 1978.

————. *History and Christianity.* Downers Grove, Ill.: Inter-Varsity, 1971.

Nash, Ronald, ed. *The Philosophy of Gordon H. Clark.* Philadelphia: Presbyterian and Reformed, 1968.

Niebuhr, H. Richard. *Christ and Culture.* New York: Harper, 1951.

Nock, A. D. *Conversion.* Oxford: Oxford University Press, 1933.

Padover, Saul K., ed. *The Complete Madison.* New York: Harper, 1953.

Pannenberg, Wolfhart. *Basic Questions in Theology,* Vol. II. London: SCM, 1971.

Pinnock, Clark. *Reason Enough.* Downers Grove, Ill.: Inter-Varsity, 1980.

Plass, Ewald, comp. *What Luther Says.* 3 vols. St. Louis: Concordia, 1959.

Polanyi, Michael. "History and Hope," *Virginia Quarterly Review* 38 (1962):177–95.

Roszak, Theodore. *The Making of a Counter Culture.* Garden City, N.Y.: Doubleday, 1969.

Rushdoony, R. J. *This Independent Republic.* Nutley, N.J.: Craig Press, 1964.

Russell, Bertrand. *Let the People Think.* London: Watts, 1941.

Sayers, Dorothy. "Creed or Chaos," in *The Necessity of Systematic Theology,* ed. John Jefferson Davis. Washington: University Press of America, 1978.

Schaeffer, Francis. *How Should We Then Live?* Old Tappan, N.J.: Revell, 1976.

Skinner, B. F. *Beyond Freedom and Dignity.* New York: Knopf, 1971.

Selwyn, E. G. *The First Epistle of St. Peter.* London: MacMillan, 1958.

Sorokin, Pitirim A. *Social and Cultural Dynamics,* Vol. II. New York: American Book Co., 1937.

Swinburne, Richard. *The Existence of God.* New York: Oxford University Press, 1979.

Van Til, Cornelius. *A Christian Theory of Knowledge.* Philadelphia: Presbyterian and Reformed, 1969.

————. *The Defense of the Faith.* Philadelphia: Presbyterian and Reformed, 1955.

Warfield, B. B. *Augustine and Calvin.* Philadelphia: Presbyterian and Reformed, 1956.

Wertonbaker, T. J. *The Puritan Oligarchy: The Founding of American Civilization.* New York: Scribner's, 1947.

Whitehead, Alfred North. *The Function of Reason.* 1929; rpt. Boston: Beacon Press, 1958.

# 5

## The Role
## of Religious Experience
## in Theology

I t has been noted by many observers that the twentieth-century
American sensibility is an experiential one. Feeling, emotion,
"sensitivity," self-awareness and "self-actualization," "born-again"
religion and self-help therapies—all in one way or another point
toward the immediacy of personal experience. This experiential
emphasis has influenced the character of American religion and
theology in both its liberal and conservative expressions. Both the
heritage of Puritan and revivalistic Christianity and the tradition
of American philosophical pragmatism have tended to reinforce
experience as an important dimension of American religious life.

The term "experience" can be a rather nebulous one. Here it is
used to refer to the affective or "feeling" dimension of human sensibility, as distinguished from the cognitive and the voluntary. "Religious experience" refers to an immediate awareness of divine
realities, which then can form the basis for reflection, analysis,
and ethical action. Religious experience points to the dimension
of the paranormal—i.e., to the realm of the supernatural, as distinguished from ordinary sense experience.

Any discussion of religious experience in relation to systematic
theology raises a number of significant questions. Do the Old and

New Testaments assign an important role to the experiential dimension of religion? What role has religious experience played in the history of the Christian church? Should religious experience play any normative role in evangelical theology? What principles for evaluating religious experiences can be derived from scripture? These are some of the issues that will be addressed in the present chapter.


## Biblical Insights

### The Old Testament

In both testaments it is clear that personal religious experience has a prominent place. The great figures of the Old Testament have immediate experiences of the divine which are influential in shaping their own understanding and that of the covenant people. God speaks to Abraham in a night vision, and a deep terror falls upon Abraham in deep sleep (Gen. 15:12). Abraham experiences the dimension of the "numinous," the *mysterium tremendum*, described by Rudolf Otto in *The Idea of the Holy*.

God reveals himself to Moses through the remarkable phenomenon of the burning bush (Exod. 3). Samuel is called to the prophetic ministry when God speaks to him at night (1 Sam. 3). Elijah hears the still, small voice of God at Mount Horeb (1 Kings 19). God speaks to Solomon in a dream (1 Kings 3). Isaiah is overwhelmed by the temple vision of God's holiness (Isa. 6). The word of God is experienced by Jeremiah as "fire" in his bones (Jer. 20:9). Ezekiel is given strange visions by God and is "lifted up" by the Spirit of God (Ezek. 2:2; 3:12; 8:3). God gives Daniel the power to interpret dreams and visions (Dan. 7:1; 8:1).

While it is certainly the case that such experiences were not everyday occurrences in the life of Israel, it is equally true that any account of Old Testament religion which takes the authority of scripture seriously must take such experiences into account. The plainly supernatural dimension of Old Testament religion is a pervasive aspect of the documents.

The Old Testament writers clearly witness to the affective side of faith. The important place of "religious affections" is especially prominent in the Psalms, though hardly limited to that portion of the Old Testament canon. The psalmist's soul longs and thirsts for the living God (Ps. 42:1—2). God is his exceeding joy (Ps. 43:4). The precepts of the Lord rejoice the heart, and to the pious believer are sweeter than honey (Ps. 19:8—10). The psalmist delights in God's statutes and his soul is consumed with longing for the law (Ps. 119:16, 20, 103). The psalmist invites the inquirer to taste and see that the Lord is good (Ps. 34:8). From these and other expressions of Old Testament piety it is clear that a personal awareness of God in his goodness and glory does stir the emotions. The psalmists of Israel would no doubt have agreed with Jonathan Edwards' estimation in *Religious Affections*: "Without holy affection there is no true religion; and no light in the understanding which does not produce holy affection in the heart" (I. ii).

### The New Testament

The New Testament no less than the Old gives abundant examples of the immediate experience of supernatural realities. Jesus of Nazareth, "God with us" and the Word made flesh, in his healings, miracles, and exorcisms manifests the power and presence of God and his kingdom among men. Saul the persecutor of the church becomes Paul the apostle to the Gentiles through a dramatic conversion experience on the road to Damascus. The Pentecostal experience of speaking in known languages and in the tongues of angels (Acts 2:11; 8:17; 10:46) manifests the immediate presence of the Spirit in the Christian community. The Pauline discussions in Romans 12 and 1 Corinthians 12—14 of such charismatic gifts as prophecy, healing, tongues, knowledge, wisdom, and interpretation presuppose the Spirit's immediacy to the church. Through a vision the apostle Peter is supernaturally directed to share the gospel with the Gentile Cornelius (Acts 10). In a dramatic series of visions John of the Apocalypse is given a stunning revelation of the risen and reigning Christ and insight into the course of the church's future history.

James Dunn, commenting on the "charismatic" dimension of the New Testament witness, notes that for all the New Testament writers, in varying degrees, the gift of the Spirit is one essential element in the conversion experience.[1] The distinctively Christian experience in the New Testament involves both Jesus and the Spirit, and such experience was influential in shaping both the theology and the life of the early church.

1. James Dunn, *Baptism in the Holy Spirit*, pp. 226—29.

It would be a mistake, however, to equate the affective dimensions of New Testament Christianity with its more spectacular charismatic expressions. Not all speak in tongues, heal, or perform miracles, but all are to be "aglow with the Spirit," never flagging in zeal (Rom. 12:11). All are to experience peace with God (Rom. 5:1) and to manifest fruits of the Spirit such as love, joy, and peace (Gal. 5:22). Such fruits of the Spirit, rather than charismatic gifts as such, are the sure signs of spiritual maturity. The believer is to constantly rejoice in the Lord (Phil. 4:4) and to sing with thankful heart unto God (Col. 3:16). The believer has personally tasted the spiritual power and reality of the word of God (Heb. 6:5). Without having seen Christ with the physical eyes, the believer, through the ministry of the Spirit, rejoices in the presence and reality of salvation with unutterable and exalted joy (1 Peter 1:8). The risen Christ tells John that lukewarm Christians are a contradiction in the life of the church (Rev. 3:16).

While many church members today are suspicious of all "enthusiasm" and emotionalism in religion, it is undeniable that in both testaments God touches the whole person, including the emotions. A religion without "holy affections" in the proper sense is not the religion of the Bible, but some pale and atrophied imitation of it.

## Religious Experience in History

### Ancient and medieval church

The mystical and charismatic stream is an ancient one in the history of the church. The Montanist movement in the second century was a notable expression of enthusiastic and experiential religion. Montanus created a stir in Asia Minor around the year 172, claiming that God spoke directly through him: "Man is a lyre, and I move over him like a plectrum." Two prophetesses, Maximilla and Priscilla, called for asceticism and rigorous church discipline, and claimed to have experienced visions and the gift of tongues. Maximilla is reputed to have said, "After me there will be no more prophecy, but the end." According to Epiphanius, an early church father, Priscilla claimed that "Christ came to me in the likeness of a woman and revealed that here Jerusalem comes down from heaven."

The Montanists were reacting to what they believed to be spiritual deadness and worldliness in the church of their day. The prophecies concerning the imminence of the end, presumably based on new revelatory experiences, proved to be mistaken. The authorities of the catholic church saw the movement as a threat to the unity and order of the church—a reaction to many later enthusiastic movements in history.

During the sixth century the mystical ideas of Pseudo-Dionysius the Areopagite achieved wide circulation in the church. In his *Mystical Theology* and other writings Pseudo-Dionysius advocated a process of spiritual purification, illumination, and vision culminating in union with God. The God thus experienced was claimed to be utterly beyond the normal human categories of predication—neither darkness nor light, neither negative nor positive. According to this mystical theology union with God can be experienced, but not conceptualized or expressed. The works of Pseudo-Dionysius were translated into Latin by John Scotus Erigena and became influential in the Latin church.

During the thirteenth century the "Brotherhood of the Free Spirit," a German mystical movement, advocated a pantheistic type of mysticism, teaching that God was the being or essence of all beings.

Meister Eckhart (d. 1328) was one of the more notable medieval mystics. According to Eckhart, when "a person has a true spiritual experience, he may boldly drop the spiritual disciplines. . . . As St. Paul says, 'The letter kills, but the Spirit makes alive.' " Eckhart was reacting to the ritualism and institutionalism of the Roman Catholic Church. Like others in the mystical tradition he was seeking for the immediate presence of God apart from priesthood, liturgy, and sacrament. Such a spiritual program was inevitably perceived by the ecclesiastical leadership as anti-authoritarian and subversive for church discipline.

### Reformation and post-Reformation developments

Luther, Calvin, and other mainstream Reformers were careful to insist upon the balance of word and Spirit in the Christian life, with the written word having priority as the authority for faith and practice. The "radical" or "left-wing" Reformers, as represented by the Anabaptist tradition, at times tended to give the Spirit priority over the word in matters of religious authority. Thomas Münzer

(1490–1525), a religious enthusiast and fanatic who contested Luther's spiritual leadership, advocated mystical views and called for a radical reformation of church and state by the standard of his "inner light." Münzer even came to advocate violence as a means of reformation: "We must exterminate with the sword, like Joshua, the Canaanitish nations."

According to Kaspar Schwenckfeld (ca. 1490–1561), a somewhat less extreme Anabaptist leader, the Spirit defined the word, not the word the Spirit. Scripture was seen as a confirmation of one's own spiritual experience.

George Fox and his Quaker followers appealed to the "inner light" as the primary source of religious truth. According to Quaker theologian Robert Barclay, "the Spirit, and not the Scripture, is the foundation and ground of all truth and knowledge, and the primary rule of faith and manners."[2] In the United States, Elias Hicks (1748–1830), in a dispute with "evangelical" Quakers, championed traditional Quaker positions. Hicks believed that the Bible was a source of spiritual knowledge and inspiration, but denied that it was the only rule of faith and practice.

On the continent evangelical pietism emerged as a strong current of spiritual renewal during the seventeenth and eighteenth centuries. Pietist leaders such as August Hermann Francke (1663–1727) and P. J. Spener (1635–1705) promoted a fresh discovery of Christianity as a living experience within continental Lutheranism. Spener and Francke stressed personal repentance, Bible study, lay responsibility, and small fellowship groups as essential elements of church renewal. Count Nikolaus von Zinzendorf (1700–1760) and his Moravian followers promoted an intimate devotion to the grace of Christ in the cross. For the Moravians the faith of the heart transcended barriers of creed and denomination. Zinzendorf and his followers were deeply concerned for world mission and for the cause of Christian unity. Their evangelical pietism was a significant influence in the life of John Wesley, who shared with them a concern for the rediscovery of a warm, experiential Christian faith.

In America, Jonathan Edwards, a representative of the Puritan and Reformed stream of Protestantism, was both an instrument of religious awakening and a keen analyst of its dynamics. In his

2. H. D. McDonald, *Theories of Revelation*, p. 72.

*Treatise Concerning Religious Affections* (1746), Edwards, in the wake of the Great Awakening, set about to answer the question, How can true piety be distinguished from mere emotionalism? According to Edwards there were a number of "distinguishing signs of truly gracious and holy affections." Genuine religious affections are based on a perception of the moral excellency of divine things; they produce a sense of spiritual humility; they promote a spirit of love; they lead to consistency and obedience in the practice of the Christian life. Love, and not the intensity or novelty of the experience as such, is the hallmark of a genuine work of divine grace. Edwards' work, although over two centuries old, is still valuable today, especially in light of similar issues raised in our own day by the resurgent neo-pentecostal movement.

### Liberal Protestantism

In evangelical pietism religious experience provided vitality and renewal for faith; in liberal Protestantism it tended to replace scripture as the norm of faith and practice. Kant's *Critique of Pure Reason* was a philosophical landmark in the development of liberal Protestantism. Kant argued that God was not a possible object of sense experience, and hence that no theoretical knowledge of his existence or attributes was possible. The traditional theistic proofs, Kant concluded, were invalid. God could only be conceived as the necessary postulate of human moral experience, the Cosmic Lawgiver behind the moral law.

While Kant was correct in believing that God was not an object of sense experience, he was mistaken in denying that God is manifest through the world of space, time, and sense to the spiritual sensibility of mankind. Kant asserted but did not prove the impossibility of God's immanence in human experience. His understanding of God's relation to the world was one-sided in the direction of transcendence and was deistic rather than biblical at this point. Both the Bible and the common religious experience of mankind testify against Kant's claim that there is no spiritual faculty in man by which God can be experienced.[3] Nevertheless,

---

3. For a more detailed criticism of Kant's epistemology, see John Jefferson Davis, "Kant and the Problem of Religious Knowledge," in *Perspectives on Evangelical Theology,* ed. Kenneth S. Kantzer and Stanley N. Gundry (Grand Rapids: Baker, 1979). On the evidential value of religious experience in relation to theistic proofs, see Richard Swinburne, *The Existence of God,* pp. 244ff.

Kant's viewpoint was vastly influential in Protestant theology and undercut the authority of scripture as a deposit of divine revelation given to human experience.

Friedrich Schleiermacher accepted the Kantian critique of religious knowledge and attempted to reformulate Christian theology upon a new basis. Perhaps God could not be *known*, but he could still be *experienced*. In *On Religion: Speeches to Its Cultured Despisers*, Schleiermacher turned to an experiential basis for Christian theology. "The contemplation of the pious," he suggested, "is the immediate consciousness of the universal existence of all finite things, in and through the Infinite, and of all temporal things in and through the eternal."[4] This intuitive sense of the dependence of all finite things upon the Infinite was, thought Schleiermacher, the essence of the religious experience.

This line of thought was developed more systematically in Schleiermacher's *The Christian Faith*. "Christian doctrines," he stated, "are accounts of the Christian religious affections set forth in speech."[5] In other words, Christian theology is nothing more or less than the articulation of the content of Christian piety. In this view the Bible is not a collection of divinely revealed doctrines but a record of human religious experience. Christian doctrines in all their forms "have their ultimate grounds so exclusively in the emotions of the religious self-consciousness, that where these do not exist the doctrines cannot arise."[6]

Schleiermacher was correct, of course, in seeing an integral relation between Christian doctrine and Christian religious experience. By making religious experience primary, however, and by denying the cognitive dimension of divine revelation, he dissolved the classical substance of Christian doctrine into a mist of pantheistic piety.

The nineteenth century in America also witnessed theological experiments that shifted the basis of religious authority to experience. Ralph Waldo Emerson was a leader of the transcendentalists or "left wing" Unitarians, who called for a religion based on the "immediate reception of spiritual truth." Emerson was unhappy with the rationalism of the conservative Unitarians who, while being severe critics of Calvinism, still held to a form of Chris-

4. Friedrich Schleiermacher, *On Religion: Speeches to Its Cultured Despisers*, p. 28.
5. Schleiermacher, *The Christian Faith*, vol. I, p. 76.
6. Ibid., p. 78.

tianity based on divine revelation in the Gospels and attested by the biblical miracles. In a famous address delivered in 1838 to the graduating class of Harvard Divinity School, Emerson told these future Unitarian ministers that "historical Christianity destroys the power of preaching, by withdrawing it from the exploration of the moral nature of man, where the sublime is, where are the resources of astonishment."[7] Preaching that takes as its source the doctrines of the Bible overlooks the splendid resources of the soul and human self-consciousness. As a result, stated Emerson, the "true Christianity—a faith like Christ's in the infinitude of man— is lost."[8] Emerson's "true Christianity" was hardly more than a pantheistic humanism. His optimistic faith in the goodness and infinitude of the human soul was a thoroughgoing abandonment of historic Christianity.

The experiential focus in American religious liberalism is also found in the modernist theologies of such men as Harry Emerson Fosdick and Shailer Mathews. In *Christianity and Progress*, Fosdick declared that the "one vital thing in religion is first-hand, personal experience."[9] And what is the essence of Christianity? It is not "a creed, nor an organization, nor a ritual. ... They are the leaves, not the roots; they are the wires, not the message. Christianity itself is a life."[10]

In a different context Fosdick's words could have very evangelical meaning. Evangelicals agree that Christian faith is not *just* assent to doctrine, and that true religion must have an experiential component. Fosdick's modernism, however, had the fatal defect of allowing the "modern mind" to exercise veto power over what counted for valid religious experience. The result in modernism was a naturalistic reduction of the content of historic Christian faith. There was no room for miracles, spirits, demons, incarnation, and resurrection in Fosdick's reconstruction of the faith.

The theology of Douglas Clyde Macintosh, professor at Yale for many years, represented a somewhat different form of experiential theology in America. Macintosh attempted to recast Christian theology according to the methodology of the natural sciences. In

7. Ralph Waldo Emerson, *Collected Works*, vol. I, pp. 87–88.

8. Ibid., p. 89.

9. In William R. Miller, ed., *Contemporary American Protestant Thought, 1900–1970*, p. 192.

10. Ibid., p. 194.

*Theology as an Empirical Science* he expressed the belief that "it is possible to rest theology upon valid evidence and sound reasoning."[11] An appeal to "valid evidence and sound reasoning" certainly seems commendable. Where, however, does Christian theology find its basic source and starting point? According to Macintosh, not in the Bible, but in religious experience. The "scientific" theologian, using the inductive methods of the natural sciences, will "select from the manifold of religious experience those elements which give knowledge of God, just as the physicist selects from the multitude of the elements of sense experience those which are of importance for the understanding of nature and matter and energy."[12] The result of Macintosh's "scientific" method was a diminishing of the Chalcedonian understanding of the deity of Christ, agnosticism on the preexistence of Christ and the possibility of prayerful communion with the risen Christ, and silence on the virgin birth, bodily resurrection, and parousia.

At the University of Chicago, Henry Nelson Wieman, a forerunner of contemporary process theologians, was developing his own brand of empirical theology. In works such as *Religious Experience and Scientific Method* (1926), *Normative Psychology of Religion* (1935), and *Intellectual Foundations of Faith* (1961), Wieman propounded a naturalistic empiricism which insisted that God was not a personal mind but rather a creative process. Wieman's reductionism was an unsuccessful attempt to adapt Christianity to the "modern mind."

In recent years experience has played a large role in the construction of various forms of liberation theology. According to James Cone, "There can be no black theology which does not take the black experience as a source for its starting point"; for black theology "the categories of interpretation must arise out of the thought forms of the black experience itself,"[13]

Related sentiments are voiced are voiced by feminist theologian Letty M. Russell. As an advocate of an inductive method she believes that Christian thinkers must draw out "the material for reflection from their life experiences as it relates to the gospel

---

11. Douglas Clyde Macintosh, *Theology as an Empirical Science*, p. 25.
12. Ibid., p. 26.
13. James Cone, *God of the Oppressed*, pp. 17–18.

message."[14] The gospel is good news "only when it speaks concretely to their particular needs of liberation."

It is certainly the case that Christian theology must be situated or contextualized adequately in terms of the life experiences of the people whom it seeks to address. The danger in liberation theology, however, is that the contemporary context can come to dominate the biblical content, and in fact become a substitute for it. Concern for various forms of temporal liberation must not be allowed to displace the biblical insistence on the necessity of regeneration, the root of all lasting social transformation.

Human experience has played a large role in the formulation of recent process theologies. John B. Cobb has proposed a Christian natural theology that appeals for its justification to the "general experience of mankind."[15] More recently, Cobb and David Griffin have stated that Christian doctrines are "relatively adequate explications of truths that are universally apprehended at the preconscious level of experience."[16]

Many people have found process theology's appeal to human experience and its emphasis on dynamism and change to be attractive features. Such aspects of process thought seem to be in resonance with important dimensions of the American temperament. In appealing to the general experience of mankind, however, process theology is in danger of eroding the particularity of biblical revelation and glossing over the very real differences that exist in the world views of the various religious traditions. In Buddhism, for example, the reality and permanence of the individual soul is denied. In Western religions, on the other hand, the reality of the soul is a basic tenet. What does the "general experience of mankind" teach in such a case? Is the Ultimate Reality behind the world of appearances personal or impersonal in nature? Again, the great religious traditions of mankind are divided on even such a fundamental issue as this. Apart from a normative divine revelation, how are such conflicting truth claims to be adjudicated? By assigning a philosophy of experience (largely based on the philosophy of Alfred North Whitehead) priority over biblical revelation, process theology introduces an inescapable relativism into the heart of its system. Historic points of Christian doctrine,

---

14. Letty M. Russell, *Human Liberation in a Feminist Perspective*, p. 53.

15. John B. Cobb, *A Christian Natural Theology*, p. 277.

16. Cobb and David Ray Griffin, *Process Theology*, p. 37.

such as the certainty of God's ultimate and complete triumph over evil, are muted, and the uniqueness of the Christian claims in relation to other world religions is compromised. Biblical revelation, attested by historical evidences and credentials open to rational inspection, provides a far more adequate means than religious experience *per se* of adjudicating the conflicting truth claims of the various world religions.

Another school of recent American theology, sometimes known as the new liberalism, is represented in the writings of David Tracy and Langdon Gilkey, both of the University of Chicago Divinity School. Like the older nineteenth-century liberalism of Schleiermacher it sees human experience as a basic source for the construction of Christian theology. According to Tracy, in his *Blessed Rage for Order: The New Pluralism in Theology*, the two principal sources for theology are the Christian texts and "common human experience and language."[17] Theology finds a point of contact in everyday and scientific language where the experience of "limits" signals a "religious dimension."[18]

All theologies, of course, are influenced by "common human experience and language" as well as by Christian texts. The crucial question, however, is, Which of the two influences is normative? Is the bottom line of authority the Bible or the modern mind? In Tracy's case the modern sensibility seems clearly to have the upper hand. As a result, much of the content of historic Christian supernaturalism is jettisoned in the process.

Tracy's colleague, Langdon Gilkey, likewise appeals heavily to experience in his theological method. In *Naming the Whirlwind: The Renewal of God-Language*, Gilkey argues that the task of theology is to "thematize" or bring to conscious awareness the "dimensions of ultimacy" in secular experience. Writing in the late 1960s, Gilkey assumed that secularity was a cultural given and shaped his theology accordingly. Language referring to any "transcendent, sacred ultimate, or essential dimension of reality or of process is, in both its metaphysical and its revelational forms, meaningless for any modern men who share the secular experience of our age."[19]

The upsurge of religious interest in the United States in the

17. David Tracy, *Blessed Rage for Order*, p. 43.
18. Ibid., p. 47.
19. Langdon Gilkey, *Naming the Whirlwind*, p. 180.

1970s and 1980s—in its evangelical, charismatic, cultic, heterodox, and Eastern forms—has shown that the spirit of secularity was neither as monolithic nor as permanent as Gilkey and liberal theologians had believed. The basic problem with accommodationist theologies that try to restructure and reduce orthodox Christianity to dimensions presumably acceptable to the modern mind is that the "modern mind" is notoriously changeable. A theology married to the modernity of one decade can be widowed in the next.

Gilkey's theological method took secularity too seriously; it gave modernity a hermeneutical veto over biblical revelation that it did not deserve. Christian theology, if it is to preserve its own integrity and spiritual vitality, must not content itself with presenting the gospel on the culture's own terms, but must challenge the root assumptions of the culture in terms of the gospel itself. The spirit of secularity is nothing other than mankind's ageless flight from God, the attempt to suppress the truth in unrighteousness (Rom. 1:20–21). Any theology which compromises the supernatural dimension of the faith will not ultimately succeed in influencing a humanistic culture, and will be in grave danger of preaching another gospel altogether.

### Cultic and heterodox traditions

Religious experience has functioned as a theological norm not only in liberal Protestantism but also in many of the cultic and heterdox religious groups that have arisen in America since the nineteenth century. The appeal to experience has manifested itself both in pantheistic mysticism and in new revelation claims through dreams and visions.

Mormonism is one of the more important of the native American religions. Joseph Smith (1805–1844), while seeking divine guidance alone in the forest, claimed to have been led by an angel to discover the golden plates of the Book of Mormon. In 1830 Smith published the plates and founded a new church, the Church of Jesus Christ of Latter-day Saints. After further alleged revelations, a plurality of gods and of wives were introduced into Mormonism.

New revelation claims have been made more recently by Sun Myung Moon, founder of the Unification Church. In a 1974 meeting at Madison Square Garden in New York City, Moon announced the "new future of Christianity": "I have come to reveal something new," he said. "I want to share with you a new revelation from God." Moon has also been quoted as saying privately, "God is now throwing Christianity away and is now establishing a new religion, and this new religion is Unification Church."[20] It is obvious from such statements that for Moon the authority of scripture has been superseded by his own new "revelations."

Another prominent stream in native American religion is represented by the self-help and "positive-thinking" schools. In 1897 Ralph Waldo Trine published a book titled *In Tune with the Infinite; or, Fullness of Peace, Power, and Plenty.* The book has since gone through many printings and has been translated into over twenty languages. Trine told his readers, "Within yourself lies the cause of whatever enters your life in exact accord with what you would have it." The point of such religious exercises and meditation was to realize one's unity with the "infinite life and power" within. Such language betrays a blurring of the crucial distinction between the creature and the Creator, and the personality of God has been lost in an impersonal process or power. The affinity of Trine's thought with Eastern mysticism is apparent. The real issues of life, according to Trine, lie beyond our normal rational powers: "There are certain faculties that we have that are not part of the active, thinking mind. . . . Through them we have intuitions, impulses, leadings, that instead of being merely the occasional, should be the normal and habitual."[21] Orthodox Christians believe, of course, that the infinite reality of the triune, personal God far transcends man's ability to completely grasp the divine fullness. The problem with Trine's experientialism, however, is that it emasculates the rational ability to distinguish between genuine and spurious religious experiences. Not all "intuitions, impulses, leadings" are from God. The world, the flesh, and the devil, as well as the God of the Bible, can speak through our inward subjectivity. Without the normative and rationally comprehensible doctrines of scripture we are left defenseless against the seductions of alien spirits, ideologies, and forces.

Charles Fillmore's Unity School of Christianity is representative of the self-help, positive-thinking groups. According to Unity teachings the Bible, while it is constantly used, is not considered

20. Sun Myung Moon, in "The Secret Sayings of 'Master' Moon," p. 49.
21. Ralph Waldo Trine, *In Tune with the Infinite*, p. 223.

the sole or final authority in faith and practice. Man must be in direct, personal communion with God and not be dependent upon secondary sources such as the scriptures. This experiential, positive-thinking orientation is also found today in such prominent religious figures as Norman Vincent Peale and Robert Schuller. Any shift away from the normative role of scripture toward experience as religious authority inevitably leads to a slighting or abandonment of crucial biblical doctrines such as original sin and the necessity of a substitutionary atonement. As a consequence, various schemes of self-salvation, while retaining the language and imagery of the Bible, replace the biblical content with what amounts to a different gospel.

### Humanistic psychology, humanism, "life after life"

The experiential emphasis in modern American culture is hardly limited to organized religion. It is found prominently in the humanistic psychologies of Carl Rogers and Abraham Maslow. These secular therapies, stressing feeling, experience, and self-realization, can function as a substitute religion for their practitioners.

Rogers is very explicit about the normative role of human experience in his own world view. "Experience is, for me," he says, "the highest authority. . . . No other person's ideas, and none of my own ideas, are as authoritative as my experience. It is to experience that I must return again and again, to discover a closer approximation to truth as it is in the process of becoming in me. Neither the Bible nor the prophets, . . . neither the revelations of God nor man—can take precedence over my own direct experience."[22]

Rogers can hardly be accused of stating his position in ambiguous terms. The issue is quite clear: for Rogers, the bottom line for truth is personal experience. Evangelical Protestantism, on the other hand, standing in the Reformation tradition of *sola scriptura,* has insisted on the normative priority of scripture over both ecclesiastical or private experience as the test of truth. The two competing views of truth have vast consequences for the shape of a culture. In our own day humanism and biblical Christianity are pressing rival conceptions of truth in political and social battles concerning abortion, homosexuality, sex education, and other

---

22. Carl Rogers, *On Becoming a Person,* pp. 23–24.

moral issues. The outcome of the struggle for moral leadership in the society is not yet apparent.

The experiential focus in Rogerian psychology stresses feelings rather than facts. "Objective facts are quite unimportant," he writes. "The only facts which have significance for therapy are the feelings which the client is able to bring into the situation."[23] If this is the case in one's philosophy, the inevitable result is situationism and relativism in morals. My feelings replace an objective divine law outside the self as the criteria of right and wrong. The slogan "If it feels good, do it" is a crude but not inconsistent deduction from the philosophy of self-realization. As Paul Vitz, a former practitioner of humanistic psychology, has noted in his *Psychology as Religion: The Cult of Self-Worship*, such humanistic therapies involve "no duties, denials, inhibitions, restraints—only rights, privileges, and opportunities for change."[24] It is little wonder that the effect of such psychologies has been largely to contribute to the moral anarchism and permissiveness of the age.

An experiential norm for truth is succinctly expressed in the second *Humanist Manifesto* (1973): "We affirm that moral values derive their source from human experience. Ethics is autonomous and situational. ... Life has meaning because we create and develop our futures." The infinite, personal God of the Bible does not exist; man creates his own values and determines what is "right" and "wrong." There is no transcendent, absolute, and eternal moral law because there is no transcendent, absolute, and eternal God to give such a law. Man has replaced God as the moral center of the universe. The humanistic faith expressed somewhat guardedly by John Dewey in *A Common Faith* (1934) is now, a generation later, being promoted with no such reticence. Such "humanism," it now appears, is merely a form of man's self-worship and a polite name for atheism.

The denial of the biblical God by various humanistic ideologies not only involves an exaltation of human experience, but also has opened a doorway into the world of the occult. Man, made in the image of God, cannot live for long in a spiritual vacuum. The longing for transcendence, if not satisfied through authentic biblical religion, may seek its satisfaction in the realms of darkness. Such

23. Rogers, *Counseling and Psychotherapy*, p. 244.
24. Paul Vitz, *Psychology as Religion*, p. 38.

has been the case with a number of those involved in the "death and dying" movement of recent years.

Raymond A. Moody, Jr., author of *Life After Life*, stimulated the public's interest in so-called "near death" or "out-of-body" experiences. According to Moody the typical subject of a near-death experience reported glimpses of "the spirits of relatives and friends who have already died, and a loving, warm spirit of a kind he has never encountered before—*a being of light*—appears before him." The theological implications of such experiences are not lost on the author. He notes that frequently in the case of persons having such experiences, "the reward-punishment model of the afterlife is abandoned and disavowed, even by many who had been accustomed to thinking in those terms."[25] In other words, the biblical doctrines of heaven, hell, and final judgment are superseded by the near-death experience. Here is a clear example of personal experience being given priority over divine revelation as a norm of truth.

From a Christian perspective it appears that certain forms of experience in the area of death and dying can open the doorway to the occult. As Albrecht and Alexander have commented, "It becomes more and more evident that people like ... Moody and Kübler-Ross are very available and influential pawns in a cosmic chess game."[26] For secular man death may appear to be the "last frontier" in a two-dimensional universe. But that very secularity can disarm and deceive the unwary in the face of the very real and dangerous spiritual influences that exist beyond the realm of the five senses.

## Religious Experience: Theological Evaluation

### Dangers

Despite what Joseph Smith or Mary Baker Eddy or Sun Myung Moon may claim, it is clear from scripture that the church is not to expect any new revelations from God. During the apostolic age the definitive and utterly sufficient deposit of doctrine and morals was delivered to the church. In most emphatic terms Paul declares to the Galatians, "But even if we, or an angel from heaven, should

25. Raymond A. Moody, Jr., *Life After Life*, p. 70.
26. Mark Albrecht and Brooks Alexander, "Thanatology," p. 11.

preach to you a gospel contrary to that which we preached to you, let him be accursed" (Gal. 1:8). An ecstatic experience or an angelic visitation—no matter how subjectively impressive—is not to be allowed to contradict the authority of the apostolic gospel. The church has already been established upon the firm foundation of the New Testament apostles and prophets, Jesus Christ himself being the cornerstone (Eph. 2:20). Once the foundation of any building has been laid, no further foundation needs to be built upon it. Jude urges his readers, facing a situation characterized by the spread of heterodox teaching, to "contend for the faith which was once for all [ἅπαξ] delivered to the saints" (v. 3). Jude's language presupposes that the apostolic faith is a finished, complete, and recognized body of doctrine. It is "once for all" committed to the church, and no new doctrine is to be expected or needed.

The New Testament asserts not only the completeness and sufficiency of the apostolic doctrine, but also the necessity of being alert to spiritual counterfeits generated by Satan and his cohorts. "Beloved, do not believe every spirit, but test the spirits to see whether they are of God; for many false prophets have gone out into the world" (1 John 4:1). Many antichrists are even now at work in the world (1 John 2:18). Prophesying is not to be despised, but all teachings are to be tested (1 Thess. 5:20—21). Spectacular spiritual powers such as the ability to prophesy, cast out demons, and perform acts of healing are not necessarily a sign of a saving relationship with Christ (Matt. 7:21—23). False prophets and false messiahs can perform deceptive signs and wonders (Matt. 24:24; cf. 2 Thess. 2:9, of antichrist). A prophet or dreamer of dreams may be able to perform signs and wonders, and successfully predict future events, and yet be guilty of teaching false doctrine (Deut. 13:1—3). In the face of claims based on near-death experiences, the believer needs to remember that Satan, the liar (John 8:44) and deceiver (Rev. 20:3,8), can disguise himself as an angel of light (2 Cor. 11:14).

In all cases the test of Christian belief is not to be experience, paranormal or otherwise, but conformity to the apostolic doctrine of scripture. The rule is *sola scriptura*. Other revelation claims are to be rejected; no new doctrines or morals are to be received. The spiritual counterfeits which are appearing today are somewhat reminiscent of the pagan claims faced by the early church. In the Hellenistic religious environment of the New Testament claims of revelatory appearances of pagan gods such as Apollo, Zeus, Asclepius, and Sarapis were not uncommon. The worshipers of these pagan gods claimed to experience healings, and at times believed themselves commanded to build a shrine to the god in question.

According to the New Testament the reality of one's relationship to the true God is not based on the intensity of subjective experience, but on abiding in the apostolic teaching. "What you have heard from the beginning, let that abide in you; if what you have heard from the beginning abides in you, you also will abide in the Son and in the Father" (1 John 2:24). Abiding in the doctrine means obedience to the commandments of of God. "By this we know that we have come to know him, if we keep his commandments" (1 John 2:3). This emphasis on keeping the commandments is found in various forms twelve times in the Gospel of John and six times in 1 John. The message is clear: "By their fruits you shall know them" (Matt. 7:20). A true experience of God produces not antinomianism and a life of disobedience, but a life characterized by Christian grace and love. The Spirit of God points the believer to Jesus Christ (John 15:26); demonic spirits and fallen fleshly impulses draw attention to human personalities and leaders.

Appeals to personal religious experience or feelings rather than scripture can be dangerous in seeking God's will in matters of guidance. Luther, Calvin, and other mainstream Reformers insisted on the integral link of word and Spirit in the Christian life. In matters of knowledge the teaching of scripture was given clear priority over subjective experience.

John Wesley, who certainly was not one to minimize the legitimate role of vital religious experience, insisted that "secret impulses" were no indication of God's will apart from scripture. "I have declared again and again," he said, "that I make the word of God the rule of all my actions; and that I no more follow any 'secret impulse' instead thereof, than I follow Mohamet or Confucius."[27] Wesley's term "secret impulse" could include dreams, visions, or a sense of being led by the Spirit. All such impulses were to be tested by scripture. Wesley knew that a fallen human

---

27. McDonald, *Theories of Revelation,* p. 259.

nature was capable of pious self-deception. Cases, unfortunately all too common in our own day, where professing Christians feel "led" to seek a divorce on nonbiblical grounds are sad examples of such self-deception. God's Spirit does not "lead" the believer in ways that contradict the express commands of scripture.

In some charismatic circles there is a dangerous tendency to wait for a special word or "leading" from the Spirit in circumstances where the scriptures give very explicit guidance. "Certain directives are so clear in Scripture that to wait for a verbal directive amounts to just plain old disobedient laziness," notes Ken Thomas; the commands to make disciples (Matt. 28) or to feed the hungry (Matt. 25) "need not to be reiterated daily by the Holy Spirit."[28] There is a danger here that the believer will allow dependence on "secret impulses" to displace the normative priority of the written word of God. The only infallible rule of faith and practice is the Holy Spirit speaking *in scripture*—not apart from it. As Frederick Dale Bruner has noted, the moment any rite, any experience, becomes a supplement to faith or a condition for fullness before God, then spiritual danger is at hand.

It has been previously noted that religious experience plays a significant role in both evangelical and liberal theologies. In the evangelical tradition religious experience is a medium but not the norm of theological truth. In liberal and modernistic theologies, however, experience tends to become the norm as well as the medium of truth. P. T. Forsyth, in *The Principle of Authority*, preserved this necessary distinction between the medium and the norm. "A real authority is indeed *within* experience, but it is not the authority *of* experience, it is an authority *for* experience, it is an authority experienced."[29]

Likewise, J. Gresham Machen, in *The Origin of Paul's Religion*, noted that theology, as it appears in Paul, "is not a product of Christian experience, but a setting forth of those facts by which Christian experience has been produced."[30] For Paul, the experience of the "rise of the Easter faith in the hearts of the disciples" (Bultmann) has no basis apart from the objective reality of the bodily resurrection of Jesus as a historical event. For the evangelical, the power and presence of the Spirit of God is experienced

28. Kenneth Thomas, "Social Action in the Charismatic Renewal Movement," p. 12.
29. P. T. Forsyth, *The Principle of Authority*, p. 75.
30. J. Gresham Machen, *The Origin of Paul's Religion*, pp. 168–69.

through the word of biblical revelation, but the locus of authority is not in the experience as such but in the written word of God beyond the experience—the written word which points to the divine realities themselves.

Theologies which appeal to experience as the highest norm open the door to heresy, moral anarchism, narcissism, and cultural impotence. Modernist theologies, ostensibly drawing from both scripture and the "modern sensibility" as sources, inevitably have given the latter veto power over the former. The result has been a reductionistic version of the faith which jettisons such historic biblical doctrines as the virgin birth, the substitutionary atonement, and the bodily resurrection—in the name of "credibility" and "relevance." Such apologetic strategies have experienced repeated failure in their attempts to appease the demands of the "modern mind" and have frequently been little more than temporary stops on the road to a full-fledged secularism.

Granting to personal experience the final test of truth can lead to the moral anarchism so characteristic of the "me generation." After all, how can I be the judge of someone else's sense of self-realization? It may not feel right for me, but who is to say that it may not be right for someone else? Such an experientialism is subversive of a stable social order. The experientialism of the situation ethic, with its antinomian tendencies, has been a major contributor to the anarchism and permissiveness of late twentieth-century American culture.

A preoccupation with personal experience can also lead to what social critic Christopher Lasch has called the "culture of narcissism." Even the most authentic piety must guard against the subtle dangers of narcissism and self-absorption. The medieval monastics and the Puritans were aware of these dangers, even if they were not always successful in avoiding them.

The chief end of man, as stated in the Westminster Shorter Catechism, is to "glorify God and to enjoy him forever." Seeking the glory of God does have as its legitimate fruit the enjoyment of God, but the proper focus is on God, not on our personal experiences. Biblical religion is theocentric rather than anthropocentric in its fundamental orientation.

The "culture of narcissism" can contribute to the cultural impotence of the church. Authentic Christian spirituality is not an ecclesiastical hot-tub but the dynamo of kingdom action. A heart on fire for the glory of God and for the extension of his kingdom will spend much time in private with God, but will then go forth into the world to fight God's battles and do God's work. "Work *and* pray": both are essential to spiritual vitality and the mission of the church.

### Positive values

While it is certainly the case that religious experience has its dangers, it is equally true that there can be no living New Testament faith without it. The evangelical tradition has consistently pointed to authentic faith in terms of a living relationship with the living Christ, and not merely in terms of intellectual assent or institutional affiliation. Evangelicals would agree with the assessment of Jonathan Edwards that "true religion, in great part, consists in holy affections." In a similar vein John Wesley affirmed that Christianity is no mere speculative belief, but a "feeling possession of God in the heart, wrought by the Holy Ghost."[31]

As previously noted, the Protestant Reformers sought to maintain a proper balance between word and Spirit in the Christian life—i.e., between the cognitive and the experiential dimensions. Reflecting on the history of Puritanism and pietism, Richard Lovelace concluded that the key to a "live orthodoxy" is a "proper balance between the Spirit and the Word with appropriate attention given to the role of each."[32] Here Lovelace is simply continuing the emphasis of the Reformers.

In our own day the most controversial examples of "vital religious experience" have been found in the charismatic or neo-Pentecostal movement. Some conservative groups look upon the charismatic movement with suspicion and disfavor, holding that the supernatural gifts of the Spirit such as tongues, prophecy, and miracles ceased with the apostles or with the closing of the canon. It is argued that such supernatural gifts were given solely to accredit the apostolic revelation (Heb. 2:4), and that once the body of apostolic revelation was complete, there was no further need for such signs. Sometimes 1 Cor. 13:10 is cited in this connection: "When the perfect comes, the imperfect will pass away." It is argued that "the perfect" refers to the completed New Testament canon and "the imperfect" to the Pentecostal gifts.

31. McDonald, *Theories of Revelation*, p. 259.
32. Richard F. Lovelace, *Dynamics of Spiritual Life*, p. 279.

While it is true that the Pentecostal gifts did serve to accredit revelation (Heb. 2:4), it would be incorrect to identify this as their sole and exclusive function in the New Testament. Such gifts were also given as aids to worship: "To each is given the manifestation of the Spirit for the common good" (1 Cor. 12:7), i.e. for the edification of the community. He who speaks in a tongue edifies himself (1 Cor. 14:4). In such a case there is no reference to public revelation. The one who prophesies edifies the entire church (1 Cor. 14:4b). That "the perfect" in 1 Cor. 13:10 refers to the canon is hardly convincing; in the context of the passage the more likely reference is to the perfection of love in the eternal state (cf. vv. 8, 12, 13).

While the case for the cessation of the Pentecostal gifts does not seem convincing, it is also the case that charismatic experiences do not constitute new doctrines or new moral teachings. The body of apostolic doctrines is complete (Gal. 1:8; Eph. 2:20; Jude 3). The Spirit is not revealing new doctrines, but fresh applications of the doctrines delivered once for all to the church. Paul's advice to the Thessalonian church is quite relevant to the modern situation: Do not quench the Spirit, and do not despise prophesying, but test everything, hold fast the good, and abstain from every form of evil (1 Thess. 5:19–22).

Religious experience also has a role to play in the understanding of scripture. One who has never been regenerated by the Holy Spirit cannot understand the spiritual truths of the word of God. The unspiritual man does not receive the gifts of the Spirit of God; they are foolishness to him, and he is unable to understand them because they require spiritual discernment (1 Cor. 2:14). As a natural man Nicodemus is puzzled by Christ's teachings concerning the new birth (John 3). It is only after our own personal conversion experience that the Bible "comes alive" for us. It is no longer merely an ancient religious book, it becomes the living word, actively discerning the thoughts and intentions of the heart (Heb. 4:12). God speaks directly to our hearts through his word. Our religious experience is not the norm of truth, but it is the medium or channel through which that truth becomes real and personal to us.

As Edward Schillebeeckx has observed, "Language only communicates meaning when it expresses an experience that is shared."[33] The biblical language comes alive for us when the Holy Spirit creates an experiential bond between us and the spiritual realities attested by the biblical authors.

Experience in the broader sense of cultural awareness may also contribute to our understanding of scripture. As various liberation theologians have argued, the experience of oppression from cultural settings differing from our own may sensitize us to aspects of the biblical text that we otherwise might have missed. Similar observations could be made in relation to feminist and Third World theologies. In all such cases, however, the evangelical will insist that the subcultural experience in question function as the medium and not the norm for biblical revelation.

Finally, it needs to be said that vital religious experience is necessary for the successful prosecution of the church's mission to the world. If it is the case that zeal without knowledge can be destructive, it is also the case that knowledge without zeal can lead to spiritual sterility and cultural impotence. Those who know their God in a vital way will stand firm and do brave deeds (Dan. 11:32); they will join the battle against the enemies of Christ and his church. "This is the victory that overcomes the world, our faith" (1 John 5:4). Living faith in the risen and reigning Christ produces lively religious affections and a robust, confident outlook that enlists the believer in kingdom-extending action.

## Bibliography

Albrecht, Mark, and Alexander, Brooks. "Thanatology: Death and Dying," *Spiritual Counterfeits Project Journal*, April, 1977, pp. 5–11.

Alexander, Brooks. "The Rise of Cosmic Humanism," *Spiritual Counterfeits Project Journal*, Winter, 1981–82, pp. 1–6.

Barrett, C. K. *The Holy Spirit and the Gospel Tradition*. London: SPCK, 1966.

Berger, Peter L. *A Rumor of Angels*. Garden City, N.Y.: Doubleday, 1970.

Bretall, Robert W. *The Empirical Theology of Henry Nelson Wieman*. New York: Macmillan, 1963.

Bruner, Frederick Dale. *A Theology of the Holy Spirit*. Grand Rapids: Eerdmans, 1970.

33. Edward Schillebeeckx, *The Understanding of Faith*, p. 15.

Cobb, John B. *A Christian Natural Theology.* Philadelphia: Westminster, 1965.

Cobb, John B., and Griffin, David Ray. *Process Theology.* Philadelphia: Westminster, 1976.

Cone, James. *A Black Theology of Liberation.* Philadelphia: Lippincott, 1970.

_____ . *God of the Oppressed.* New York: Seabury, 1975.

Cunliffe-Jones, Hubert. *Christian Theology Since 1600.* London: Duckworth, 1970.

Dunn, James. *Baptism in the Holy Spirit.* Philadelphia: Westminster, 1970.

_____ . *Jesus and the Spirit.* Philadelphia: Westminster, 1975.

Edwards, Jonathan. *Religious Affections,* ed. John E. Smith. New Haven: Yale University Press, 1959.

Emerson, Ralph Waldo. *Collected Works,* Vol. I. Cambridge: Harvard University Press, 1971.

Forsyth, P. T. *The Principle of Authority.* 2nd ed. London: Independent Press, 1912.

Gilkey, Langdon. *Naming the Whirlwind: The Renewal of God-Language.* Indianapolis: Bobbs-Merrill, 1969.

Grant, Frederick C., ed. *Hellenistic Religions.* New York: Liberal Arts Press, 1953.

Handy, Robert T. *Religion in the American Experience.* Columbia: University of South Carolina Press, 1972.

James, Williams. *The Varieties of Religious Experience.* New York: Longman, Green, 1902.

Kant, Immanuel. *Critique of Pure Reason.* Chicago: Britannica, 1952.

Kantzer, Kenneth S., and Gundry, Stanley, eds. *Perspectives on Evangelical Theology.* Grand Rapids: Baker, 1979.

Kelsey, Morton T. *The Christian and the Supernatural.* Minneapolis: Augsburg, 1976.

Lasch, Christopher. *The Culture of Narcissism: American Life in an Age of Diminishing Expectations.* New York: Norton, 1979.

Lovelace, Richard F. *Dynamics of Spiritual Life.* Downers Grove, Ill.: Inter-Varsity, 1979.

Machen, J. Gresham. *The Origin of Paul's Religion.* New York: Macmillan, 1923.

McDonald, H. D. *Theories of Revelation.* Grand Rapids: Baker, 1979.

Macintosh, Douglas Clyde. *Theology as an Empirical Science.* New York: Macmillan, 1919.

Miller, William R., ed. *Contemporary American Protestant Thought, 1900–1970.* Indianapolis: Bobbs-Merrill, 1973.

Moody, Raymond A., Jr. *Life After Life.* Atlanta: Mockingbird Books, 1975.

Moon, Sun Myung. In "The Secret Sayings of 'Master' Moon," *Time,* June 14, 1976, p. 49.

_____ . "The New Future of Christianity," *New York Times*, Sept. 20, 1974, p. 44c.

Nock, A. D. *Conversion.* London: Oxford University Press, 1933.

Otto, Rudolf. *The Idea of the Holy.* London: Oxford University Press, 1931.

Rogers, Carl. *Counseling and Psychotherapy.* Boston: Houghton Mifflin, 1942.

_____ . *On Becoming a Person.* Boston: Houghton Mifflin, 1961.

Russell, Letty M. *Human Liberation in a Feminist Perspective.* Philadelphia: Westminster, 1974.

Schleiermacher, Friedrich. *The Christian Faith,* Vol. I. New York: Harper Torchbooks, 1963.

_____ . *On Religion: Speeches to Its Cultured Despisers.* New York: Frederick Ungar, 1955.

Schillebeeckx, Edward. *The Understanding of Faith.* London: Sheed and Ward, 1974.

Swinburne, Richard. *The Existence of God.* New York: Oxford University Press, 1979.

Sweet, William Warren. *Religion in the Development of American Culture.* New York: Scribner's, 1952.

Thomas, Kenneth. "Social Action in the Charismatic Renewal Movement," paper for Theology 104, Gordon-Conwell Theological Seminary, April, 1981.

Tracy, David. *Blessed Rage for Order: The New Pluralism in Theology.* New York: Seabury, 1975.

Trine, Ralph Waldo. *In Tune with the Infinite; or, Fullness of Peace, Power, and Plenty.* Indianapolis: Bobbs-Merrill, 1947.

Vitz, Paul. *Psychology as Religion: The Cult of Self-Worship.* Grand Rapids: Eerdmans, 1977.

# 6

# Scripture:
# Word of the Great King

## Authority

"The principal cause of modern theological sickness," according to Clark Pinnock, "is a crisis of valid authority." In our own day the "authority of scripture is the watershed of theological conviction . . . The central problem for theology is its own epistemological base."[1] John Warwick Montgomery concurs in this evaluation. According to Montgomery, "The doctrinal problem which, above all others, demands resolution in the modern church is that of the authority of Holy Scripture."[2]

The contemporary evangelical insistence on the primacy of biblical authority for the church's theology is rooted in the tradition of the great Protestant Reformers of the sixteenth century. Martin Luther, in his unequivocal insistence on the *sola scriptura* principle, was reasserting the rights of the Word of God above all merely human words, whether those of Aristotle, Renaissance humanism, or ecclesiastical tradition. The *sola scriptura* principle was the reassertion and rediscovery of the plenary authority of the risen and reigning Christ, the sole King of the church, an

1. Clark Pinnock, *Biblical Revelation*, pp. 10–11.
2. John Warwick Montgomery, ed., *God's Inerrant Word*, p. 15.

authority mediated through the inspired and infallible word of scripture. The Reformation was in a real sense a victory over the humanistic thinking which had infiltrated the medieval church. In the latter part of the twentieth century the question of biblical authority again represents a conflict between the authority of the risen and reigning Christ in the church and the authority claims of the "modern mind" of Enlightenment humanism. The issue again is whether the Word of God or the word of man shall reign supreme in faith and life.

Luther was hardly alone among the Reformers in his insistence on scripture as the supreme authority for the Christian church. In his *Institutes* John Calvin wrote that "the Scriptures obtain full authority among believers only when men regard them as having sprung from heaven, as if there the living words of God were heard" (I.vii,1). For Calvin the scriptures were no mere historical records of actual religious experience, but the very oracles of God.

The Calvinistic heritage was mediated in America through the lasting influence of the Westminster Confession of Faith. According to this confession, "The Supreme Judge, by which all controversies of religion are to be determined, and all decrees of councils, opinions of ancient writers, doctrines of men, and private spirits, are to be examined, and in whose sentence we are to rest, can be no other but the Holy Spirit speaking in the scripture" (I.x). Here it is notable that the Holy Spirit speaks not apart from scripture or contrary to scripture, but *in* scripture. Scripture is thus the final written authority for the Christian church.

In our own day inerrancy (pp. 186–199) has become a major focus of evangelical discussions concerning the authority of scripture. As evangelicals continue to wrestle with the various dimensions of this debate, it is important to insist on the comprehensiveness of the Bible's authority. There is a danger that excessive concentration on problematic details of the biblical text will cause the evangelical community in the United States to suffer from "tunnel vision" theologically and lose the impulse to apply in practice the authority of the Word of God to all of life. The cultural mandate to subdue the earth (Gen. 1:26–28) and the Great Commission to disciple the nations (Matt. 28:19–20) set forth the mission of God's people in the broadest terms. Not only the church as an ecclesiastical organization but also the family, education, government, economic life, the arts—all domains of human culture—are to be permeated with the principles and precepts of the Word of God. The risen and reigning Christ is King not only of the church but of the entire universe (Eph. 1:20–23). The crown rights of King Jesus are to be proclaimed in every area of human life, until the knowledge and glory of God cover the earth as the waters cover the seas. In the closing decades of the twentieth century, as the institutions built upon the values of Enlightenment humanism continue to face crises, it is imperative that Christians seize the opportunities to present biblical alternatives. The task of the church will increasingly become one of reconstructing the foundations of a dying humanistic culture—but upon the enduring principles and values of the Word of God. This was the task of the Christian church in the waning days of the Roman Empire, and it is again the church's task in the twilight years of a declining Enlightenment culture.

## Inspiration

### Definition; distinction; nature

In his *Systematic Theology* Charles Hodge, the great Princeton theologian, defined inspiration as "the supernatural influence of the Holy Spirit on selected individuals which rendered them the instruments of God for the infallible communication of his mind and will."[3] Hodge's definition recognizes, of course, that divine inspiration operates through persons, but the central concern is not with individuals as such but with the products of that influence, the scriptures. The point is that the Spirit's inspiration produced an "infallible *communication* of his *mind* and *will.*"

Inspiration is to be distinguished from revelation and illumination. Revelation refers to the original act or word of God by which God communicates his mind and will. Inspiration refers to the process by which this original revelation is recorded and transmitted to God's people. Illumination refers to the work of the Holy Spirit in opening the believer's mind to understand the meaning and significance of the written word. Thus, in the sixth chapter of Isaiah the prophet refers to a revelatory experience of God in the Jerusalem temple. Chapter 6 represents the inspired

3. Charles Hodge, *Systematic Theology*, vol. I, p. 154.

record of this experience. In subsequent generations the Holy
Spirit has witnessed to this written account, applying it in the
faith and life of the people of God.

Over the centuries various attempts have been made to construct theories of the "mechanics" of inspiration. In Hellenistic
Judaism and the early church writers such as Philo, Athenagoras,
and Tertullian suggested a "mantic" or "ecstatic" theory of inspiration. This theory suggested the image of the writer of scripture
as a religious mystic in a state of ecstasy or trance, with rational
faculties suspended. This rather one-sided theory, with its emphasis solely on the divine aspect of scripture, was rejected by
the mainstream church.

Reference is often made to "dictation" theories of inspiration.
Here the model is that of the human author as the "stenographer"
of the Holy Spirit. Such language was used in a metaphorical sense
by Chrysostom and Augustine, and is commonly attributed to
evangelicals, but is not in fact representative of the evangelical
tradition.[4]

The nineteenth-century Roman Catholic writers J. Bonfrère and
J. Jahn suggested a "negative assistance" theory. Here it was supposed that the writers of scripture were substantially on their
own, but were supervised and occasionally corrected by the Spirit
when in danger of committing an error. This theory, which attempted to account for the manifest signs of individual personality
and style, failed to assert the Spirit's integral involvement in the
process of inspiration, and was condemned by the First Vatican
Council in 1870.

### Evangelical view of inspiration

The evangelical view of inspiration can be expressed by means
of the terms *verbal, plenary,* and *confluent.* Inspiration is *verbal* in
that the very words of the canonical text, and not merely the
writers or the general concepts, are the subjects of the Holy Spirit's
special influence. For the writers of scripture the canonical text
is a supernatural product of the Spirit of God. This is quite evident
in a text such as 2 Tim. 3:16, πᾶσα γραφὴ θεόπνευστος. Here
it is the γραφὴ, the scripture, which is θεόπνευστος, "God-

---

4. Cf. J. I. Packer, *"Fundamentalism" and the Word of God,* pp. 78–79, 178–79.

breathed."[5] The German scholar G. Schrenk, commenting on the view of inspiration held in the early church and characteristic of the New Testament writers, concluded that the "implication of the doctrine of inspiration is that the revealed truth of God characterizes every word." According to Schrenk early Christianity did not free itself from this "Judaistic" conception of scripture.[6] Even though Schrenk does not himself hold such a view, he does admit that it is found in the New Testament.

Evangelicals hold that inspiration is *plenary*—i.e., that it extends to all parts of the canon, from Genesis to Revelation. This view is to be contrasted with views of "partial" inspiration, which may consider certain parts of the canon—e.g., Isa. 40–66, Amos, the Decalogue, the Sermon on the Mount—as "authentic" Word of God and truly inspired. The second-century heretic Marcion considered the Old Testament to be an inferior revelation of the creator God to the Jews, and composed a New Testament canon including only expurgated versions of the Gospel of Luke and most of the Pauline epistles. Nineteenth-century Protestant liberals such as Adolf Harnack tended to see in the ethical ideals of the eighth-century prophets and the Sermon on the Mount the "essence" of Christianity.

For the evangelical, all scripture is inspired by God and hence useful for instruction, correction, reproof, and for the training of the people of God for the work of ministry. This is not to deny, of course, that certain parts of the canon are more crucial than others. It is not accidental that the book of Romans has played a larger role in church history than has 2 Chronicles. Nevertheless, the various parts of the canon are like the instruments of a symphony orchestra: some may be more prominent than others, but each contributes to the harmony of the whole. Discerning the whole counsel of God requires listening attentively to the canon of scripture as a whole.

The evangelical view of inspiration is that the process is *confluent.* The divine and human interaction "flow together." The influence of the Holy Spirit on the canonical authors was such that the individual personalities and styles were not suppressed but

5. For a detailed exegetical discussion of the significance of the term θεόπνευστος see B. B. Warfield, "God-Inspired Scripture," in *The Inspiration and Authority of the Bible,* pp. 245 – 96.

6. G. Schrenk, "γραφή," I, 755, 757.

rather made vehicles of the divine purpose. The personalities of David, Jeremiah, Isaiah, John, Paul, and the other biblical writers shine through their works.

The analogy of the incarnation is not an inappropriate one to draw in relation to the Bible. The Bible was given through truly human instruments, with a truly divine result. God in his sovereignty worked through the personalities and circumstances of the writers to produce the desired messages. Unlike the person of Jesus Christ, however, the text of scripture is not an extension or embodiment of the divine essence; it is a product of the divine purpose and control. Charges that evangelicals "worship the Bible" and are guilty of "bibliolatry" are simply not true. Evangelicals worship the God revealed in the Bible and attempt to obey his will as recorded in scripture.

The process of inspiration—verbal, plenary, and confluent— should be understood in relation to the doctrine of providence. All events that take place in history are under the guidance and control of the sovereign will and plan of God (Eph. 1:11). Not even a sparrow falls to the ground apart from the Father's will (Matt. 10:29). Consequently, every event that ultimately led to the formation of the scriptures—original revelation, inspiration, periods of oral transmission, gathering of source documents, final canonization (pp. 199–205)—was occurring not by chance but under the supervision of the sovereign Lord of history. This biblical concept of the all-encompassing providence of God will be pertinent to subsequent discussions of biblical criticism (pp. 206–214) and canonicity.

### History of the doctrine of inspiration

The evangelical view of inspiration is not a novelty, but is rooted deeply in the history of the church. Clement of Rome, writing in the first century, calls the scriptures the "true utterances of the Holy Spirit" (*Epistles* 1.45). In the second century Irenaeus calls the scriptures "divine" and "perfect," being uttered by God (*Against Heresies* 2.41.1; 2.28.2). Origen, a third-century father, refused to accept a third testament because it would not be "divine" (*Lev. hom.* 5). Cyril of Jerusalem declared in the fourth century that the "certitude of our faith does not depend on reasoning based on whim, but on the teachings drawn from the scriptures" (*Catech.* IV; *De Spiritu Sancto*, n. 17). In the fifth century Augustine stated that

"I believe most firmly that no one of these authors has erred in any respect in writing" (*Epistles* 82.1.3). These citations, which could be multiplied many times over, indicate clearly that the early fathers believed without hesitation in the divine origin and inspiration of the scriptures.

In the medieval church Anselm affirmed that he would preach nothing other than what scripture, produced by a miracle of the Spirit, contained (*De conc. proesc. Dei*, q.3, c.6). Bonaventure declared that "all our knowledge ought to have its basis in the knowledge of Holy Scripture" (*Brevil. prol.*). During the medieval period church tradition continued to encroach upon the authority of scripture, but the formal authority of the inspiration of scripture was maintained.

The Protestant Reformers recognized the divine inspiration and authority of the Bible in no uncertain terms. According to Luther, "The entire Scriptures are assigned to the Holy Ghost." Calvin wrote that scripture has "come down to us from the very mouth of God" (*Inst.* I.vii,5). The English Reformer Thomas Cranmer held that scripture was "a most sure ground and an infallible truth" (*Works*, 1.24).[7] The Lutheran Formula of Concord taught that scripture was God's "pure, infallible, and unalterable Word."

In the seventeenth century both Reformed and Lutheran theologians refined the Reformation teachings on the authority of Scripture. Quenstedt, a Lutheran, affirmed that "in the canonical sacred scripture there is no lie, no falsehood, not even the smallest error either in words or in matter ... whether it be a matter of dogma or of morals or of history or chronology or of topography or nomenclature" (*Theologia did.-pol.*, 1685). Quenstedt also held that the Hebrew vowel points of the Masoretic text were inspired, but later developments in text criticism rendered this view untenable.

In a classic article titled "Inspiration" appearing in 1881 in the *Presbyterian Review*, A. A. Hodge and B. B. Warfield articulated a position which has remained standard for much of conservative Protestantism in America since that time. "The writers of this article," they stated, "are sincerely convinced of the perfect soundness of the great catholic doctrine of biblical inspiration, i.e., that

---

7. For a response to recent attempts to attribute neo-orthodox views of inspiration to Luther and Calvin, see John Warwick Montgomery, ed., *God's Inerrant Word*, pp. 95—114.

the scriptures not only contain, but *are the Word of God,* and hence that all their elements and all their affirmations are absolutely errorless. . . . We affirm that a candid inspection of all the ascertained phenomena of the original text of scripture will leave unmodified the ancient faith of the church. In all their real affirmations these books are without error."

Hodge and Warfield stressed the affirmations of scripture. This took into account the circumstances that occasionally the scripture writers report statements by others—e.g. Satan—that are clearly false. Inspiration and inerrancy were posited of the autographs, in recognition of the fact that in some cases the text had been damaged in transmission.

The liberal scholar Kirsopp Lake, writing in 1926, candidly admitted that church history was on the side of the conservatives in the matter of the doctrine of inspiration. "It is a mistake often made by educated persons who happen to have but little knowledge of historical theology," he wrote, "to suppose that fundamentalism is a new and strange form of thought. . . . How many were there, for instance, in the Christian churches of the eighteenth century, who doubted the infallible inspiration of all Scripture? A few perhaps, but very few. No, the fundamentalist may be wrong; I think that he is. But it is we who have departed from the tradition, not he. . . . The Bible and the *corpus theologicum* of the church is [*sic*]on the fundamentalist side."[8] Written in the midst of the modernist-fundamentalist controversy, this is a striking admission indeed: "The Bible and the *corpus theologicum* of the church is [*sic*] on the fundamentalist side." Though he himself rejected the historic doctrine of inspiration, he had to admit that the testimony of church history and the Bible itself witnessed against his position.

### Biblical basis of inspiration

The verbal inspiration of the Old Testament can be established by examining the claims of the Old Testament itself, the use of the Old Testament by the apostles, and the use of the Old Testament by Christ.

Phrases such as "Thus says the Lord" and "Hear the word of the Lord" recur constantly in the Old Testament. God says to Jeremiah, "I have put *my words* in your mouth" (1:9); "I am making *my words*

8. Kirsopp Lake, *The Religion of Yesterday and Tomorrow,* p. 61.

in your mouth a fire" (5:14). God tells Moses that after him he will raise up "a prophet like you. . . . I will put my words in his mouth" (Deut. 18:18). Balaam is constrained to be the mouthpiece of God, even contrary to his intention (Num. 22:38; 23:12; 24:16). The preface to the Decalogue asserts that "God spoke all these words" (Exod. 20:1). According to Exod. 21:18, the Decalogue was "written with the finger of God." False prophets are guilty of substituting the contents of their own minds for the speech of God (Ezek. 13:2–3, 7). Jeremiah redictates all the words of the scroll burned by King Jehoiakim (Jer. 36:2, 4, 28). Here it is clear that the words of the scroll are identified with the words of God. The foregoing citations, and many similar ones that could be mentioned, show clearly that the Old Testament itself asserts that God spoke to his chosen messengers and that these very words have been recorded as scripture. The distinction between an authentic message from God and the products of one's own imagination is made within the Old Testament itself (Ezek. 13:2–3, 7). Only an *a priori* belief that God does not or cannot speak to man would prevent the reader from taking seriously the Old Testament's own claims to verbal inspiration.

In the New Testament the apostolic writers clearly consider the text of the Old Testament to be inspired. In Acts 4:25 Peter declares that the Lord "by the mouth of our father David . . . did say by the Holy Spirit." The words of David from Ps. 2:1 are attributed to the Holy Spirit. In Rom. 9:17 Paul says, "For the scripture says to Pharaoh." The citation is from Exod. 9:16, where God is the speaker. There is such an identification in the mind of Paul of what scripture says and what God says that the terms are interchangeable in the apostle's usage.[9] To Paul the entire Old Testament canon represents the oracles of God—i.e., the living voice of God (Rom. 3:2).

For John the details of the crucifixion were divinely predicted in the words of the Old Testament (John 19:24, 28). For James the inclusion of the Gentiles in the plan of salvation was predicted by the words of the prophets (Acts 15:15). The writer of Hebrews identifies the words of the psalmist with the words of the Holy Spirit:

9. For a fuller discussion of this point, see Warfield, "It Says:" "Scripture Says:" "God Says," in *The Inspiration and Authority of the Bible*, pp. 299 – 348.

"As the Holy Spirit says, 'Today, when you hear his voice' " (Heb. 3:7; Ps. 95:7).

This apostolic usage is that of Christ himself. Everywhere the Lord Jesus considers the Old Testament to be the inspired Word of God. During the temptation Christ quotes from the Book of Deuteronomy four times, declaring that man lives not by bread alone, but by every word that proceeds from the mouth of God (Matt. 4:1–11). According to Jesus even a messenger raised from the dead could not have greater authority than Moses and the prophets (Luke 16:19–31). The words of David in Ps. 110:1 are inspired by the Holy Spirit (Matt. 22:43). In defense of his claim to be one with the Father—a claim considered blasphemous by the Jews—Jesus points to one word ("gods") in Ps. 82:6, a psalm of Asaph, to make his point (John 10:34). "Scripture cannot be broken," he declares, expressing his complete confidence in the sublime authority of the Old Testament (John 10:35). After the resurrection Christ chides the disciples for being slow of heart to believe all that the prophets had spoken of him (Luke 24:25–26, 44).

Christ's complete confidence in the inspiration and authority of the Old Testament is found in all four Gospels and in every stratum of New Testament tradition, however those strata might be distinguished. John W. Wenham, in *Christ and the Bible*, ably summarizes the Savior's view: "To Christ the Old Testament was true, authoritative, inspired. To him the God of the Old Testament was the teaching of the living God. To him, what scripture said, God said."[10]

The argument for the inspiration of the New Testament is more indirect. The analogy of the Old Testament would lead one to expect that God would give the people of the new covenant authoritative written documents to regulate their faith and life in the same way that he gave such documents to the people of the old covenant. Paul contrasts the two dispensations in the following manner: "For if what faded away came with splendor, what is permanent must have much more splendor" (2 Cor. 3:11). The New Testament economy is not only more glorious than the Old; it is also more permanent. Hence, in order to guard this permanency, it seems most reasonable to expect that God would have estab-

10. John W. Wenham, *Christ and the Bible*, p. 37.

lished permanent, canonical documents to serve as the constitution of the new community.

An explicit argument for the inspiration of our present New Testament writings can be set forth along the following lines: first, from the nature of Christ's teachings; second, from the specific promise of Christ to the church; third, from the specific claims of the apostles; and fourth, from New Testament statements concerning the witness of the Holy Spirit to the Word of God in the church.

First of all, consider the permanent nature of Christ's teachings. According to Christ, not a jot or tittle of the Old Testament law would pass away without being fulfilled while heaven and earth remained (Matt. 5:18). The Savior claims the same degree of permanence for his own teachings: "Heaven and earth will pass away, but my words will not pass away" (Matt. 24:35). The permanence of Old Testament law was ensured through its preservation in written form; one would expect the same process to have been applied in the case of Christ's words. In the Gospel of John, Jesus declares that "the word that I have spoken will be his judge at the last day" (12:48). If the word of Christ is to be the basis for the universal and public eschatological judgment, one would expect that word to have been made generally available to mankind in written form. And what is said concerning the permanence of Christ's teaching applies by implication to the teachings of the apostles, who are the Lord's specially commissioned spokesmen. "Christ speaking in me" (2 Cor. 13:3): the Pauline claim is the apostolic claim generally.

In the second place, the New Testament records specific promises of Christ to his disciples concerning the recollection and preservation of his teachings. Prior to the resurrection Jesus promises his disciples that "he that heareth you, heareth me" (Luke 10:16). If they are required to bear testimony during times of persecution, they are to take courage from the assurance that "it is not you that speak, but the Spirit of your Father who speaks in you" (Matt. 10:20). Looking forward to the period of postresurrection mission, Jesus assures the Twelve that "the Counselor, the Holy Spirit, whom the Father will send in my name, he will teach you all things, and bring to your remembrance all that I have said to you" (John 14:26). Likewise, John 15:26: "When the Counselor comes, whom I shall send to you from the Father, even the Spirit of truth, who proceeds from the Father, he will bear witness to me." Similarly, John 16:13,15: "When the Spirit of truth comes, he will guide you into all the truth. . . . He will take what is mine and declare it to you." These texts clearly indicate that Jesus did not intend to leave his disciples to their own devices in the preservation of his teachings. The supernatural aid of the Holy Spirit was promised for the task.

In the third place, we find in the New Testament specific apostolic claims to inspiration. These are most numerous in the Pauline epistles, but by no means limited to them. Paul claims that his teaching is not on the authority of human wisdom, but on the authority of the Spirit (1 Cor. 2:13). He reminds the Corinthians that his written instructions are commandments from the Lord (1 Cor. 14:37). He is consciously aware that Christ speaks through him to the churches (2 Cor. 13:3). Paul gives thanks that the Thessalonians received the gospel which he preached not merely as a human word but as the very Word of God (1 Thess. 2:13). Even if an angel from heaven should preach a different message, that message should be rejected on the basis of the gospel that Paul had already preached (Gal. 1:8). The apostles and prophets are the foundation of the New Testament church (Eph. 2:20).

The apostle Peter declares that the gospel was preached in the power of the Holy Spirit sent from heaven (1 Peter 1:12). According to 2 Peter 3:16 the Pauline epistles are to be considered in the same category with the Old Testament scriptures.

In the fourth place, the New Testament speaks of the witness of the Spirit to the Word of God in the church. According to 1 John 2:27 the believers have an anointing of the Spirit which enables them to discern truth and error. Elsewhere, in John 7:17, Jesus says that if anyone is *willing* to do the will of God, he will be able to know whether the doctrine is truly from God. And the sheep hear the voice of the shepherd and follow him (John 10:27). There is a spiritual affinity between the believing community and the teachings of the Master. It is indeed a remarkable fact that over the course of church history, with its multitude of doctrinal disagreements, a virtual unanimity has emerged among the Christian churches that the twenty-seven books of our present New Testament do in fact represent the authoritative and inspired Word of God. We have good reason to believe that such a consensus is no accident of history, but that the sovereign Lord of history has, in his providential control of all events, caused the truly inspired

testimonies to the gospel of Christ to be received and acknowledged in the churches.

### Objections

Various objections have been raised against the foregoing lines
of argument for the inspiration of the New Testament. One objection of a philosophical nature claims that the entire procedure is
circular. How can one establish the authority of the New Testament
by appealing to the New Testament itself? At this point it is worth
noting that such an objection was raised against Christ himself
during his earthly ministry. According to the Pharisees, his testimony was not true because he bore witness concerning himself
(John 8:13). Not so, Jesus replied. "Although I give testimony of
myself, my testimony is true" (8:14). By the very nature of the case,
if God speaks, if a true prophet delivers a word from God, that
word, as to its authority, is self-authenticating. God cannot and
does not need to appeal to any higher authority beyond himself
to establish his authority. God may condescend to corroborate his
message with miracles, but he is not bound to do so. John the
Baptist performed no miracles but he truly spoke for God, and
those who were willing recognized the divine authority of the
message. The willing creature is given the ability, by the grace of
God, to recognize the voice of the Creator. The voice of God is as
clear and self-evidencing in itself as is the noonday sun or table
salt to sight or taste. How can one convince another that salt is
"salty"? Invite him to taste the salt, and the salt will evidence its
intrinsic qualities in his experience. This is not to say that historical evidences have no role to play in the confirmation of a
message. The point, however, is that the primal clarity is produced
not by the evidences, but by the self-evidencing power of the Word
of God itself. The charge of circularity is thus seen to be somewhat
misplaced. All argument must begin with a "given," with some
premises considered evident in themselves. In this case, the Word
of God presents itself as the ultimate given of all human thought,
the basis for the most comprehensive world view possible. If God
does exist, then his word must be the ultimate framework for all
human meaning and the ultimate frame of reference for all human
factuality.

It could be objected that a good number of the New Testament
books make no explicit claims to inspiration. This is certainly the

case, but the same is true for many parts of the Old Testament which are received as inspired by the New Testament authors. In Matt. 22:43 Christ quotes from Ps. 110, attributing it to the Holy Spirit even though there is no such explicit claim in the psalm itself. In John 10:34 Christ quotes Ps. 82:6 as an authoritative and inspired text, and again there is no explicit claim to inspiration in the text itself. These examples show that the absence of an explicit claim to inspiration does not imply the absence of inspiration. The inspiration or lack of it for a given text can be established on other grounds. If one were to remove from the Old Testament all passages not claiming direct inspiration, there would be little of the Old Testament canon left.

Certain statements of Paul are sometimes adduced as arguments against verbal, plenary inspiration. In 1 Cor. 7:10, in the context of a discussion of marriage, Paul distinguishes between his own teaching and that of the Lord. In 7:25 he states that he has no commandment from the Lord, but gives his own opinion in the matter. Is such an expression of "opinion" consistent with divine inspiration? Here it is important to realize that inspiration is expressed through a variety of forms and moods: commands, questions, promises, declarative statements, expressions of praise— and advice. In 1 Cor. 7 the proper distinctive is not inspired vs. noninspired, but apostolic *commands* vs. apostolic *advice.* In some matters of Christian conduct it is not a matter of sinning or not sinning but a matter of discretion, advisability, or expediency. Such is the case in the matter treated by the apostle in 1 Cor. 7:25. It is helpful to remember in this regard that an entire book of the Old Testament canon—the Book of Proverbs—falls into this category of "inspired advice."

### Nonevangelical views of inspiration

Since the rise of modern biblical criticism there has been a widespread revolt in theology against the classical doctrine of verbal inspiration. Most Protestant theologians continue to give lip service to the authority of the Bible in some fashion, but deny that authority to the specific words of the text.

The nineteenth-century liberalism of Schleiermacher saw Christian theology as a whole as a verbalization of religious experience. This stress on religious experience as the locus of authority is also found in the Protestant modernist Shailer Mathews. In *The Faith of Modernism* (1924), Mathews states that the Bible "when properly arranged on the basis of satisfactory evidence is a trustworthy record of human experience of God."[11] Being "properly arranged" implies a reconstruction of the Bible along critical and evolutionary lines. Even if the Bible is then accepted, it is not apparent why, if experience is the norm, Jeremiah's or Paul's experience of God should be considered more authoritative than Mohammed's, Mary Baker Eddy's, or Joseph Smith's. A *subjective* theory of biblical inspiration and authority erodes the uniqueness of Christianity's truth claims.

According to Gordon Kaufman of the Harvard Divinity School, the Bible "is a human book like any other, written and transcribed by human hands. ... The Bible's authority derives from the revelatory events of which it contains the primary reports."[12] This stress on revelatory events is also found in the "biblical theology" movement represented by Oscar Cullmann, Alan Richardson, and G. Ernest Wright.[13] This point of view reflects the impact of the Barthian stress on the "event" character of revelation itself.

The view of authority espoused by Kaufman and others has serious weaknesses, and is in the last analysis untenable. In the first place, it is clear that such a view is not that of Christ and the writers of the New Testament. They cited the words of the canonical text, and not merely the events described, as being of divine authority. In the second place, this view drives an illegitimate wedge between event and interpretation. Evidently Kaufman believes that the modern reader of the Bible can find "revelatory events" in the Bible apart from "inspired interpretation" as it has been traditionally understood. But how is one to know, for example, that the crucifixion of Jesus of Nazareth by the Romans was anything more than the execution of another political criminal? How is one to discern the *religious* meaning of such an event without the apostolic and inspired *interpretation* of the event— that here in fact the Son of God was dying for the sins of the world? "Revelatory events" have no authority apart from a revelatory and inspired interpretation. There are no raw, uninterpreted facts; "facts" do not speak for themselves. Furthermore, how can

11. Robert L. Ferm, ed., *Issues in American Protestantism*, p. 283.

12. Gordon Kaufman, *Systematic Theology*, p. 63.

13. For a discussion of the biblical theology movement, its problems, and demise, see Brevard Childs, *Biblical Theology in Crisis*, (Philadelphia: Westminster, 1970), chs. 1–4.

one know that there were any revelatory events at all, if the inspiration and authority of the text are denied? Why accept the accounts of the exodus and the resurrection at all? Perhaps they represent no more than the overheated religious imaginations of the writers. Not only the revelatory character of the text but also its "event" character is undermined by the view in question.

Another alternative, equally problematic, is presented by John Macquarrie in his *Principles of Christian Theology.* Inspiration, Macquarrie believes, "does not lie in the words ... but belongs to the scriptures only as they are set in the context of the whole life of faith in the community." Here verbal inspiration is transmuted into the community's *experience* of faith in relation to the text. "The belief that the Bible is infallible is one that dies hard in some parts of the Christian world," Macquarrie tells us. "The Christian revelation comes in a person, not in a book."[14] One can certainly agree that God intended the Bible to be proclaimed and heard in the context of a community of faith. The point is, however, that the authority rests in the Bible, and not in some vague and amorphous experience of faith in the community. And evangelicals would certainly agree that Jesus Christ in his person was a divine revelation. The difficulty for Macquarrie's view is an epistemological one: What access to that revelatory person is available except through the words of the New Testament? The existence of Jesus as a historical person is attested in Tacitus and the Talmud, but their interpretation of the significance of that person is quite different from that of the New Testament. Mohammed acknowledges the existence of Jesus, but denies him as the unique incarnation of God and the only savior of mankind. By rejecting the inspiration of the words of the New Testament, Macquarrie demolishes the epistemological basis for the revelatory character of Jesus' person which he desires to retain.

## Inerrancy

### A definition

The inerrancy of scripture is a consequence of its verbal, plenary inspiration. Scripture is free from error in all its teachings and

14. John Macquarrie, *Principles of Christian Theology,* p. 9.

affirmations because it is in·its entirety the product of an infinite, all-wise, and all-powerful God who cannot err.

The doctrine of inerrancy is a hallmark of evangelical Christianity. It finds expression in a variety of doctrinal statements. The basis of faith of the Evangelical Theological Society is that "the Bible alone, and the Bible in its entirety, is the Word of God written, and hence free from error in the autographs." The doctrinal statement of Gordon-Conwell Theological Seminary states that "the sixty-six canonical books of the Bible as originally written were inspired of God, hence free from error. They constitute the only infallible guide in faith and practice." In this latter statement it might be noted that the concepts of inerrancy and infallibility are used in a synonymous fashion.

In recent theological discussions the meaning of the term "inerrancy" has been carefully refined to avoid a number of misunderstandings. In matters of precision of detail and the like, it is important to note that scripture sets its own standards of accuracy, according to the purpose and particular literary genre employed by the authors. Article XIII of the Chicago Statement on Biblical Inerrancy reflects such refinements: "We deny that it is proper to evaluate Scripture according to standards of truth and error that are alien to its usage or purpose. We further deny that inerrancy is negated by Biblical phenomena such as a lack of modern technical precision, irregularities of grammar or spelling, observational descriptions of nature, the reporting of falsehoods, the use of hyperbole and round numbers, the topical arrangement of material, variant selections of material in parallel accounts, or the use of free citations."

The recognition that standards of accuracy in reporting are relative to the context and purpose of the writer or speaker is not unique to theological discussions. This point has been stressed in recent discussions in the philosophy of language. In *Philosophical Investigations* Wittgenstein asked, "Am I inexact when I do not give distance to the sun to the nearest foot, or tell a joiner the width of a table to the nearest thousandth of an inch?" (sect. 88). Clearly the standards of accuracy in the physical sciences and in ordinary discourse are different.

An examination of biblical usage of the term πλάνη, "error," will help to prevent an overly precisionist concept of exactitude from being imposed on the scripture from without. This term is used

in Matt. 27:64, "so the last error shall be worse than the first"; Rom.
1:27, "the recompense of their error"; James 5:20, "who converts
a sinner from the error of his ways"; 2 Peter 2:18, "escaped from
them who live in error"; 3:17, "being led away with the error of the
wicked." Similarly, the usage of πλανάομαι, to "err, wander," should
be considered in Matt. 22:29; Mark 12:24; 12:27; Heb. 3:10; James
1:16; 5:19. In these texts it is evident that "error" in scripture refers
to matters of major import, a "wandering from the truth" in significant fashion. This is not to minimize the importance of details,
but it is helpful in keeping such matters in proper proportion.

The philosopher Michael Polanyi has made some useful observations on the process of understanding a complex whole, whether
it happens to be a written text, a work of art, or a problem in
science or mathematics. In order for the details of the whole to
be properly comprehended, our attention must rest upon them
not in an atomistic fashion but *subsidiarily*, in terms of their joint
bearing upon the focal meaning of the whole. "To be aware of
something subsidiarily means that we are not aware of it in itself,
but as a clue or instrument pointing beyond itself."[15] Or again,
"When we comprehend a particular set of items or parts of a
whole, the focus of our attention is shifted from the hitherto un-
comprehended particulars to the understanding of their joint
meaning."[16] If one stands too close to a painting by an impres-
sionist master and focuses on a few strokes of color, the meaning
of the whole is lost. Similarly, if one focuses on small details of a
Gospel pericope in isolation from the focal meaning of the whole—
as can be easily done in critical exegesis and "scientific" commentaries—the meaning of the text dissolves. Sight of the forest is
lost by limiting attention to particular leaves. The details of the
biblical text are to be comprehended subsidiarily as tools or instruments which point beyond themselves to the joint meaning,
the "hermeneutical center" intended by the human and divine
authors. This way of understanding the relationship of parts and
whole in a text can help to avoid some false issues in discussions
of inerrancy.

### "Limited" inerrancy

All evangelicals recognize that the concept of inerrancy needs
careful qualifications in terms of the actual usage and purposes

---

15. Michael Polanyi, *The Study of Man*, p. 44.
16. Ibid., p. 29.

of the scriptural authors. Some, however, have suggested a view that has come to be known as "limited inerrancy." According to this view, the inerrancy of scripture is limited to matters of faith and practice. Matters of historical detail, geography, cosmology, and natural science are not necessarily free from error.

It can be readily seen that this view is faced with a number of considerable problems. In the first place, it seems inconsistent with the attitude of Christ and the apostles, who were not hesitant to argue crucial points of doctrine on the basis of details of the Old Testament text (e.g. John 10:34). In the second place, there is the problem of subjectivism. Who decides what parts of scripture are relevant to faith and practice, and which parts are not? This would seem to open the door to a "canon within the canon," with all the hermeneutical problems thereby entailed. In the third place, specific biblical texts indicate that the distinction between matters of faith and practice and other presumably nonrevelatory matters is a rather artificial one. Consider the messianic prophecy of Micah 5:2: "But you, O Bethlehem Ephrathah, ... from you shall come forth for me one who is to be ruler in Israel." Here a christological point is made in relation to a specific geographic detail, Bethlehem. In Deut. 18:22 a specific test for discerning false prophets is given: "If the word does not come to pass, ... that is a word which the Lord has not spoken." Here the correlation between an inspired word and specific historical events in the future is set forth. The proposal of limited inerrancy, which presumably would relieve some of the pressure on the evangelical doctrine of inspiration from the side of historical criticism, would seem to concede too much and to raise as many problems as it solves.

### Historical considerations

It has been suggested that the evangelical view of inerrancy is a novelty, being read back into church history by Hodge and Warfield during the nineteenth century. This is hardly the case. The antiquity of the doctrine is admitted by candid scholars of varying theological persuasions. "That scripture is inerrant is a constant element in Christian tradition," notes the Roman Catholic scholar Richard F. Smith, writing in the *Jerome Biblical Commentary*. "The inerrancy of Scripture is ... a teaching common to all the early Christian writers."[17]

---

17. Richard F. Smith, in *Jerome Biblical Commentary*, p. 513.

In his *Introduction to New Testament Thought,* F. C. Grant points out that everywhere in the New Testament "it is taken for granted that what is written in Scripture is the work of divine inspiration, and is therefore trustworthy, infallible, and inerrant. . . . No New Testament writer would dream of questioning a statement contained in the Old Testament."[18] Rudolf Bultmann, in *Jesus and the Word,* observes that "Jesus agreed always with the scribes of his time in accepting without question the authority of the Law. . . . Jesus did not attack the Law but assumed its authority and interpreted it."[19] Grant and Bultmann, neither of whom holds the inerrantist view, yet recognize that it is embedded in the New Testament writings themselves.

Long before the formulations of Hodge and Warfield, John Robinson, pastor to the Pilgrims of Plymouth, could write, "Who is able to understand the manner of God's working in giving the Holy Ghost to man, and in directing the tongues and pens of the prophets infallibly, and so they could not err?"[20] Likewise Timothy Dwight, president of Yale, defending biblical authority in debates with students during the 1790s, held that with respect to the apostles, "each inspired man was, as to his preaching or his writing, absolutely preserved from errors."[21]

It is worthwhile to recall again the statement of the modernist scholar Kirsopp Lake cited earlier (p. 178). In regard to the history of the doctrine of inspiration, "the fundamentalist may be wrong; I think that he is. But it is we who have departed from the tradition, not he . . . The Bible and the *corpus theologicum* of the church is on the fundamentalist side." Hodge and Warfield did specify the doctrine of inerrancy in relation to the autographs, in the light of textual studies, but the essentials of the doctrine were present from the time of the New Testament itself.

### Biblical basis: types of argument

However strong the testimony of tradition, the crucial question for evangelicals is, of course, the testimony of scripture itself. Do the biblical data support the doctrine of inerrancy? Here there are two main lines of argument to be considered. The first is based

18. Frederick C. Grant, *An Introduction to New Testament Thought,* p. 75.
19. Rudolf Bultmann, *Jesus and the Word,* p. 61.
20. In Frank Foster, *A Genetic History of the New England Theology,* p. 13.
21. In John Woodbridge, Mark Noll, and Nathan Hatch, *The Gospel in America,* p. 108.

on a consideration of Christ's attitude toward and actual usage of the Old Testament scriptures. The argument could be stated as follows: Christ trusted the Old Testament scriptures without reservation or qualification; the attitude of Christ should determine that of his disciples; hence we should trust scripture without qualification or reservation. This line of argument is presented quite ably by John W. Wenham in *Christ and the Bible*; the reader is referred to that work for a detailed discussion of the evidence and for responses to various objections.

A second line of argument moves from the nature of God to the nature of scripture. This argument can be stated in the following way: God by his very nature is not subject to error; the scriptures in their entirety are a communication from God; hence the scriptures are in their entirety free from error. The first premise is self-evident, for God is not limited with respect to his knowledge, power, or goodness. It is the second premise that is the point of contention.

In the first place, there are the direct biblical statements on inspiration: 2 Tim. 3:16, "All scriptures are inspired by God"; 2 Peter 1:21, "No prophecy ever came by the impulse of man, but men moved by the Holy Spirit spoke from God"; Rom. 3:2, "The Jews are entrusted with the oracles of God."

In the second place, there is the interchangeability in biblical usage of the phrases "it says," "scriptures says," and "God says"—an equivalency previously noted in the discussion of inspiration. Warfield examines one class of texts (e.g., Gal. 3:8; Rom. 9:17) where the scripture is spoken of interchangeably with God. There is a second class of texts (e.g., Matt. 19:4–5; Heb. 3:7; Acts 4:24–25) where God is spoken of as if he were the scriptures. If scripture speaks, God is speaking. The actual use of the Old Testament by the writers of the New Testament makes "an irresistible impression of the absolute identification . . . of the Scriptures in their hands with the living voice of God," notes Warfield.[22] "The very essence of the case is, that, under the force of their conception of the Scriptures as an oracular book, it was all one to the New Testament writers whether they said 'God says' or 'Scripture says.' "[23]

The data cited by Warfield, together with the texts cited in re-

---

22. Warfield, *Inspiration and Authority,* p. 299.
23. Ibid., p. 348.

lation to the discussion of inspiration, strongly support the second premise of the argument: scripture in its entirety is a communication from God. Hence, the scripture in its entirety is free from error in all its teachings.

### Problem texts

Almost all serious students of the Bible recognize its claims to inspiration and the high view of the authority of the Old Testament held by Christ and the apostles. It is the presence of various "problem" texts that raises questions about the doctrine of inerrancy in the minds of many whose general theological position is quite conservative. In this section we will attempt to treat a representative sample of such difficulties that might present themselves to the careful reader.

There are a number of different approaches that might be taken in the face of such problems. One unsatisfactory approach is simply to ignore the problem and to pretend that it does not exist. This "ostrich" approach is not intellectually honest and is no solution at all. A second unsatisfactory approach, from an evangelical perspective, is to acknowledge the problem and to conclude that an error must exist. This is the approach in liberal and neo-orthodox theologies. According to Barth, with respect to the scriptures, "The men whom we hear as witnesses speak as fallible, erring men like ourselves" (*Church Dogmatics*, I/2, 507). The problem here is that to be certain that an error exists, one would need virtually exhaustive knowledge of all circumstances relating to the matters described by the texts, and in the very nature of the case such knowledge is unavailable to us.

A third approach is to acknowledge the difficulty and to attempt a harmonization. This is the traditional evangelical approach. Attempts at harmonization are consistent with the plenary inspiration, and hence doctrinal coherence, of the Bible as a whole. J. I. Packer is surely correct in arguing that "our methods of interpreting Scripture must be such as express faith in its truth and consistency as God's Word. Our approach must be harmonistic, for we know at the outset that God's utterance is not self-contradictory."[24]

A fourth approach is to acknowledge the difficulty and, where

24. Packer, *"Fundamentalism,"* pp. 109–10.

no plausible harmonization is apparent, to leave the matter temporarily in suspense. Again Packer notes that what "we cannot harmonize by a plausible and natural hypothesis is best left unharmonized, with a frank admission that in our present state of knowledge we do not see how these apparent discrepancies should be resolved."[25] This is quite consistent with practices in the natural sciences. Accepted theories are not abandoned at the first sign of evidence that appears contradictory.[26] Historian of science Thomas S. Kuhn has noted that "to be accepted as a paradigm, a theory must seem better than its competition, but it need not, and in fact never does, explain all the facts with which it can be confronted."[27] In the matter of the inspiration and inerrancy of the Bible, the paradigm is Christ's attitude toward the Old Testament, and isolated difficulties do not outweigh the mass of evidence that supports the paradigm.

The general range of biblical difficulties encompasses four main categories: scientific, moral, historical, and internal. Several examples from each category will be examined.

Since the seventeenth century and the rise of modern science questions relating to science have been common. In Matt. 13:32, for example, it is stated that the mustard seed is the "smallest of all seeds." Strictly speaking, this is not the case: orchid seeds are smaller. The key here is to note the context of the language. The speaker and his audience are not located in a botany class but in some Palestinian village. The language is relative to the experience and environment of the audience. The statement, "There is usually frost on the ground by the first of October," will be correct if spoken in Vermont, but not in southern Florida. All language presupposes a context and an environment and should be evaluated accordingly.

Many biblical statements seem to presuppose a geocentric view of the solar system. "Its rising [the sun] is from the end of the heavens, and its circuit to the end of them" (Ps. 19:6). Does this in fact *teach* a geocentric solar system? Not really; it simply affirms that a person looking into the sky will see the sun describing such a path. The choice of a frame of reference for statements about the physical universe is relative to the needs of the observer. James

25. Ibid., p. 110.
26. For examples from the history of science, see Michael Polanyi, *Personal Knowledge* (Chicago: University of Chicago Press, 1958), pp. 12–13.
27. Thomas S. Kuhn, *The Structure of Scientific Revolutions*, pp. 17–18.

Rutherford, in the widely used text *The Project Physics Course*, states that "physicists now generally agree that all systems of reference are in principle equally valid for describing phenomena, although some will be easier and others more complex to use or think about. ... We should not speak of reference systems being right or wrong, but rather as convenient or inconvenient."[28] To this very day navigators use a geocentric coordinate system for their calculations, as do astronomers in locating stars.

As Bernard Ramm has pointed out, the language of the Bible in relation to natural phenomena is popular, not scientific. "The language of the Bible is phenomenal, ... 'pertaining to appearances.' ... Scripture ... uses the words of everyday life: it describes natural objects as they appear."[29] A recognition of the phenomenological nature of biblical language will help to prevent misreadings of scripture such as that of Cosmas Indicopleustes, a sixth-century monk, who insisted that the earth was flat on the basis of a literalistic reading of Isa. 40:22; "It is he who sits above the circle of the earth."[30]

A second category of difficulties is moral in nature. At times attitudes or actions are attributed to God which, to the modern reader, seem ethically substandard or even morally repugnant. A well-known example here concerns the command in Deut. 7:1–16 to slaughter the Canaanites. It should be noted that scripture describes the Canaanite culture of that day as degenerate and hardened in sin, guilty of gross idolatry, sexual perversion, child sacrifice, and witchcraft. They were sinning against the light of nature and conscience (Rom. 1:18–19; 2:14–15). Righteous Canaanites (e.g., Rahab, Josh. 2) could have saved themselves and their families. God is utterly holy, and our view of sin can be all too shallow (cf. John W. Wenham, *The Goodness of God*). God's patience has its limits; at times he executes capital punishment on entire societies that have become irremediably hardened in apostasy and sin (e.g., the generation of the flood; Sodom and Gomorrah). There is yet a more fearful judgment awaiting a faithless and sinful human race (2 Thess. 1:9). Those who openly reject the revelation of Jesus Christ face more severe judgment than the Canaanites (cf. Matt. 10:15). The "problem" in this case is not in the

28. James Rutherford, *The Project Physics Course*, p. 40, unit 2.
29. Bernard Ramm, *The Christian View of Science and Scripture*, pp. 46–47.
30. In John Dillenberger, *Protestant Thought and Natural Science*, p. 21.

text or in the character of God, but in our shallow understanding of sin, holiness, and divine judgment.

A third category of problems concerns historical details, where there appears to be a conflict between biblical statements and extrabiblical sources. The historical accuracy of the Old Testament in particular has been the focus of attention by biblical critics for the last several centuries. In this connection the biblical archaeologist William F. Albright has written, "The excessive scepticism shown toward the Bible by important historical schools of the eighteenth and nineteenth centuries ... has been progressively discredited. Discovery after discovery has established the accuracy of innumerable details."[31] According to Albright, it is "sheer hypercriticism to deny the substantially Mosaic character of the Pentateuchal tradition."[32]

Kenneth A. Kitchen notes the contributions made to the understanding of the Old Testament by ancient Near Eastern comparative studies. "Where problems have been raised in Old Testament studies, the information available from ancient Near Eastern sources can ... cut down the scope of these problems considerably, and sometimes solve them outright."[33] "The theories current in Old Testament studies ... were mainly established in a vacuum with little or no reference to the ancient Near East, and initially too often in accordance with *a priori* philosophical and literary principles."[34]

In the New Testament, Luke's historical accuracy has been frequently challenged. For example, Luke's use of the term πολιτάρχας to describe a city official in Thessalonica (Acts 17:6) has been questioned, since the term was not known in the classical literature. Subsequently, however, says F. F. Bruce, "some clear inscriptions have been found that make use of the title. Interestingly enough, five of these are in reference to Thessalonica."[35]

Sir William Ramsay, a noted archaeologist of the last century, began with a skeptical attitude toward Luke's historiography, but his own research led him to reverse his initial position. "Luke is a historian of the first rank," he concluded. "Not merely are his

31. William F. Albright, *The Archaeology of Palestine*, pp. 127–28.
32. Ibid., p. 224.
33. Kenneth A. Kitchen, *Ancient Orient and Old Testament*, pp. 168–69.
34. Ibid., p. 172.
35. F. F. Bruce, "Archaeological Confirmations of the New Testament," p. 325.

statements of fact trustworthy; he is possessed of the true historic sense."[36]

Similar conclusions have been reached more recently by the classical historian A. N. Sherwin-White. "For Acts the confirmation of historicity is overwhelming. . . . Any attempts to reject its basic historicity even in matters of detail must now appear absurd. Roman historians have long taken it for granted."[37] Sherwin-White notes the peculiar fact that classical historians treat their documents with far less skepticism than do critical New Testament scholars, even though the manuscript basis for the New Testament is far wider than for any other similar documents from the classical world.

Internal difficulties probably constitute the largest single category, especially where the ordinary reader is concerned. Such difficulties may involve New Testament quotations from the Old Testament or apparent discrepancies in parallel accounts of the same event.

In Heb. 11:21 the writer refers to a "staff." In the Masoretic text of Gen. 47:31, the Old Testament passage cited, the reading is "bed." It should be noted that the Hebrew consonants אטה can be translated either "bed" (אִטָּה, MT) or "staff" (אַטֶּה, LXX), according to the vowel pointing selected. In this case Philip Hughes has suggested that the Septuagint translator probably preserved the better reading. Where the Masoretic text and the Septuagint disagree, the Septuagint may actually in some cases preserve the better reading, since the vowel points were added to the Masoretic only during the sixth to eighth centuries A.D.

At times the New Testament writers quote from the Old Testament in a way that corresponds exactly neither to the Masoretic Text nor the Septuagint, nor, for that matter, to any known text form. T. W. Manson has commented in this regard, "We are long accustomed to distinguish carefully between the text which . . . is sacred, and the commentary upon it. . . . Odd as it may seem to us, the freedom with which they handled the Biblical text is a direct result of the supreme importance which they attached to it."[38] Similarly Earle Ellis, commenting on Paul's use of the Old

---

36. William Ramsay, *The Bearing of Recent Discovery on the Trustworthiness of the New Testament*, p. 222.

37. A. N. Sherwin-White, *Roman Law and Roman Society in the New Testament*, p. 189.

38. T. W. Manson, "The Argument From Prophecy," p. 135.

Testament, notes that his idea of a quotation was not one of " 'parroting' the text; neither was it an eisegesis which arbitrarily imposed a foreign meaning upon the text. It was rather . . . a quotation-exposition, a *midrash pesher*, which drew from the text the meaning originally implanted by the Holy Spirit, and expressed that meaning in the most appropriate words and phrases known to him."[39]

In Matt. 23:9–10 the quotation applied to the death of Judas is assigned to Jeremiah (cf. 32:6–9) instead of to Zech. 11:12–13, which seems to be the correct reference. The comments of Berkeley Mickelsen on this problem are worth citing at length:

> In Matthew 27:7–8 the word "field" occurs three times. The chief priests purchased the field with Judas' money—the thirty pieces of silver. In the original Old Testament passage Zechariah is talking about the value which the people put upon himself and the Lord. Using typology, Matthew applies this to Jesus. Zechariah said nothing about the purchase of a field. But Jeremiah does (see Jer. 32:6–9, 10–15, 25, 43–44). For Jeremiah the purchase showed God's concern for his people. Jeremiah said that after the exile God would bless his people in their land. Using typology, Matthew connects the field purchase of Jeremiah with the thirty pieces of silver and the potter spoken of by Zechariah. So the three words "for the field" are the reason for Matthew's formula: "through the prophet Jeremiah, saying" (27:9). If we judge Matthew by the standards of his own time, this is an acceptable way of doing it. He wanted to stress the field so he located the passage where the field was mentioned."[40]

In short, a better understanding of the writer's literary conventions—in this case, a typological use of the Old Testament—can lead to a resolution of the difficulty.

There are many examples of apparent discrepancies in parallel accounts. For example, the king lists in Kings and Chronicles frequently vary as to the length of reigns of certain kings. In an important study, *The Mysterious Numbers of the Hebrew Kings*, E. R. Thiele showed that in many instances the differences could be accounted for in terms of periods of co-reigns and differing methods of computing regnal years in the northern and southern

39. Earle Ellis, *Prophecy and Hermeneutic in Early Christianity*, p. 180.
40. Berkeley Mickelsen, "The Bible's Own Approach to Authority," p. 86.

kingdoms. Here is a case where a more accurate understanding of the original historical context and cultural practices helped to resolve difficulties.

The Synoptic Gospels abound with variant accounts of the same incident or sayings. The words of institution of the Lord's Supper are variously reported by Mark and Luke, for example: Mark 14:22, "this is my body"; Luke 22:19, "this is my blood which is given for you"; Mark 14:24, "this is my blood of the covenant"; Luke 22:20, "this cup is the new covenant in my blood." Leon Morris has observed that the inerrancy which the Bible teaches "is compatible with variant reports of the words used on a given occasion."[41] Paraphrases rather than exact quotations would be quite in harmony with the evangelists' general purposes.

In a similar vein John Wenham, commenting on the relationship between variant sayings in Matthew and Luke, observes that it is "quite improbable that the great sayings which find a place both in Matthew and Luke ... were uttered only once by Jesus. ... He would have repeated them again and again."[42]

What of variant accounts of the same event, as in Matt. 21:18—22, where the cursing of the fig tree takes effect immediately, whereas in Mark 11:20—25 it takes effect over a longer period of time? In such cases, suggests R. T. France, the evangelical should not attempt a hasty harmonization before considering the possibility that differing literary styles and purpose might account for the different treatments. The Gospels may well be thought of more along the lines of paintings rather than snapshots. The analogy of art would suggest that different styles—e.g., naturalism or impressionism—could give equally valuable, though differing, representations of the same historical events. To extend the analogy to the realm of film making, the difference between an ordinary news clip and time-lapse photography is suggestive. Perhaps in the case of the cursing of the fig tree the "film" in Matthew's "camera" was running faster, in order to dramatize the miraculous element of the event. In any case, it seems clear that the historical substratum is essentially the same in both accounts.

The foregoing examples represent only a small sample of the texts which might have been discussed. While such discussions

41. Leon Morris, "Biblical Authority and the Concept of Inerrancy," p. 36.
42. John W. Wenham, "Synoptic Independence and the Origin of Luke's Travel Narratives," p. 513.

of detailed problems are necessary and valuable, especially in an academic context, the larger issues of biblical authority need to be kept in focus. Detailed defenses of biblical inerrancy are quite fruitless if that authority is never applied in practice to the broad range of issues facing the church. As R. J. Rushdoony has argued, the doctrine of inerrancy or infallibility is not "simply an ecclesiastical doctrine. It is basic to life. To limit the scriptures to the role of a church book is to deny them and then to substitute man's word as law for everyday life."[43]

In a similar vein Carl F. H. Henry has noted that while for liberals the danger is to forget that "no movement can speak powerfully and definitively to the world if its leaders continually undermine the authority of its charter documents," the danger for conservatives is to forget that "no movement can speak powerfully and persuasively if it exhausts its energy by defending those documents instead of thrusting them into the world."[44]

## Canonicity

### Definition

If the Bible is to be the final written authority for faith and practice, it is evident that the following question must be answered: What books are properly part of the Bible? This is the question of canonicity. The "canon" is a list of divinely authoritative books read in the churches. In classical Greek κανών (cf. Hebrew קָנֶה, a "reed") means literally a reed or cane, a straight rod; metaphorically a testing rule or norm. Hence the canon of Holy Scripture is the list of divinely authorized books which constitute the norm for the church's teaching, faith, and life.

### Bibliographic resources

The main concern of pp. 199–205 will be with the theological issues related to the process of canonization rather than the historical details pertaining to the canonicity of the various biblical books. For further information on historical questions the reader is referred to the following works: F. F. Bruce, "New Light on the

43. R. J. Rushdoony, *Infallibility: An Inescapable Concept*, p. 65.
44. Carl F. H. Henry, "American Evangelicals in a Turning Time," p. 1060.

Origins of the New Testament Canon," in Longenecker and Tenney, eds., *New Dimensions in New Testament Study* (1974), pp. 3—18; J. N. Birdsall, "Canon of the New Testament," *New Bible Dictionary*, pp. 194—99; Feine, Behm, and Kümmel, *Introduction to the New Testament* (1965), pp. 334—59; W. H. Green, *General Introduction to the Old Testament* (1905); R. Laird Harris, *Inspiration and Canonicity of the Bible* (1957); R. K. Harrison, *Introduction to the Old Testament* (1969), II, 74—85; N. H. Ridderbos, "Canon of the Old Testament," *New Bible Dictionary*, pp. 186—94; J. Turro and R. Brown, "Canonicity," *Jerome Bible Commentary* (1968); John W. Wenham, *Christ and the Bible* (1972), ch. 6, "Extent of the Canon"; B. F. Westcott, *The Bible in the Church* (1905); E. J. Young, "Canon of the Old Testament," in C. F. H. Henry, ed., *Revelation and the Bible* (1957), pp. 153—85.

For those with little previous background in this area, the treatments in the *New Bible Dictionary*, together with the chapters by Wenham and Young, would be a good introduction to the entire topic.

### General considerations

It should be noted at the outset that the canon is not itself a matter of direct revelation. That is, although God gave a collection of inspired books, there is no inspired "table of contents" as such. The church's reception of the canon is ultimately and inescapably a judgment of faith rather than a matter of "necessary proofs." This is not to say, however, that historical evidences and arguments are superfluous. The general approach taken here is that the church's reception of the canon was due to a combination of objective factors (authorship, orthodox content) and subjective factors (Spirit's witness to the believing church), overruled and superintended by the sovereign providence of God (cf. Wenham). More will be said concerning the theological significance of divine providence in the process of canonization on pp. 201—205.

### Formation of the Old Testament canon

In general, the canon of the Old Testament depends, in a theological sense, on the witness of the New Testament. Very simply, the believer today accepts the Old Testament as authoritative because Christ and the apostles did so. Some of the historical details of the process of its formation need to be reviewed.

From the beginning Israel had a conception of authoritative books. Recall the words of Deut. 31:24–25: "When Moses had finished writing the words of this law in a book, to the very end, Moses commanded the Levites . . . , 'Take this book of the law, and put it by the side of the ark of the covenant of the Lord your God, that it may be there for a witness against you.' " As M. G. Kline has pointed out, the making of a covenant implied the existence of authoritative covenant documents—i.e., a canon—which contained the stipulations and sanctions of the covenant.[45] Joshua and the kings of Israel were to test their conduct by this written law (Josh. 1:8; Deut. 17:18; 1 Sam. 15; 1 Kings 3:14; 14:7–8).

It is difficult to reconstruct in detail the various stages of the formation of the Old Testament canon. Brevard Childs has observed that the "Jewish canon was formed through a complex historical process which is largely inaccessible to critical reconstruction."[46] Nevertheless, there is considerable evidence for the view that the canon of the Old Testament was recognized as substantially complete by the Jews after the work of Ezra and Nehemiah. Josephus, writing around A.D. 95, states that "from Artaxerxes [Persian king; reigned 465–425 B.C.] until our time everything has been recorded, but has not been deemed worthy of like credit with what preceded, because the exact succession of the prophets ceased. . . . No one has dared either to add anything to them, or to take anything from them. . . . It is instinctive in all Jews at once from their very birth to regard them as commands of God, and to abide by them, and if need be, cheerfully to die for them" (*Against Apion* 1.8.41, 42). Philo, as quoted by Eusebius (*De praeparatio evangelica* 8.6), speaks in similar fashion. Thus Josephus and Philo considered the Jewish canon to have been completed during the fifth century B.C. Wenham has concluded that there is "no reason to doubt that the Canon of the Old Testament is substantially Ezra's canon, just as the Pentateuch was substantially Moses' canon."[47]

That the Jewish canon was the same as our present list of thirty-nine books can be deduced from statements in the Talmud, Mishnah, and apocryphal writings. The Talmudic tractate *Baba Bathra* 14b gives the following account:

45. See M. G. Kline, *The Structure of Biblical Authority.*
46. Brevard Childs, *Introduction to the Old Testament as Scripture*, p. 67.
47. Wenham, *Christ and the Bible*, p. 134.

Moses wrote his own book [the five], as also the chapter of Balaam's prophecy and parables, and the book of Job. Joshua wrote his own book and the last eight verses of the Pentateuch. Samuel wrote his own book [1 and 2 Samuel], and also Judges and Ruth. David wrote the book of Psalms through the ten elders, Adam, Melchizedek, Abraham, Moses Heman, Jeduthan, Asaph, and the three sons of Korah. Jeremiah wrote his own book, as also the Kings and the Lamentations. Hezekiah and his company wrote [edited] the book of Isaiah, Proverbs, Canticles, and Ecclesiastes. The men of the great synagogue [Council of Jamnia, *ca.* A.D. 95?] wrote [edited] the book of Esther. Ezra wrote his own book [Ezra — Nehemiah] and joined on the Chronicles.

The Talmud was compiled around A.D. 500 but contains many older traditions. Many of the ascriptions of authorship in this passage are, or course, quite fanciful, but it is significant that the books enumerated correspond with our present list.

According to R. D. Wilson, "All the books of the Old Testament are cited as scripture in one or another tractates of the Mishna."[48] Like the Talmud the Mishnah, compiled around A.D. 200, preserves many older traditions.

A passage in the apocryphal book 2 Esdras (14:37—47), around A.D. 100, refers to twenty-four sacred books. It can be seen that the number twenty-four corresponds to our present thirty-nine, according to the Jewish method of enumeration: 39 — 11 (minor prophets = 1) — 1 (1, 2 Sam.) — 1 (1, 2 Kings) — 1 (1, 2 Chron.) — 1 (Ezra — Nehemiah) = 24.

During the first century A.D. the use of the Old Testament by Christ and the apostles presupposes the recognition of a definite body of authoritative books by Jews. A text such as Luke 24:44 assumes the common threefold division of the canon: "These are my words which I spoke to you, while I was still with you, that everything written about me in the law of Moses and the prophets and the psalms (= "writings") must be fulfilled." Jesus had many disputes with the scribes and Pharisees, but there is no evidence of any disagreement whatsoever on the extent of the canon.

According to the apostle Paul the Jews were, in the providence of God, entrusted with the task of transmitting the scriptures. "Then what advantage has the Jew? Or what is the value of cir-

---

48. R. D. Wilson, "The Book of Daniel and the Canon," p. 363.

cumcision? Much in every way. To begin with, the Jews are entrusted with the oracles of God" (Rom. 3:1–2). If this is the case, the determination of the Old Testament canon becomes a matter of historical investigation; i.e., what books were received as authoritative by the Jews during the time of Christ and the apostles? As we have seen, the evidence indicates that the Jewish canon of the first century and our present canon are the same.

Several questions may occur at this point. What of the fact that a number of books—e.g., Ruth, Ezra, Nehemiah, Esther, Ecclesiastes, Song of Solomon, and Lamentations—are not explicitly quoted in the New Testament? Here it should be recalled that the question of canonicity is to be distinguished from that of quotation by the New Testament. The key question is, Were these books received as canonical by the Jews in the first century? In each case the answer is yes.

A second question involves the apocryphal books such as Tobit, Judith, Ecclesiasticus, Baruch, 1 and 2 Maccabees, and the story of Bel and the Dragon, found in codices of the Septuagint. These were evidently popular among the Jews of Alexandria, found their way into the Vulgate, and were affirmed in the face of Protestant criticism by the Council of Trent in 1546. It should be noted that the codices containing these books date from the fourth or fifth century; what the first-century copies of the Septuagint may have contained is not clearly known. However, Brevard Childs has observed that from "the Jewish perspective the Greek Bible never had an independent integrity which could contest the Hebrew. Thus the Greek was continually brought into conformity with the Hebrew, and never the reverse."[49]

Jerome, the greatest Old Testament scholar in the Latin church, clearly distinguished between the authority of the Palestinian canon and that of the apocryphal writings. The Council of Trent had no Hebrew scholars of the stature of Jerome and bypassed his criticisms.

The apocryphal books contain teachings out of harmony with the rest of biblical revelation. A doctrine of justification by faith plus works can be found in Tobit 12:9 and 1 Macc. 2:52. The doctrine of purgatory is supported by 2 Macc. 12:41 ff. Creation out of preexisting matter is found in Wisdom 11:17. Thus on both his-

---

49. Childs, *Introduction*, p. 99.

torical and theological grounds the Protestant Reformers were justified in rejecting the apocryphal books and reaffirming the ancient Palestinian canon of the Jews.

### Formation of the New Testament

Our present list of twenty-seven canonical books is mentioned explicitly in the thirty-ninth Festal Letter of Athanasius in A.D. 367. Athanasius was apparently the first to use the term κανών specifically of this fixed body of writings. The complete canon of the New Testament as we now know it was ratified at the third council of Carthage in A.D. 397 and accepted throughout the Latin church, though occasional doubts about Hebrews still lingered. Considerations of apostolic authorship or sponsorship, orthodox content, and acceptance in the churches were the prime elements in the long process of the formation of our present New Testament canon. For discussion of questions relating to particular New Testament books, the reader is referred to the sources listed on pp. 199–200.

The views of Adolf Harnack and B. B. Warfield represent two contrasting pictures of the process of canonization. In *The Origin of the New Testament* (1925), Harnack argued that it is to Marcion that we owe the idea of a new canon and to the Montanists the idea of a closed canon. In this view the canon is the church's response to heresies. This construction, however, begins the process of canonization too late. The discovery of the Gnostic *Gospel of Truth*, originating during the middle of the second century, probably in Rome, gave evidence of acquaintance with the four Gospels, the Pauline epistles, Hebrews, Revelation, traces of Acts, 1 John, 1 Peter, and perhaps others. W. C. van Unnik comments: "Before the books could be used in the way they are used in the *Gospel of Truth*, they must have already enjoyed authority for a considerable time. . . . Moreover, we should notice that this all took place before the condemnation of Marcion."[50]

If Harnack places the canonization of the New Testament too late, Warfield probably places it too early. Warfield's views are presented in "The Formation of the Canon of the New Testament," in *The Inspiration and Authority of the Bible*. According to Warfield

50. Wenham, *Christ and the Bible*, p. 154.

the New Testament books were *known* to be inspired from the beginning. "The principle of canonicity was not apostolic authorship, but imposition [of certain books] by the apostles as law." In this view the New Testament writings were received as scripture from the beginning. While this view may accord with the early reception of the Gospels, the Pauline epistles, 1 John, and 1 Peter, it is not in accord with the doubts concerning 2 Peter, Jude, James, 2 and 3 John, and Revelation that persisted for a considerable time. A more accurate picture of the actual historical process would represent something of a compromise between the views of Harnack and Warfield.

The following argument for the canon of the New Testament explicitly parallels the argument for its inspiration: (1) the analogy of the Old Testament leads us to expect a canon for the new covenant community; (2) the disciples of Jesus were promised guidance of the Spirit in their official teaching duties (John 14:26; 15:2; 16:13); (3) the New Testament writers are aware of their divine authority (1 Cor. 14:37; 1 Thess. 2:13; 2 Thess. 3:14; 2 Cor. 13:3; 1 Peter 1:12); (4) the apostles class one another's writings as scripture (2 Peter 3:16); (5) New Testament believers are promised the ability to recognize God's truth (John 7:17; 10:27; 1 John 2:27); (6) the present twenty-seven books have won virtually unanimous consent from believers throughout the ages and throughout the world.

The conclusion is that the canonical books are those inspired books which by the providence of God have been recognized by the people of God as the true teaching of God. The church did not *create* the canon; God in his sovereign providence caused it to be *recognized.* The same sovereign God who guides all events of history (Eph. 1:11) according to his infinite power and wisdom, apart from whose will not even a sparrow falls to the ground (Matt. 10:29), who guided and controlled the process of revelation and inspiration, also guided the process of canonization. In the last analysis the church's confidence in the canon of the New Testament rests in the reality of God's sovereignty and providence. The same God who brought the church into being through the life, death, and resurrection of Jesus Christ and the sending of the Holy Spirit also gave to the church twenty-seven authoritative books as a norm of its teaching, faith, and life.

## Biblical Criticism

### Introduction

George Bancroft was an American who pursued biblical studies in Germany during the nineteenth century. He was quite disillusioned by the religious skepticism which he found widespread among the professors. "I never heard anything like moral or religious feeling manifested in their theological lectures," Bancroft observed. "There is a great deal more religion in a few lines of Xenophon, than in a whole course of Eichhorn. ... The Bible is treated with very little respect, and the narratives are laughed at as an old wife's tale, fit to be believed in the nursery."[51]

Bancroft's observations confirm suspicions widely held in evangelical circles that the entire project of biblical criticism arose in a spiritual and intellectual atmosphere hostile to orthodox Christianity. These suspicions, while not completely justified, nevertheless have a great measure of truth. Biblical criticism as we know it today betrays its roots in two traditions that have long been in tension with each other: the humanism and rationalism stemming from the Renaissance and the Enlightenment, and the biblicism stemming from the Reformation. Both streams represented a new interest in studying the original texts of scripture, but with different religious motives. The Renaissance-Enlightenment stream became the dominant influence in academic circles and produced the estrangement between biblical scholarship and piety that is so common today. In this section we will examine some of the major areas of biblical criticism and attempt to evaluate theologically some of their strengths and limitations.

### Types of biblical criticism

It is customary to distinguish between biblical criticism in its "lower" and "higher" forms. "Lower" criticism is usually referred to as "text criticism," the effort to carefully establish the original text of scripture from a comparative analysis of extant manuscripts. This discipline has not generally been seen as hostile to faith, although some very conservative proponents of the King James Version have thought it to be so. The real problems and major controversies have involved the so-called "higher" criticism,

51. Jerry Wayne Brown, *The Rise of Biblical Criticism in America*, p. 42.

which involves critical reconstructions of the sources, literary genres, events, and religious ideas behind the canonical text. When such studies have been pursued with skeptical and naturalistic presuppositions, the results have been consistently disruptive of faith.

It can be readily seen that text criticism might raise questions quite vital for evangelical faith. Has the text of the Bible become so corrupted as to make the doctrine of verbal inspiration untenable? A review of the evidence concerning the state of Old Testament and New Testament manuscripts will show that this is not in fact the case.

With respect to the text of the Old Testament, before the discovery of the Qumran scrolls the earliest copies of the Masoretic text dated from A.D. 916. But there were earlier witnesses to the Hebrew text: Jerome's Vulgate, translated from the Hebrew *ca.* A.D. 400; the Talmud, *ca.* A.D. 350–500; the Mishnah, *ca.* A.D. 200; fragments from the Greek translation of Aquila, *ca.* A.D. 130; first-century quotations by Josephus and Philo.

Study of the Qumran manuscripts has confirmed the high reliability of the Masoretic text. Where the Samaritan Pentateuch (*ca.* fourth century B.C.) and the Septuagint (*ca.* third century B.C.) are found to agree against the Masoretic text, Qumran indicates that these two preserve earlier forms of the text and constitute an independent textual tradition.

Modern research in the area of philology should be noted. Studies in comparative Semitic languages such as Arabic, Akkadian, and Ugaritic have shed light on problem texts and lessened the tendency of many scholars to emend the Masoretic text. The general thrust of these modern studies has been to strengthen the confidence in the text of the Old Testament as we now have it.

In regard to the New Testament, the manuscript tradition is very strong. There are some 5,255 manuscripts of all or part of the New Testament, a manuscript witness unrivaled by any comparable document from the ancient world.

What of the fact that there is no complete manuscript of the New Testament before the fourth century? To put this question in proper perspective the situation with respect to the texts of classical writers should be examined. In the case of the Roman author Livy the gap between the time of writing and the earliest extant manuscript is 500 years. In the case of Plato, the gap is 1,300 years;

in the case of Euripides, 1,600 years. Yet classical scholars in such cases do not hesitate to place confidence in their texts. The temporal gap between the writing of the Gospels and the great uncial manuscripts such as ℵ and B is around 250 years. Some papyri such as $P^{66}$ and $P^{75}$ are dated around A.D. 200, if not earlier.

Is it not the case that there are over 100,000 different variants in the 5,255 Greek manuscripts? This is true, but the vast majority of these variants are quite trivial. F. J. Hort's assessment of the situation made in 1885 is still valid: "If comparative trivialities, such as changes of order, the insertion or omission of the article with proper names, and the like, are set aside, the words in our opinion still subject to doubt can hardly amount to more than a thousandth part of the whole New Testament." Even here it is the case that no significant point of Christian doctrine or morals depends primarily for its support on a disputed text. Consequently, textual studies can certainly be seen as aids to, and not enemies of, a truly biblical faith.

For further background on matters relating to text criticism, the reader can profitably consult F. F. Bruce, *The New Testament Documents: Are They Reliable?* Bruce M. Metzger, *The Text of the New Testament*; John W. Wenham, *Christ and the Bible*, pp. 164–87; R. D. Wilson, *A Scientific Investigation of the Old Testament*.

It is the so-called "higher criticism" that has been the source of so much controversy in the church, especially since the nineteenth century. The term "higher criticism" was used as early as 1782, in the preface to J. G. Eichhorn's *Einleitung an das Alte Testament*.

Much of the energy of eighteenth- and nineteenth-century biblical critics was directed toward reconstructing the presumed written and oral sources behind the canonical texts of the Old Testament, especially the Pentateuch, and the Gospels. Much of this scholarship impugned the inspiration and the historical reliability of the biblical text.

In retrospect it has become increasingly clear that much of the older source criticism was of limited value for understanding the sacred text as it had actually functioned in the church. The never-ending search for hypothetical sources behind the text deflected attention away from the canonical text as a literary and religious whole, with a consequent loss of understanding. The limitations of such source-critical studies have been noted by scholars in relation to literature in general. "To learn about the literary ancestry of say, *Hamlet*," writes Montgomery Watt, "is interesting and leads to insights of various kinds; but it does not show us wherein the greatness of *Hamlet* lies. ... Studies of sources and origins satisfy our intellectual curiosity ... but the essential creative work of genius eludes such studies."[52]

In the area of New Testament studies the search for the sources behind the Gospels has been frustrating for recent investigation. Wenham, commenting on recent work in the Synoptic Gospels, concludes that "synoptic studies, in spite of two centuries of intensive research, have reached something of an impasse. Our own Society for New Testament Studies Synoptic Problem Seminar after eight years of discussion seems no nearer agreement."[53]

In an article published in *Novum Testamentum* S. Petrie reviewed the confusing and contradictory conclusions of New Testament scholars regarding the "Q" document, the hypothetical sayings-source allegedly used by Matthew and Luke, and possibly by Mark: "Q is a single document; it is a composite document, incorporating earlier sources; it is used in different redactions; it is more than one document. The original language of Q is Greek; the original language is Aramaic; it is used in different translations; Q is the Matthean logia; it is not the Matthean logia. ... Q is a gospel; it is not a gospel. Q includes the Crucifixion story; it does not include the Crucifixion story. ... Matthew's order is the correct order; Luke's is the correct order; neither order is correct; Q is used by Mark; it is not used by Mark."[54]

Such scholarly theorizing may be intriguing in an academic context, but the seminary graduate quickly discovers that such speculation has little relevance for the actual work of parish ministry. Few parish members are concerned about the relative priority of Matthew or Mark or the existence of some hypothetical "Q" document.

For further discussions on questions of authorship, dating, and source criticism from a conservative theological perspective, the reader is referred to Colin Brown, ed., *History, Criticism, and Faith*; Donald Guthrie, *New Testament Introduction*; R. K. Harrison, *Introduction to the Old Testament*; Kenneth Howkins, *The Challenge of*

---

52. W. Montgomery Watt, *What Is Islam?* p. 12.
53. Wenham, "Synoptic Independence," p. 507.
54. S. Petrie, " 'Q' Is Only What You Make It," pp. 29–30.

*Religious Studies*; Kenneth A. Kitchen, *Ancient Orient and Old Testament*; George Ladd, *The New Testament and Criticism*; E. J. Young, *Introduction to the Old Testament*.

During the twentieth century form criticism, pioneered by Rudolf Bultmann and Martin Dibelius in New Testament circles, moved to the forefront of scholarly interest. Form critics argued that the primitive oral and written traditions were reshaped or even created by the early church in its varied context of worship and mission. Bultmann, Dibelius, and their followers injected large doses of historical skepticism into their studies of the Gospel pericopes. More recently, redaction criticism has continued in this general vein, stressing the creative role of the evangelists as theologians and final redactors of the Gospel traditions. A basic issue in both form and redaction studies is the relationship of history and theology in the Gospels. The more radical critics have undermined the church's traditional belief that the Gospel writers reflected truly historical traditions in their writings.

Norman Perrin, a New Testament scholar in the Bultmannian school, has posed the issue sharply in *What is Redaction Criticism*: "We must take as our starting point the assumption that the Gospels offer us directly information about the theology of the early church and not about the teachings of the historical Jesus, and that any information we may derive from them about Jesus can only come as a result of the stringent application of the very carefully contrived criteria for authenticity."[55]

Perrin makes a number of very questionable assumptions in his approach. He assumes that the early church had little or no interest in a biography of Jesus, but only in what the "Christ of faith" was saying to the church. This assumption is contradicted in a number of ways. The existence of numerous apocryphal gospels which attempted to supply biographical details of the life of Jesus, especially concerning his childhood, testifies to the widespread interest in the early church in this type of biographical material. Much of this gospel material was not especially relevant to the Gentile churches—e.g., debates on sabbath observance. On the other hand, other issues of immediate relevance to the Gentile churches—e.g., circumcision and eating meat sacrificed to idols— is not discussed at all. If the gospel material was "created on the

55. Norman Perrin, *What Is Redaction Criticism?* p. 69.

spot" to satisfy theological concerns, one would expect the composition of the Gospels to be different in the foregoing aspects from what one actually finds.

Perrin assumes that a theological motivation for writing the Gospels excludes concern for historical authority. This reflects a very prejudiced view of the relationship of faith and history and is not consistent with statements in the New Testament such as Luke 1:1–4 and 1 Cor. 15:3–6, 12–19. Historian A. N. Sherwin-White has maintained that "those who had a passionate interest in the story of Christ, even if their interest in events was parabolical and didactic rather than historical, would not be led by that very fact to pervert and utterly destroy the historical kernel of their material."[56] A less prejudiced view than Perrin's will recognize more than a "kernel" of historicity in the Gospels.

Perrin assumes that the supernatural element in the Gospels cannot be historical. This is nothing more than sheer philosophical prejudice. A naturalistic Christianity is not the Christianity of the New Testament.

Perrin would use a "criterion of dissimilarity" to discern the authentic sayings of the historical Jesus. Only sayings which are dissimilar to the teachings of the early church and contemporary Judaism can be accepted as authentic logia of Jesus, Perrin would have us believe. This assumption is rather preposterous, for it requires us to believe that Jesus, surely one of the most influential personalities of all time, had virtually no influence on his followers in the early church and was not influenced at all by his Jewish environment! The criterion of dissimilarity is based on arbitrary, *a priori* assumptions about what Jesus could or could not have said, and reveals more about Perrin's philosophical and theological prejudices than about the character of the New Testament documents.

There are yet further problems with the methods of radical form and redaction criticism. The relatively short time—one generation—between the historical Jesus and the writing of the Gospels does not allow for elaborate modification of the oral tradition. A. N. Sherwin-White offers a parallel from the study of classical history: "Herodotus enables us to test the tempo of myth-making and the tests suggest that even two generations are too short a

56. Sherwin-White, *Roman Law*, p. 191.

span to allow the mythical tendency to prevail over the hard historic core of the oral tradition."[57]

The apostles and other eyewitnesses were present to guard the authenticity of the tradition (cf. Gal. 2:1–2; 1 Cor. 15:6). Creative ideas and great literature are the products of creative individuals, not anonymous committees, whether in the early church or elsewhere.

These criticisms do not imply that there is no room for form and redactional approaches in an evangelical study of the scriptures. They do indicate, however, that such approaches must be carefully purged of their naturalistic prejudices and artificial oppositions of history and theology before they can be truly fruitful tools for biblical study. Otherwise they become merely one more sophisticated method for imposing the exegete's theological prejudices upon the text.

### An evaluation

Any evaluation of the impact of the historical-critical study of the Bible will recognize both positive and negative aspects. On the positive side, the historical study of the Bible has rightly emphasized the necessity of letting the text speak in its own integrity out of its own historical situation rather than being forced to speak through some theological tradition—whether the allegorical hermeneutic of the medieval church or the dehistoricizing existentialist hermeneutic of our own day. Exegetical honesty is an attempt to discern "what it meant" before insisting on an answer to our question of "what it means."

The historical study of scripture has also led to the recognition that our own understanding of scripture has its own historical context. Consequently, since we read the Bible under the conditions of history, we should always be open to new insights from the scripture, rather than insisting that our present degree of understanding is unsurpassable.

On the other hand, the negative results of the historical-critical method have been both numerous and pervasive. Even liberal practitioners of the method are recognizing some of the problems it has created for the church. "I am now convinced," says Old Testament scholar Brevard Childs, "that the relation between the

57. Ibid., p. 190.

historical-critical study of the Bible and its theological use as religious literature within a community of faith and practice needs to be completely rethought." He speaks of the "deep-seated confusion" with biblical studies on this matter, and of the inability to relate many of the results of historical research to communities of faith.[58]

James D. Smart laments the situation in which biblical illiteracy seems to be increasing in the churches, in spite of the enormous research in biblical studies during the last two centuries. He thinks that it is "striking that in the years during which biblical interpretation has become ever more complex ... the church's life has fallen into a pattern that provides a diminishing amount of time for the study of scripture."[59] From an evangelical perspective, causes for this situation are not hard to find. Biblical research that is characterized as "complex" by Smart in many cases is more accurately characterized as *irrelevant* to the ministry of the church. And why should persons taught to disbelieve the divine authority of the Bible wish to spend a great deal of time on such an ancient book?

Walter Wink is even more openly critical of the established historical-critical orthodoxy. "Historical biblical criticism is bankrupt," he declares.[60] The method has separated the concerns of the scholar from the church: "The outcome of biblical studies in the academy is a trained incapacity to deal with the real problems of actual living persons in their daily lives."[61] Too many biblical scholars use the Bible to write papers for their academic colleagues, and not to serve the community of faith.

Gerhard Maier argues that practitioners of the historical-critical method, by seeking a "canon within the canon" and by seeking to separate the human and the divine in the biblical text, have ended with a mass of contradictions and arbitrariness, producing estrangement between the scholars and the congregations.

Unbelieving approaches to the biblical text have led to a loss of spiritual substance and power in preaching in churches infected with the critical methodologies. Donald E. Miller, writing in the *Christian Century*, observes that "many a liberal minister appears

58. Childs, *Introduction to the Old Testament*, p. 17.
59. James D. Smart, *The Strange Silence of the Bible in the Church*, p. 17.
60. Walter Wink, *The Bible in Human Transformation*, p. 1.
61. Ibid., p. 6.

as a reed in the wind, his or her sermons being virtually reviews of books championing the latest cultural fad. No claims to ultimacy issue from these pulpits."[62]

From an evangelical perspective it is encouraging to see such frank recognitions from liberals of the problems produced by the excesses of biblical criticism. Only time will tell, however, whether this scholarly unrest signals a meaningful return to the classical understandings of biblical inspiration and authority.

## The Cultural Impact of the Bible

### Church

In recent years it has become increasingly evident that denominations that have abandoned the classical doctrines of the inspiration and authority of the Bible have suffered spiritual decline. The erosion of the authority base upon which the church's message and mission rest has led to a decline in the power of preaching, decreases in membership, a weakened commitment to world missions, and an accommodation of the church to the world's agenda. On the other hand, churches and denominations which have held to a high view of the authority of scripture—in theory and in practice—have experienced spiritual vitality and growth.

The debilitating effects of biblical skepticism and criticism have been notable in the area of theological education. Edward Farley of the Divinity School of Vanderbilt University has admitted that mainline theological education has been trapped in a cul-de-sac because the basis on which it used to rest—biblical authority—has been shattered.[63] Modernist seminaries have been unable to impart to their students any confidence in either the unity or authority of the Bible. As a consequence of the confusion within modernist theological faculties, the graduates of such institutions have largely lacked the theological convictions and spiritual power necessary for life-giving ministry in the church.

### Society

At the beginning of this chapter it was stated that evangelical Christians need to understand the authority of scripture in a com-

---

62. Donald E. Miller, "The Future of Liberal Christianity," p. 267.
63. In Clark Pinnock, "Mainline Theological Education: A Loss of Focus," p. 15.

prehensive fashion, as an authority for every aspect of human life. It is fitting to conclude this discussion by recalling the broad impact which the Bible, understood as a divinely originated and authoritative book, has actually had on human civilization.

After tracing the expansion of Christianity over some two thousand years, Kenneth Scott Latourette concluded that "more than any other religion, or indeed, than any other element in human experience, Christianity has made for the intellectual advance of man in reducing languages to writing, creating literatures, promoting education from primary grades through institutions of university level, and stimulating the human mind and spirit to fresh explorations into the unknown."[64] This great impetus to intellectual advance came from the conviction that the Bible was indeed a written revelation of divine origin and authority. Christianity, a "religion of the book," fostered literacy and education on the most comprehensive scale.

The Protestant Reformers were vigorous promoters of education. Martin Luther promoted the establishment of schools from 1523 onward, and, notably, for both males and females. Karl Holl points out that Calvin "made the tie of the church with the school an even closer one. He counted the doctor, i.e., the teacher, among the four officers of the church. Thus even more definite expression was given the position that the organization of the church cannot be counted as complete unless provisions are made at the same time for a school."[65] The commitment of the Reformers to the *sola scriptura* principle was translated into a practical concern to apply that authority to all of life in the education of the succeeding generations.

The Reformation's rediscovery of biblical authority bore fruit in the growth of constitutional freedom and self-government. It is no accident that nations such as Switzerland, the Netherlands, Scotland, England, and the United States, with long traditions of civil freedom, are nations where the Protestant Reformation, and in particular Calvinism, made a deep impact upon the life of society. Holl writes that "without the impetuous power with which Calvinism, and only Calvinism, could endow the resistance, parliamentary government would have gone under not only in the Low

64. Kenneth Scott Latourette, A History of the Expansion of Christianity, vol. VII, pp. 480–81.

65. Karl Holl, The Cultural Significance of the Reformation, p. 111.

Countries, but also in the England of the Stuarts, as it did in the rest of Europe."[66] The Puritan and Reformed tradition, with its strong confidence in the sovereignty of God and biblical authority, had a theological basis of evaluating all human laws and governments by a divine standard. Reformed theology thus provided a strong basis for constitutional freedom and limited government. All human kings were subject to the higher authority of Jesus Christ, the only true and unlimited sovereign over both church and world.

The contribution of the biblical world view to the rise of modern science has already been noted (pp. 106—108). It is no exaggeration that the development of science, education, and government as we have come to know them in the West could hardly have taken place apart from the influence of the Bible and its authority. If the declining societies of the West continue to reject that authority, they will not forever be able to enjoy the cultural fruits produced by biblical revelation. If the foundation be destroyed, the superstructure will not long endure.

## Bibliography

Albright, William F. *The Archaeology of Palestine.* Baltimore: Penguin Books, 1949.

Barr, James. *The Semantics of Biblical Language.* London: Oxford University Press, 1961.

Barth, Karl. *Church Dogmatics,* I/2. New York: Scribner's, 1956.

Brown, Jerry Wayne. *The Rise of Biblical Criticism in America.* Middletown, Conn.: Wesleyan University Press, 1969.

Bruce, F. F. "Archaeological Confirmations of the New Testament," in Carl F. H. Henry, ed., *Revelation and the Bible.* Grand Rapids: Baker, 1958.

Bultmann, Rudolf. *Jesus and the Word.* 1926; rpt. New York: Scribner's, 1958.

Childs, Brevard. *Introduction to the Old Testament as Scripture.* Philadelphia: Fortress, 1979.

Dillenberger, John. *Protestant Thought and Natural Science.* Garden City, N.Y.: Doubleday, 1960.

Ellis, Earle. *Prophecy and Hermeneutic in Early Christianity.* Grand Rapids: Eerdmans, 1978.

Ferm, Robert L., ed. *Issues in American Protestantism.* Garden City, N.Y.: Doubleday, 1969.

66. Ibid., p. 68.

Foster, Frank. *A Genetic History of the New England Theology.* Chicago: University of Chicago Press, 1970.

France, R. T. "Inerrancy and New Testament Exegesis," *Themelios* 1 (1975):12–18.

Grant, Frederick C. *An Introduction to New Testament Thought.* New York: Abingdon-Cokesbury, 1950.

Henry, Carl F. H. "American Evangelicals in a Turning Time," *Christian Century,* Nov. 5, 1980, pp. 1058–62.

————. ed. *Revelation and the Bible.* Grand Rapids: Baker, 1957.

Hodge, A. A., and Warfield, Benjamin B., "Inspiration," *Presbyterian Review* 2 (1881):225–60.

Hodge, Charles. *Systematic Theology.* 1873; rpt. Grand Rapids: Eerdmans, 1960.

Holl, Karl. *The Cultural Significance of the Reformation.* 1911; rpt. Cleveland: World, 1959.

Hughes, Philip E. *Commentary on the Epistle to the Hebrews.* Grand Rapids: Eerdmans, 1977.

Kaufman, Gordon. *Systematic Theology: A Historicist Perspective.* New York: Scribner's, 1968.

Kelsey, David H. *The Uses of Scripture in Recent Theology.* Philadelphia: Fortress, 1975.

Kitchen, Kenneth A. *Ancient Orient and Old Testament.* Downers Grove, Ill.: Inter-Varsity, 1966.

Kline, Meredith G. *The Structure of Biblical Authority.* Grand Rapids: Eerdmans, 1972.

Kuhn, Thomas S. *The Structure of Scientific Revolutions.* Chicago: University of Chicago Press, 1962.

Lake, Kirsopp. *The Religion of Yesterday and Tomorrow.* Boston: Houghton Mifflin, 1925.

Latourette, Kenneth Scott. *A History of the Expansion of Christianity,* vol. VII. New York: Harper, 1945.

Leith, John H., ed. *Creeds of the Churches.* Richmond: John Knox, 1973.

Maier, Gerhard. *The End of the Historical-Critical Method.* St. Louis: Concordia, 1977.

Manson, T. W. "The Argument From Prophecy," *Journal of Theological Studies* 46(1945):135.

Macquarrie, John. *Principles of Christian Theology.* New York: Scribner's, 1966.

Mickelsen, Berkeley. "The Bible's Own Approach to Authority," in Jack Rogers, ed., *Biblical Authority.* Waco, Tex.: Word, 1977.

Miller, Donald E. "The Future of Liberal Christianity," *Christian Century,* Mar. 10, 1982.

Montgomery, John Warwick, ed. *God's Inerrant Word*. Minneapolis: Bethany, 1974.

Morris, Leon. "Biblical Authority and the Concept of Inerrancy," *Churchman* 81 (1967):

Packer, James I. *"Fundamentalism" and the Word of God*. Grand Rapids: Eerdmans, 1958.

Perrin, Norman. *What Is Redaction Criticism?* Philadelphia: Fortress, 1969.

Petrie, S. " 'Q' Is Only What You Make It," *Novum Testamentum* 3(1959):29 f.

Pinnock, Clark. *Biblical Revelation*. Chicago: Moody Press, 1971.

————. "Mainline Theological Education: A Loss of Focus," *TSF Bulletin*, Jan./Feb., 1982.

Polanyi, Michael. *The Study of Man*. Chicago: University of Chicago Press, 1959.

Ramm, Bernard. *The Christian View of Science and Scripture*. Grand Rapids: Eerdmans, 1954.

Ramsay, William. *The Bearing of Recent Discovery on the Trustworthiness of the New Testament*. London: Hodder and Stoughton, 1920.

Rushdoony, R. J. *Infallibility: An Inescapable Concept*. Vallecito, Calif.: Ross House, 1978.

Rutherford, F. J., *et al., The Project Physics Course*. New York: Holt, Rinehart, and Winston, 1970.

Schrenk, G. "γραφή," *TDNT*, ed. Gerhard Kittel, tr. G. Bromiley. Grand Rapids: Eerdmans, 1964. I,749—61.

Sherwin-White, A. N. *Roman Law and Roman Society in the New Testament*. New York: Oxford University Press, 1963.

Smart, James D. *The Strange Silence of the Bible in the Church*. Philadelphia: Westminster, 1970.

Smith, Richard F. In *Jerome Biblical Commentary*, ed. Raymond E. Brown etal. Englewood Cliffs, N.J.: Prentice-Hall, 1969.

Stuhlmacher, Peter. *Historical Criticism and Theological Interpretation of Scripture*. Philadelphia: Fortress, 1977.

Thiele, Edwin R. *The Mysterious Numbers of the Hebrew Kings*. Grand Rapids: Eerdmans, 1951.

Warfield, Benjamin B. *The Inspiration and Authority of the Bible*. Philadelphia: Presbyterian and Reformed, 1948.

Watt, W. Montgomery. *What Is Islam?* London: Longman, 1979.

Wenham, John W. *Christ and the Bible*. Downers Grove, Ill.: Inter-Varsity Press, 1972.

————. *The Goodness of God*. Downers Grove, Ill.: Inter-Varsity Press, 1974.

————. "Synoptic Independence and the Origin of Luke's Travel Narratives," *New Testament Studies* 27(1981):507—15.

Wilson, R. D. "The Book of Daniel and the Canon," *Princeton Theological Review* 13(1915):363.

Wink, Walter. *The Bible in Human Transformation.* Philadelphia: Fortress, 1973.

Woodbridge, John D.; Noll, Mark A.; and Hatch, Nathan O. *The Gospel in America.* Grand Rapids: Zondervan, 1979.

# 7

# Tradition as
# Theological Authority

In their recent study, *The Search for America's Faith*, George Gallup, Jr. and David Poling reported that the Catholic clergy "were firm in their trusting of 'what the church says' for their final authority (by some 70 percent)." The Protestant clergy, on the other hand, "by almost the identical majority, 76 percent, stated that 'what the Bible says' is the trustworthy authority in one's faith."[1] Thus it appears that the basic question of scripture versus church and tradition as the highest norm of faith—a question posed in classic fashion at the time of the Protestant Reformation—is still a very live one for the American church today. No question in theology is more fundamental than the question of authority; hence the issue of scripture, tradition, and church is of perennial concern to the evangelical community.

The term "tradition" has been used in quite diverse ways. In the broadest sense tradition can refer to the sum total of doctrines, moral teachings, customs, and liturgical practices that have been handed down from the church's past. In this broad sense tradition includes scripture itself, since the church's faith and life were in existence prior to the completion of the canon as we now know

---

1. George Gallup, Jr., and David Poling, *The Search for America's Faith* (Nashville: Abingdon, 1980), p. 141.

it. For the purpose of this discussion, however, tradition is used in the narrower sense influenced by the Reformation and post-Reformation debates—i.e., a body of doctrinal and moral teachings in distinction from scripture. It is the question of the existence and authority of any such traditions that will be the primary focus of this chapter.

## Tradition in the Early Church

### Judaism and the New Testament

The question of tradition and its authority is posed in the New Testament in relation to rabbinic Judaism. Tradition in a self-conscious sense, with a developed terminology, emerged within Judaism through its confrontation with Hellenism during the last two centuries B.C. and with Christianity in the first century A.D. The Hebrew term מָסַר ("handed down, handed over") refers to a carefully controlled process of handing down received expositions of the law (cf. *Pirke Aboth* 1:1). Philo and Josephus use παράδοσις to refer both to the process of "handing down" and "that which is handed down." Josephus uses the term τὴν πατερῶν παράδοσιν, "the tradition of the fathers," for the scribes' oral teaching (*Antiquities* 12.409; cf. 10.51; 13.297; Philo, *Spec. Leg.* 4. 150.)

Already in the Talmudic tractate *Pirke Aboth* Moses is portrayed as the first to pass on the oral tradition expounding the Torah, a tradition that is considered to be divinely revealed: "Moses received the Law [oral law] from Sinai and committed it to Joshua, and Joshua to the elders, and the elders to the Prophets; and the Prophets committed it to the men of the Great Synagogue." The reference to the "men of the Great Synagogue" refers to a regularizing of the tradition which is alleged to have occurred during the time of Ezra.

In later Judaism the oral tradition in practice tended to usurp the authority of scripture itself. It was said that "the voice of the rabbi is the voice of God." The tractate *Erubin* 216 in the Babylonian Talmud stated, "My son, be more careful in [the observance of] the words of the Scribes than in the words of the Torah, for in the laws of the Torah there are positive and negative precepts [and the penalties vary]; but as to the laws of the Scribes, whoever transgresses any of the enactments of the scribes incurs the penalty of death."

To become a rabbi, and to be eligible for a seat on the Sanhedrin, required a particularly subtle mind and a dexterous ability to manipulate the biblical text. Rab Judah is cited as declaring, "None is to be given a seat on the Sanhedrin unless he is able to prove the cleanness of a reptile" from biblical texts.[2] Such perversions of the plain meaning of the text were sharply condemned by Christ in relation to the practice of "Corban" (Mark 7:9–13). The rabbis were "making void the word of God" through their inherited traditions (vs. 13). The danger that the authority of scripture can in practice be voided by traditional interpretations is not, of course, limited to rabbinic Judaism. The danger can arise even in those evangelical circles where the doctrine of inerrancy and the principle of *sola scriptura* are explicitly and officially endorsed. Traditional interpretations tend, in the mind of the holder, to become fused with the text itself, and thus to be given a spurious legitimacy and authority.

In the New Testament the normal word for tradition, occurs thirteen times. Nine occurrences refer to *halakah*, or the rabbinic elaborations on the law (Matt. 15:2–3, 6; Mark 7:3, 5, 8–9, 13; Gal. 1:14). Three occurences refer to Christian tradition or traditions (1 Cor. 11:2; 2 Thess. 2:15; 3:6). The usage in Col. 2:8 is uncertain. In all these cases παράδοσις refers to that which is handed on rather than to the agent or the process.

It is noteworthy that the traditions of rabbinic Judaism are eclipsed in the New Testament, especially since the early church received the Jewish scriptures as authoritative.[3] Tradition as such is not abolished; however, the older rabbinic traditions which had failed to perceive the true meaning of the Old Testament are abandoned, and replaced with the apostolic traditions concerning the life, death, and resurrection of Jesus and the fulfillment of the Old Testament scriptures in him. The words of the Lord Jesus establish a new tradition, and from the first were received by the early

2. R. J. Rushdoony, *Infallibility: An Inescapable Concept*, p. 63.

3. While it is true that at certain points—e.g., the use of midrash and pesher by Matthew and Paul in Old Testament exposition—the New Testament writers reflect rabbinic practices, the crucial point is that such techniques have been quite transformed through the new hermeneutical focus provided by the life, death, and resurrection of Jesus. The older expository techniques are placed in the service of an entirely new frame of reference—not the Law, but the fulfillment of God's saving purposes through Jesus the Messiah.

Christian community as having an authority like that of the Old Testament (cf. Matt. 5:22, 28, 32, 34, 39, 44, "But I say to you").

In the early church, during the period from around A.D. 60 to around 160, written and oral traditions circulated side by side. By about the year 170, however, the New Testament, substantially in the form in which we now know it, began to be widely recognized in the church as authoritative scripture, comparable to the scriptures of the Old Testament. The new oral traditions of Christ and the apostles were being brought together in a collection of new canonical documents.

### The patristic period

The relationship between scripture and tradition during the patristic period merits closer examination. Is there any clear evidence that the church fathers acknowledge unwritten doctrinal and ethical traditions that were independent of the scriptures? This question bears directly, of course, on the Protestant–Roman Catholic debate on the place and authority of tradition in the church. Only with Irenaeus, near the middle of the second century, does the issue of the relationship of scripture, tradition, and church come into clear focus. During the earlier period of the apostolic fathers the relationship of these various doctrinal norms was somewhat fluid and undefined.

In the second and third centuries Gnostic teachers appealed to "secret traditions," allegedly derived from Christ and the apostles, in support of their heretical positions. In *Against Heresies* 1.20.3 Irenaeus writes that the followers of Carpocrates "allege that Jesus spoke in a mystery privately to his disciples and apostles and required of them that they should hand these doctrines on to those who were fit for them and who were disciples." Such "secret traditions" of the Gnostics contained eccentric interpretations of Genesis, cosmology, the law, and esoteric sayings of Jesus. Needless to say, the claims of such traditions to apostolic origin are not convincing.

In the face of such heterodox teachings the church during the patristic period developed "rules of faith," which were summaries of the main points of the church's teaching and preaching. Such rules of faith are found during the period from about 170 to 270 in the writings of such fathers as Irenaeus, Tertullian, Hippolytus,

Origen, Cyprian, Novatian, and Dionysius of Alexandria, and were used as tests of orthodoxy. These rules of faith in general reflected the doctrinal structure of what later came to be known as the Apostles' Creed.

The question arises at this point as to whether such rules of faith were considered to be normative independently of—or in addition to—scripture. The evidence points to a negative answer. Origen, in the preface to *Peri Archon*, states that the teaching of the church is based upon "either the evidence to be found in the sacred Scriptures, or that to be discovered by the investigation of the logical consequences of the scriptures and adherence to accuracy." Irenaeus, in his *Demonstration of the Apostolic Preaching*, demonstrates the rule of faith from the Bible. Novatian, in *De trinitate*, clearly regards the rule of faith as derived from scripture. At times Irenaeus and Tertullian appeared to speak of the rule of faith as an autonomous norm, but such statements can be easily misinterpreted. As Hanson has noted, it is "meaningless to regard them as 'subordinating' Scripture to the rule of faith because they, with all the other fathers of the period ... consistently prove the rule of faith from scripture."[4]

The oral traditions circulating in the patristic period which were independent of scripture had, by the middle of the third century, come to be recognized as having little or no doctrinal significance. These scattered traditions included such miscellaneous stories as the following: Jesus' manger was said to have been located in a cave (Origen, *Contra Celsum* 1.56); the apostle Matthew ate seeds, berries, and vegetables but no meat (Clement of Alexandria, *Paedagogos* 2.1.16.1); John died in Ephesus; Peter was crucified head downward in Rome; Paul was martyred in Rome (Eusebius, *Ecclesiastical History* 3.1.1–3); the transfiguration took place on Mount Tabor (Origen, *Commentary on Psalm 89*, vs. 12). Whatever one might conclude concerning the historical value of such traditions, it is clear that no matter of doctrinal importance is involved. By the middle of the third century it had become increasingly apparent that scripture, and only scripture, could be the final court of appeal for establishing the church's doctrine.

4. R. P. C. Hanson, *Tradition in the Early Church*, p. 238.

## Tradition in Protestantism

### Sola scriptura and the Reformation

The principle of *sola scriptura*, a hallmark of the Protestant Reformers, emerged in Luther's debate with Johann Eck at Leipzig in 1519. Luther argued that scripture and scripture alone was to be the standard by which councils, creeds, and all ecclesiastical traditions were to be measured. In the seventeenth century the principle was epitomized in the well-known statement of the Englishman William Chillingworth: "The *Bible*, I say, the *Bible* only, is the religion of Protestants."[5]

Luther was not the first to voice this "Protestant" principle. John Wyclif, one of the forerunners of the Reformation in England, stated, "Even though there were a hundred popes and though every mendicant monk were a cardinal, they would be entitled to confidence only in so far as they accorded with the Bible." As J. Loserth has noted, "In this early period it was Wyclif who recognized and formulated the formal principle of the Reformation—the unique authority of the Bible for the belief and life of the Christian."[6]

The authorities of the late medieval church did not appreciate the reforming spirit of John Wyclif and his criticisms of the papal system. After his death the Council of Constance (1414–18) declared Wyclif to be a stiff-necked heretic, ordered his books to be burned and his body exhumed. This last decree was carried out some twelve years later under the authority of Pope Martin V. Wyclif's body was dug up, burned, and the ashes thrown into the Swift River flowing through Lutterworth, England.

It is important to realize that the *sola scriptura* principle did not imply for the Reformers a rejection of all church tradition. They affirmed the value and validity of the ecumenical creeds of the early church, and in fact believed that the weight of patristic authority supported the Reformation cause. As Calvin stated the point, "If the contest were to be determined by patristic authority, the tide of victory—to put it very modestly—would turn to our side." The Reformers were convinced that it was the papacy, and not they, who in fact had departed from the early Christian tra-

---

5. F. F. Bruce, *Tradition Old and New*, p. 168.
6. J. Loserth, "Wyclif, John," p. 463.

dition. Later historical scholarship has confirmed this judgment.[7]

*Sola scriptura* meant the primacy of scripture as a theological norm over all tradition rather than the total rejection of tradition. Creeds, confessions, and councils were to be received insofar as they were consistent with scripture. The *sola scriptura* principle also presupposed the essential clarity of scripture. The central saving message of the Bible was plain enough to be understood by all and needed no priestly hierarchy to explain it. The Holy Spirit, and not the Roman hierarchy, was the true illuminator of scriptural truth. This Reformation principle of the perspicuity of scripture was later articulated in classic fashion in the Westminster Confession of Faith's chapter on scripture: "All things in Scripture are not alike plain in themselves, nor alike clear unto all; yet those things which are necessary to be known, believed, and observed, for salvation, are so clearly propounded and opened in some place of scripture or other, that not only the learned, but the unlearned, in a due use of the ordinary means, may attain unto a sufficient understanding of them" (I.vii).

This Reformation emphasis on the perspicuity of scripture has unfortunately been lost in some streams of later Protestantism. Luther complained about the "Babylonian captivity of the church;" with the rise of the historical-critical method there is some reason to be concerned about a "Babylonian captivity of the Bible" at the hands of the biblical critics. Many lay people in the churches have been alienated from the simple biblical message by the imposing developments of critical scholarship.[8] By stressing the diversity or even "contradictions" of scripture, critical scholarship has obscured the essential clarity of the Bible's saving message.

In a dialogue at Harvard Divinity School on liberal and evangelical theology, Gordon Kaufman stated his belief in the Bible's obscurity. "There are many biblical positions on almost any topic you wish to take up," he said. "The Bible is a pluralist library of books, of theological ideas, of values, of points of view. ... What the biblical position is is unclear. ... Even if we could find the

---

7. E.g., it is interesting to note that the church father most frequently cited by Calvin in the *Institutes* is Augustine, the great exponent of divine grace and predestination.

8. Recall the comments made in relation to James Smart's *The Strange Silence of the Bible in the Church* in Chapter 6.

biblical position, how to interpret this as bearing on our situation is unclear."[9]

It indeed seems ironic that the brand of Protestant liberalism represented by Kaufman has essentially reverted to the position of the late medieval Roman Catholic Church on the question of scripture. The message of the Bible is not plain; it must be mediated to the people through either an ecclesiastical or scholarly elite. The result in both cases—Catholicism and Protestant modernism—is a loss of spiritual vitality in the churches and the usurpation of scripture's divine authority by various human authorities.[10]

### American Protestantism

American Protestantism has not been noted for its appreciation of church tradition. Thomas Jefferson once remarked, "As to tradition, if we are Protestants, we reject all tradition, and rely on the scripture alone, for that is the essence and common principle of all the Protestant churches."[11] Such comments need to be understood in the light of Jefferson's own Unitarian and otherwise heterodox views, but they are illustrative of a significant element in the American religious temperament. The streams of Protestantism influenced by deism and rationalism tended to appeal directly to the moral teachings of Jesus; later developments in church history—expecially the great orthodox creeds—were an "obfuscation" of the simple religion of the Sermon on the Mount. As the English Unitarian Joseph Priestly saw it, church history was little more than a "sordid history of corruptions."

Historian Kenneth S. Latourette has noted the marked tendency of nineteenth-century American Protestants "to ignore the developments which had taken place in Christianity in the Old World after the first century."[12] This low view of tradition is understandable in part in view of the frontier conditions of early American experience. For those who came to America, and who later ex-

9. Priscilla Whitehead and Tom McAlpine, "Evangelical/Liberal Theology—a False Dichotomy?" p. 10.

10. In the Harvard dialogue (1981) Kaufman prefaced his remarks by saying, "I am just speaking for myself." This is indeed the Achilles' heel of Protestant modernism: it speaks not by the authority of the Bible or tradition; it speaks merely "for itself."

11. Sidney E. Mead, "Protestantism in America," p. 293.

12. Kenneth Scott Latourette, *A History of the Expansion of Christianity*, vol. IV, p. 428.

tended its boundaries in the West, the nation represented a new beginning, even a "new Eden." Why encumber the new religious venture with the strife and controversy of the European past?

This ahistorical mentality was also reinforced by the revivalism of the nineteenth century. If the spiritual experience of the New Testament church could be reduplicated through the agency of revival preaching, what more could the believer need? Why bother with the ancient creeds? This anti-creedal mentality found expression in the work of frontier revivalist Barton Stone (1772–1844). Stone was ordained as a Presbyterian, but later rejected Calvinism and in 1804 established the Christian Church ("Disciples of Christ") through his preaching in Ohio, Kentucky, and Tennessee. The Diciples of Christ were associated with the slogan, "No creed but the Bible." Eighteen hundred years of church history were of little or no value; Stone had rediscovered the true "New Testament church."

There is undeniable value in reaffirming the theology and practice of the New Testament as an essential element of church reform. However, the problem in rejecting all church history and tradition is that the reflections of less gifted minds tend to be substituted for the wisdom of the spiritual and theological giants of the past. Evangelicals can affirm the primacy of scripture without implying that the Holy Spirit has taught nothing to the church over nineteen hundred years. A slogan such as "No creed but the Bible" does not really eliminate all church tradition; it merely substitutes new traditions—those of the denominational leader and his followers—for older ones.[13] Anti-creedal and anti-traditional attitudes can lead, theologically and ecclesiastically, to counterproductive efforts that merely "reinvent the wheel."

### Recent developments

There are signs that American evangelicalism is seeking a greater appreciation of the traditions and liturgies of the early church. In *Common Roots: A Call to Evangelical Maturity*, Robert E. Webber of Wheaton College argues that "a return to the historic church, to the great fathers of the first five centuries, is a return to evangelical foundations."[14] Evangelicalism is certainly rooted in the Reformation of the sixteenth century and the great revival movements

13. Ably pointed out by F. F. Bruce in *Tradition Old and New*.
14. Robert E. Webber, *Common Roots*, p. 22.

of the nineteenth century, but Webber is urging his fellow evangelicals to rediscover their roots in the faith and life of the ancient church. He argues that evangelical understandings of the nature of the church, of worship, of spirituality, of mission, and of theology can all be strengthened through a new study and appreciation of the patristic heritage.

In May of 1977 a group of some forty-five evangelical leaders met to draft a statement which came to be known as the "Chicago Call." The results of this conference, together with explanatory essays, was published in 1978 in a volume titled *The Orthodox Evangelicals*, edited by Robert E. Webber and Donald Bloesch, which affirmed: "We believe that today evangelicals are hindered from achieving full maturity by a reduction of the historic faith. ... There is ... a pressing need to reflect upon the substance of the biblical and historic faith and to recover the fullness of their heritage."[15] The drafters of the statement sought to recall their fellow evangelicals to a greater sense of "historic roots and continuity," "biblical fidelity," "creedal identity," "holistic salvation," "sacramental integrity," "spirituality," "church authority," and "church unity."

The new interest in the theological and liturgical heritage of the early church is not limited to evangelicals. Thomas C. Oden, a professor of theology at Drew University, has chronicled his own personal pilgrimage from theological liberalism back to "classical Christianity" in *Agenda for Theology*. Liberal theology's fascination with and subservience to the "modern mind" has reached the end of its tether, Oden concludes. It has become intellectually barren and spiritually and pastorally unsatisfying. Consequently, it is time for liberal Protestantism in America to rediscover the resources of classical Christianity—"the ancient ecumenical consensus of Christianity's first millennium, particularly as expressed in scripture and in the Seven Ecumenical Councils affirmed by Catholic, Protestant, and Orthodox traditions." Oden's aim is to "help free persons from feeling intimidated by modernity, which ... is rapidly losing its moral power, and to grasp the emerging vision of a postmodern Christian orthodoxy."[16]

The new appreciation for the patristic heritage among evangelicals (and those newly sympathetic to evangelicalism) is an en-

---

15. Robert E. Webber and Donald Bloesch, eds., *The Orthodox Evangelicals*, p. 11.
16. Thomas C. Oden, *Agenda for Theology*, p. xii.

couraging sign in the life of American Protestantism. While the early church can hardly be considered a model of either theological or spiritual perfection, nevertheless the new interest in patristics offers evangelicals some much needed historical depth and perspective. The early fathers faced a challenge much like our own—preserving and extending the Christian faith in a declining social order permeated by a decadent humanism. As evangelicals attempt to "recontextualize" the faith to meet changing social conditions, and to reconstruct a new social order on biblical foundations, there is much to be learned from the fathers of the early church.

In a somewhat different context the work of Brevard Childs in *Introduction to the Old Testament as Scripture,* also represents a renewed appreciation for the positive role of tradition in American Protestantism. Childs argues that Old Testament scholarship must take more seriously the canonical shape of the biblical text as it has actually been mediated through the life of the religious communities which have preserved it. The dominant tendency of older critical scholarship was to virtually bypass the canonical text as a literary whole in its own right in a search for the (hypothetical) sources and documents *behind* the text. On the contrary, Childs argues, where the actual text of the Old Testament is concerned, "One begins with the tradition and then seeks critically to understand it."[17] This emphasis has the value of recognizing the traditional role that the text played in the life of Israel as a religious community; the Old Testament becomes more than merely a text studied in the abstraction of a modern academic setting. The shape of the canonical text, reflecting actual religious traditions, also provides helpful clues for understanding the thematic unity of scripture as over against the fragmenting approaches of nineteenth-century scholarship.

Beyond the confines of biblical and theological scholarship there are signs of renewed interest in the role of tradition in the knowing process among twentieth-century philosophers. The German philosopher Hans-Georg Gadamer has recently issued sharp criticisms of the Enlightenment's rejection of tradition in a quest for secular, self-grounded certitude. This quest, Gadamer believes, has not been successful. In *Truth and Method,* widely read by biblical

---

17. Brevard Childs, *Introduction to the Old Testament as Scripture,* p. 101.

and theological scholars for its insights in the area of hermeneutics, Gadamer argues that tradition is in fact the "horizon" within which we do our thinking. The process of human understanding involves placing oneself "within a process of tradition in which past and present are constantly fused."[18] Tradition is the embodiment of the linguistic and intellectual heritage of a culture; one can no more think without the influence of tradition than one can think without language.

Michael Polanyi has written that "all mental life by which we surpass the animals is evoked in us as we assimilate the articulate framework of our culture."[19] Or again, "Human thought grows only within language and since language can exist only in a society, all thought is rooted in society."[20] Polanyi is arguing that the preconditions of all human knowledge are found in the linguistic heritage of a culture, a heritage which is traditional in nature.

A similar point was made by Ludwig Wittgenstein in the *Philosophical Investigations*, when he stated that the linguistic practices of a community become conditions through which we see the world.[21] These observations by Gadamer, Polanyi, and Wittgenstein, based on new insights in the philosophy of language, help to correct the Enlightenment's rejection of tradition and to restore to its rightful place the role of the intellectual labors of the past in the knowledge and discoveries of the present.

## Tradition in Roman Catholicism

### Early positions

Tradition plays a more prominent and authoritative role in Roman Catholic theology than in evangelical Protestantism. At the Second Vatican Council it was stated that "it is not from sacred Scripture alone that the church draws her certainty about everything which has been revealed. ... Both sacred tradition and sacred Scripture are to be accepted and venerated with the same sense of devotion and reverence," (*Documents of Vatican II*, p. 117).

This position, however, represents a long process of develop-

18. Hans-Georg Gadamer, *Truth and Method*, p. 258.
19. Michael Polanyi, *The Study of Man*, p. 31.
20. Ibid., p. 60.
21. Ludwig Wittgenstein, *Philosophical Investigations*, p. 116.

ment in Roman Catholicism away from an earlier one in which scripture was granted clear primacy over all church tradition. Prior to the fourteenth century the church fathers and medieval theologians generally held that the Bible was the unique and sole source of divine revelation. Aquinas, for example, could state that "arguments from scripture are used properly and carry necessity in matters of faith; arguments from other doctors of the church are proper, but carry only probability; for our faith is based on the revelation given to the apostles and prophets who wrote the canonical books of the scriptures and not on revelation that could have been made to other doctors" (*Summa Theologica* I.1,8).

In late medieval theology, however, the theologians begin to speak of church tradition as that which authorizes scripture. Duns Scotus, for example, claimed that the "books of the holy canon are not to be believed except insofar as one must first believe the church which approves and authorizes those books and their content."[22] This latter formulation represents a clear denial of what came to be known during the Reformation as the principle of the self-attesting authority and essential clarity of scripture.

### Trent and later developments

In response to the challenge of the Reformers' *sola scriptura* principle the Roman Catholic position on tradition as it had developed in the medieval church was officially formulated at the Council of Trent in 1546. "Following, then, the example of the orthodox Fathers," the council declared, "it receives and venerates with the same piety and reverence all the books of both the Old and New Testaments—for God is the author of both—together with all traditions concerning faith and morals, for they came from the mouth of Christ or are inspired by the Holy Spirit and have been preserved in continuous succession in the Catholic Church" (Denz. 1501).

The position of Trent was reiterated by the First Vatican Council in 1870, called to bolster Catholicism against the challenge of modernism. On the matter of revelation and tradition, this council declared that "this supernatural revelation, according to the universal belief of the church, declared by the Sacred Synod of Trent, is contained in the written books and unwritten traditions which

22. Donald G. Bloesch, *Essentials of Evangelical Theology*, vol. I, p. 57.

have come down to us" (Denz. 3006). Again, the reference to the "universal belief of the church" is an assertion that can hardly be sustained by careful historical examination of the patristic sources.

The Second Vatican Council (1963–65) attempted to soften the distinction between scripture and tradition as it had been developed at Trent and at Vatican I. According to this most recent council, "Sacred tradition and sacred scripture form one sacred deposit of the word of God. ... Both ... flowing from the same divine wellspring, in a certain way merge into a unity and tend toward the same end" (*Documents of Vatican* II, p. 117).

Vatican II was faced with an intramural Catholic debate between two opposing views of scripture and tradition, prompted by revisionist interpretations of the meaning of the Council of Trent.[23] The "two-source" view held that Trent had really understood scripture and tradition as separate and independent sources of revelation; the "one-source" view held that scripture alone, as interpreted by the church's tradition, was the sole source of revelation, and that this view had been the real intention of Trent. As Wells has pointed out, the revisionist "one-source" interpretation of Trent lacks credibility in that it is in fact quite new. For three centuries after Trent, Roman Catholics understood that council to support a two-source view. This seemed especially clear during the nineteenth century.[24] Vatican II did not resolve the debate but left the precise relationship between scripture and tradition somewhat open. It did, however, wish to claim both as forms of divine revelation.

Some recent Roman Catholic scholars—e.g., Karl Rahner (*The Vatican Council*) and Hans Küng (*Justification*)—have spoken of the Bible as the "primary" and "unique" source of revelation. While such expressions may signify a greater appreciation of the Reformational *sola scriptura* principle, their critical views of scripture and appeals to "church consciousness" as a source of theological authority prevent any simple identification of their views with those of the Reformers.

### Characteristic Roman Catholic traditions

Three Roman Catholic traditions in particular are held to be divinely revealed doctrines essential for salvation and represent

---

23. See G. C. Berkouwer, *The Second Vatican Council and the New Catholicism*, pp. 89 – 111; A. N. S. Lane, "Scripture, Tradition and Church: An Historical Survey."
24. David F. Wells, "Tradition," p. 59.

special obstacles for Protestant-Catholic relations: the dogma of the immaculate conception of the Virgin Mary; the dogma of papal infallibility; and the dogma of the bodily assumption of the Virgin Mary into heaven. All three dogmas lack credible biblical and historical support.

The way for the proclamation of the dogma of the immaculate conception in 1854 by Pius IX had been prepared years earlier. In an encyclical letter to the Roman Catholic bishops of February 2, 1849, Pius IX had expressed his own zealous veneration of Mary: "You know full well, venerable brethren, that the whole ground of our confidence is placed in the most holy Virgin, since God has vested in her the plenitude of all good, so that henceforth, if there be in us any hope, if there be any grace, if there be any salvation, we must receive it solely from her, according to the will of him who would have us possess all through Mary."[25]

Pius IX officially proclaimed the dogma on December 8, 1854, at St. Peter's in Rome, with over two hundred cardinals, bishops, and other ecclesiastical dignitaries present, declaring it to be a divinely revealed dogma, to be firmly believed by all the faithful on penalty of excommunication, "that the most blessed Virgin Mary, in the first moment of her conception, by a special grace and privilege of Almighty God, in virtue of the merits of Christ, was preserved immaculate from all stain of original sin." Schaff describes the response of those present at the papal proclamation: "The shouts of the assembled multitude, the cannons of St. Angelo, the chimes of all the bells, the illumination of St. Peter's dome, the splendor of gorgeous feasts, responded to the decree. Rome was intoxicated with . . . enthusiasm, and the whole Roman Catholic world thrilled with joy over the crowning glory of the immaculate queen of heaven, who would now be more gracious and powerful in her intercession than ever, and shower the richest blessings upon the Pope and his church."[26]

For biblical support of the dogma Roman Catholic apologists cite Gen. 3:15; Song of Sol. 4:7; 12; and Luke 1:28, but none of these texts will bear the weight that is placed upon them. The citation of Gen. 3:15 from the Vulgate ("*she* shall crush thy head, and thou shalt assail *her* heel") is based on a mistranslation of the Hebrew, which makes the reference masculine, not feminine. In the Cath-

---

25. Philip Schaff, *The Creeds of Christendom*, vol. I, pp. 108–9.
26. Ibid., p. 110.

olic misinterpretation, which refers the "she" to Mary, it is argued
that the enmity between Mary and Satan is an eternal one, which
would not be the case if she had ever been subject to original sin.
Poetic descriptions of the fair and spotless bride (Song of Sol. 4:7)
and references to the "garden enclosed, and fountain sealed" are
fancifully applied to Mary. The Vulgate of Luke 1:28, "Hail [Mary],
full of grace," is said to imply her immaculate conception. Schaff's
comment on this type of biblical interpretation is apt: "frivolous
allegorical trifling with the Word of God."[27] The dogma is explicitly
contradicted by texts such as Rom. 5:12, 18; 1 Cor. 15:22; and Eph.
2:3, which include all in original sin except Christ.

The dogma's rootage in ancient tradition is equally weak. Augustine, who surprisingly believed that Mary was free from actual
sin, did not believe that she was conceived without original sin.
The heretic Pelagius was apparently the first to espouse the doctrine. It was opposed by Bernard of Clairvaux, Anselm of Can-
terbury, Bonaventure, Aquinas,[28] the popes Leo I, Gregory I
Innocent III, Gelasius I, Innocent V, and Clement VI.

At the beginning of the fourteenth century the dogma was advocated by Duns Scotus, the "subtle doctor." During the medieval
period the belief became common in the church that though Mary
was conceived in sin, she was sanctified in the womb like John
the Baptist, and thus prepared to be a pure receptacle for the Son
of God. Others, however, held the view that Mary was fully sanctified only when she conceived Christ by the Holy Spirit, not at the
time of her own conception.

After the fourteenth century the question of Mary's relation to
original sin became a point of controversy between Thomists and
Scotists, and between Dominicans and Franciscans, the various
parties charging one another with heresy. Schaff notes that four
members of the Dominican order, "who were discovered in a pious
fraud against the Franciscan doctrine, were burned [at the stake]
by order of a papal court in Rome on the eve of the Reformation.
The Swedish prophetess, St. Birgitte, was assured in a vision by
the Mother of God that she was conceived without sin; while

27. Ibid., p. 115.
28. Aquinas, however, did believe that Mary, like John the Baptist, was sanctified in
the womb *after* the infusion of the soul.

St. Catherine of Siena prophesied for the Dominicans that Mary was sanctified in the third hour after her conception."[29]

Needless to say, such accounts do not bolster confidence in the credibility of the dogma of the immaculate conception. A candid examination of the exegetical and historical data reveals the inadequacy of their claims.

The doctrine of papal infallibility, also proclaimed by Pius IX, was officially defined on July 18, 1870, at the climax of the First Vatican Council, meeting at the Vatican in Rome. The dogma asserted that the Roman pontiff, when speaking from his chair (*ex cathedra*) on faith and morals, is infallible, and that such definitions are irreformable and not in consequence of the consent of the church. The pope on his own authority claimed the authority to define new and binding articles of faith, apart from either scripture or general council.

The arrangements for the Vatican Council had been carefully orchestrated by Pius IX to secure a vote in favor of infallibility. The pope had selected the committee members responsible for preparing the draft reports in such a way as to secure the preponderance of infallibilist sentiment. A revised order of business issued February 22, 1870, changed the traditional procedure requiring absolute or at least moral unanimity in definitions of faith and substituted for it a new rule requiring a mere numerical majority. The ancient rule of catholic tradition (*quod semper, quod ubique, quod ab omnibus creditum est*) was abandoned in order to secure a positive vote for infallibility despite the objections of a powerful minority. The pope also sought to control public opinion in Rome. Nothing was allowed to be printed in Rome during the council which opposed infallibility, while the proponents of the proposed dogma were given the full freedom to publish whatever they wished.

When Bishop Strossmayer, one of the most outspoken members of the opposition, during one of the debates criticized the principle of deciding matters of faith by mere majority votes, he was loudly interrupted by shouts from all sides of "Shame! Shame! Down with the heretic!" Other bishops leaped from their seats, rushed to the speaker's platform, and shook their fists in Stross-

29. Schaff, *Creeds*, 1:124.

mayer's face. The bishop was forced by the uproar to leave the platform.[30]

In a preliminary vote on infallibility eighty-eight bishops voted in the negative, including many distinguished for their learning and scholarship. Later, fifty-six of these and sixty others left Rome before the final vote was taken, rather than oppose Pius IX. As a result, when the final vote was taken on July 18, 1870, the new dogma of infallibility received an overwhelming vote of 533-2.

The procedural chicanery resorted to at the First Vatican Council reflects the intrinsic weakness of the arguments in favor of papal infallibility. The dogma is supported by the evidence of neither scripture nor tradition. The evidence of church tradition and history is decidedly embarrassing to the dogma. The four great ecumenical creeds (Apostles', Nicene, Chalcedonian, Athanasian) and the ecumenical councils of the first eight centuries have no references whatever to papal infallibility. In terms of the canon of true catholicity, "that which always, everywhere, and by all has been believed," this lack of evidence alone is a decisive strike against the doctrine.

One of the most damaging pieces of historical evidence, however, involves the famous case of Pope Honorius I (625 – 638), who was later officially condemned for teaching heresy by an ecumenical council. As Schaff has pointed out,[31] Honorius, in two letters to his heretical colleague Sergius, Patriarch of Constantinople, taught *ex cathedra* the Monothelite heresy, which was condemned by the sixth ecumenical council in 680.[32] This council was recognized as valid by both the Western (Latin) and Eastern (Greek) branches of the church. The council condemned and excommunicated Honorius as a heretic, and the seventh (787) and eighth (869) ecumenical councils repeated the anathemas of the sixth.

Subsequent popes down to the eleventh century, in a solemn oath upon their accession to the office, endorsed the canons of

30. Ibid., p. 145, n.2.

31. Ibid., pp. 178–80.

32. The Monothelites held that Christ had only one will, the divine. The orthodox position is that Christ had two wills, a human and a divine—will being an attribute of the nature rather than of the person. The Logos, the second person of the Trinity, possessed a divine will; Christ, possessing a fully human nature, also possessed a human will. The Monothelite heresy thus denied the full and true humanity of the Savior. If in the incarnation the Logos did not assume a full human nature, then the comprehensiveness of the redemption of human nature has been compromised.

the sixth ecumenical council and pronounced an anathema on the authors of the Monothelite heresy together with Pope Honorius, who had aided and abetted the doctrine. The Roman Catholic popes themselves for more than three hundred years publicly recognized the facts that an ecumenical council may condemn a pope for heresy and that Pope Honorius was actually and rightfully so condemned.

Schaff remarks that the case of Honorius is "as clear and strong as any fact in church history."[33] Attempts by infallibilists to claim that the records of the councils or the letters of Honorius are forgeries are simply desperate expedients, without historical credibility, to avoid the weight of the damaging evidence. The decisive fact remains, states Schaff, "that both Councils and Popes for several hundred years believed in the fallibility of the Pope, in flat contradiction to the Vatican Council."[34]

The doctrine of papal infallibility is also discredited by the fact that forged documents were used during the Middle Ages to advance the interests and power of the papacy. The Pseudo-Isidorian Decretals, supposedly compiled by Isidore of Seville (d. 636), are now recognized to contain forged materials. The decretals contain letters of ante-Nicene popes, all forgeries; canons of councils, mostly genuine; letters from later popes, thirty-five of which are forgeries. The decretals were intended to help free the bishops from the authority of the secular powers and to exalt the papacy. These documents, unknown before 852, contain obvious historical anachronisms, such as the use of the Vulgate in the decretals of the earliest popes. The obviousness of these historical errors has led even Roman Catholic scholars to acknowledge their spurious nature.

The so-called "Donation of Constantine" was also used to advance the claims of the papacy. This document, which was fabricated during the eighth or ninth century, probably in the Frankish empire, had a wide influence during the Middle Ages. According to this forgery, the Emperor Constantine supposedly conferred on Pope Sylvester I (314 – 335) primacy over the churches of Antioch, Constantinople, Alexandria, and Jerusalem, and dominion over all Italy, including Rome. The Donation made the pope supreme judge

33. Schaff, *Creeds*, 1:179.
34. Ibid., 1:180.

of all clergy. The document was apparently first used to support papal claims in 1054 by Leo IX, and was thereafter consistently used by his successors. The Renaissance scholars Nicholas of Cusa and Lorenzo Valla demonstrated its falsity during the fifteenth century.

The biblical texts cited in support of papal infallibility are as unimpressive as the evidence of church history and tradition. Most commonly cited are Matt. 16:18 ("You are Peter, and on this rock I will build my church"); Luke 22:32 ("I have prayed for thee, that thy faith may not fail"—paraph. of KJV); John 21:15 – 17 ("Feed my lambs. . . . Feed my sheep"). Of these, Matt. 16:18 is the most important.

With respect to Matt. 16:18, Protestants have seen the "rock" as Peter's confession and ultimately as Christ himself. Peter acknowledges Christ as the "rock" or "stone": "Come to him, that living stone" (1 Peter 2:4); cf. Eph. 2:20, the household of God "built upon the foundation of the prophets and the apostles [Peter not unique], Christ Jesus himself being the cornerstone."

In Matt. 16:19 Christ says to Peter, "I will give you the keys of the kingdom of heaven, and whatever you bind on earth shall be bound in heaven, and whatever you loose on earth shall be loosed in heaven." Note, however, that the "power of the keys" is given to all the apostles, not just Peter, according to John 20:22–23: "He breathed on them, and said to them, Receive the Holy Spirit. If you forgive the sins of any, they are forgiven" (ἀφῆτε, 2.p.pl.). And according to Matt. 18:17–18 the power of excommunication is exercised by the church as a whole, not by a single individual.

While Peter was certainly eminent as a leader in the early church, Matt. 16:18 and the related texts teach neither Peter's infallibility nor Christ's intention to establish a succession of infallible teachers. Significantly, when the comments of the church fathers on Matt. 16:18 are examined, it is striking that not one finds papal infallibility in the passage. Sixteen take the reference to the "rock" to mean Christ; forty-four, including Chrysostom, Ambrose, Hilary, Jerome, and Augustine, understand the "rock" to refer to Peter's faith or confession. The "unanimous consent of the fathers"—a hermeneutical norm for Roman Catholicism in matters of interpretation—is on this point simply nonexistent.

It is claimed that the popes, as the successors of Peter, are the true successors of the apostles. The "apostolic successors" of today, however, lack the essential qualifications of a true apostle, as specified in the New Testament. One must have been a witness to the resurrection of Jesus (1 Cor. 9:1, "Am I not an apostle? Have I not seen Jesus our Lord?"; cf. Acts 1:21–22). A true apostle possesses the power of performing miracles (2 Cor. 12:12; Rom. 15:18–19). The popes lack both qualifications.

The final Roman Catholic doctrinal tradition to be considered here is the dogma of the assumption of Mary into heaven. Pope Pius XII, on November 1, 1950, solemnly described what was believed to be the crowning event of the Virgin's life. In the papal proclamation *Munificentissimus Deus* the pope defined it to be an article of the Roman faith that the "immaculate Mother of God, the ever-Virgin Mary, having completed the course of her earthly life, was assumed body and soul into heavenly glory." The language here teaches the perpetual virginity of Mary as well.

Belief in the assumption of Mary is reflected in apocryphal traditions dating from about 400. The legend of the assumption was accepted as true by Pseudo-Dionysius and by Gregory the Great. Gregory relates the account thus: The apostles were assembled in the house of Mary to watch at her deathbed; Jesus appeared with the angels, received her soul, and gave it to the archangel Michael. On the following day the apostles were about to carry the body to the grave; Jesus again appeared and took Mary's body up in a cloud into heaven, there to be reunited with her soul. John of Damascus relates the legend in yet a more elaborate form: Not only the angels but the patriarchs were present with the apostles at the deathbed; even Adam and Eve were there, blessing Mary for removing the curse which through them came upon the world.

As Hanson has observed, if the dogma involves belief in a historical fact, "it is a fact wholly unknown to the writers of the second and third centuries."[35] In other words, the dogma's historical claims to be apostolic are nonexistent.

About the year 600 the emperor Maurice ordered the feast of the assumption to be celebrated in the Eastern church, fixing the date as August 15. About the same time Gregory the Great fixed the same date for the Latin church, where previously it had been celebrated on January 18.

At the First Vatican Council over two hundred bishops ex-

---

35. Hanson, *Tradition*, p. 238.

pressed a desire for a papal decree making the assumption an article of Roman faith. This desire was finally granted eighty years later by the pronouncement of Piux XII.

As to the possible biblical basis for this dogma, one Catholic scholar has admitted that there "is no explicit reference to the Assumption in the Bible."[36] Attempts have been made to relate the assumption to the doctrine of the resurrection, where sin and the sting of death are overcome in the victory of Jesus Christ (1 Cor. 15:53–57). Mary, being free from sin, presumably "anticipated" the final resurrection victory of all believers in her assumption into heaven. Referring to Luke 1:28, "Hail [Mary], full of grace," Pius IX suggested that the fullness of grace bestowed upon the Virgin was only finally achieved by her assumption. Perhaps Rev. 12:1, the description of the great sign in the heavens, a woman clothed with the sun, the moon under her feet, and head crowned with twelve stars, has some reference to Mary as well as to the church. Mary as the "New Eve" in some sense shared in the redemptive mission of Christ. "Christian intuition, guided by the Holy Spirit," writes Langlinais, "gradually came to see that Mary's share in Christ's victory over sin began with her conception in a state free from all sin (the state in which Eve was created), and ended with her miraculous Assumption (an immunity from death and corruption which Eve enjoyed until the Fall)."[37]

Such references to the biblical data can have no claim to be recognized as serious historical-grammatical exegesis. "Christian intuition"—in this case, the vagaries of grass-roots piety—has led away from the teachings of the New Testament, obscured the supremacy and uniqueness of the redemptive work of Christ, confused legend with historical fact, and placed the most serious obstacles in the path of Roman Catholic–Protestant relations. Evangelicals can learn much from a tradition of the patristic church, but can in no way compromise, in matters of doctrinal authority, the *sola scriptura* principle of the Protestant Reformation. The Bible, and the Bible alone, must remain the final written authority for Christian faith and practice.

## Bibliography

Berkouwer, G. C. *The Second Vatican Council and the New Catholicism*, tr. L. Smedes. Grand Rapids: Eerdmans, 1965.

36. J. W. Langlinais, "Assumption of Mary," p. 972.
37. Ibid., pp. 972–73.

Bloesch, Donald G. *Essentials of Evangelical Theology,* Vol. I. San Francisco: Harper, 1978.

Bruce, F. F. *Tradition Old and New.* Grand Rapids: Zondervan, 1970.

Childs, Brevard. *Introduction to the Old Testament as Scripture.* Philadelphia: Fortress, 1979.

Gadamer, Hans-Georg. *Truth and Method.* London: Sheed and Ward, 1975.

Gallup, George, Jr., and Poling, David. *The Search for America's Faith.* Nashville: Abingdon, 1980.

Hanson, R. P. C. *Tradition in the Early Church.* Philadelphia: Westminster, 1962.

Küng, Hans. *Justification.* New York: Nelson, 1964.

Lane, A. N. S. "Scripture, Tradition and Church: An Historical Survey," *Vox Evangelica* 9 (1975):37—55.

Langlinais, J. W. "Assumption of Mary," *New Catholic Encyclopedia.* New York: McGraw-Hill, 1967.

Latourette, Kenneth Scott. *A History of the Expansion of Christianity,* vol. IV. New York: Harper, 1941.

Leith, John H., ed. *Creeds of the Churches.* Richmond: John Knox, 1973.

Loserth, J. "Wyclif, John," *The New Schaff-Herzog Encyclopedia of Religious Knowledge.* New York: Funk and Wagnalls, 1912.

Mead, Sidney E. "Protestantism in America," *Church History* 23 (1954):291—320.

Oden, Thomas C. *Agenda for Theology.* San Francisco: Harper, 1979.

Polanyi, Michael. *The Study of Man.* Chicago: University of Chicago Press, 1959.

Rushdoony, R. J. *Infallibility: An Inescapable Concept.* Vallecito, Calif.: Ross House, 1978.

Schaff, Philip. *The Creeds of Christendom,* Vol. I. New York: Harper, 1877.

Thiselton, Anthony C. *The Two Horizons.* Grand Rapids: Eerdmans, 1980.

Webber, Robert E. *Common Roots: A Call to Evangelical Maturity.* Grand Rapids: Zondervan, 1978.

Webber, Robert E., and Bloesch, Donald, eds. *The Orthodox Evangelicals.* Nashville: Thomas Nelson, 1978.

Wegenast, K. "παραδίδωμε," *New International Dictionary of New Testament Theology.* Grand Rapids: Zondervan, 1978. III, 772—75.

Wells, David F. "Tradition: A Meeting Place for Catholic and Evangelical Theology?" *Christian Scholar's Review* 5:(1975):50—61.

Whitehead, Priscilla, and McAlpine, Tom. "Evangelical/Liberal Theology—a False Dichotomy?" *TSF Bulletin,* Mar/Apr., 1982, pp. 8—11.

Wittgenstein, Ludwig. *Philosophical Investigations.* New York: Macmillan, 1958.

Zockler, O. "Mary, Mother of Jesus Christ," *The New Schaff-Herzog Encyclopedia of Religious Knowledge.* New York: Funk and Wagnalls, 1910.

# 8

## The Interpretation
## of Scripture

The German scholar Gerhard Ebeling has argued that the history of the Christian church can be understood as the history of the interpretation of Holy Scripture. This striking suggestion, though it may well be one-sided, does highlight the strategic role that biblical interpretation has played in the life and mission of the church over the centuries. The basic question of authority in Christian theology cannot be considered apart from the question of hermeneutics, inasmuch as divine revelation and the Bible never function authoritatively in the abstract but rather in the context of some particular ecclesiastical tradition. Hence the question of the nature of the basic principles of biblical interpretation is a crucial one for evangelical theology, which affirms the primacy of the Bible for its faith, life, and work.

### Definition and Distinctions

D. A. Carson has observed that "one of the corollaries of modern 'hermeneutical' debate is that the word 'hermeneutics' is skidding around on an increasingly broad semantic field."[1] In contemporary literature one can find usages of the term "hermeneutics"

1. D. A. Carson, "Hermeneutics," p. 14.

ranging from the more narrow sense of biblical interpretation all
the way to broader senses encompassing virtually the entire range
of biblical and systematic theology. The term will be used here in
the narrower and more traditional sense of the "principles of biblical interpretation."

It is helpful to regard the distinction between hermeneutics and
exegesis as being a distinction between the theory of biblical interpretation and the application of that theory to a specific biblical
text. Hermeneutics is concerned with the critical examination of
the theological and philosophical assumptions and presuppositions which influence exegetical practice. Historical-grammatical
exegesis is concerned with the assumptions made by the biblical
writers; an informed and critical hermeneutics will be equally
concerned with the presuppositions of the contemporary interpreter of scripture. By exposing our own modern assumptions to
critical scrutiny in the light of the Bible, we enable the biblical
text to become free to speak to us with its own power, authority,
and integrity, rather than simply misusing it as a sounding board
for our own modern opinions. Exegesis is concerned with the
specifics of grammar, vocabulary, syntax, and historical context of
the biblical text. Hermeneutical theory presupposes these factors
and attempts to clarify the process of understanding at the contemporary pole of the hermeneutical trajectory by critically examining the philosophy, theology, and world view of the interpreter.
Not only the biblical writers but contemporary interpreters as well
are historically situated, and need to be understood in terms of
their particular contexts.

The term "hermeneutics" derives from the Greek ἑρμηνεία
("interpretation"). In classical Greek usage ἑρμηνεία could refer to
the act of speech itself as interpreting the contents of the mind;
to the process of translating from one language to another (cf.
1 Cor. 12:10); and to the interpretation of a text by commentary
and explanation. It is this latter aspect of the classical usage that
is most germane to our present concerns.

It is noteworthy that the process of interpretation is already
present *within* the Bible. This is the case not only with respect to
the interpretation of dreams and visions (Gen. 40; Dan. 2; Acts 11),
or riddles (Judg. 14; Dan. 5), or parables (Matt. 13), but also with
respect to the interpretation of the Old Testament by the New (e.g.,
as in Matthew and Hebrews). The new situation created by the

life, death, and resurrection of Jesus as the Messiah created a new context of interpretation for the older texts.

The modern interpreter is separated both chronologically and linguistically from the original biblical texts. These factors alone justify special attention in the study of hermeneutical principles. When the unique authority claims and the special subject matter—eternal life—are considered as well, then the hermeneutical task is seen to have special urgency and importance. If the Bible is what it claims to be—a unique, final, and supreme revelation from the Creator and Ruler of the universe—then the proper interpretation of the biblical message becomes a matter of paramount importance.

For evangelical theology the hermeneutical task is inextricably tied to the missionary mandate. Since the gospel is to be planted in every tongue and tribe and nation, the communication and interpretation of biblical truth across cultural boundaries becomes a vital concern. Evangelical hermeneutics, because of its missionary and evangelistic orientation, is intimately concerned with the cross-cultural dimensions of biblical interpretation (pp. 276–279).

## Highlights in the History of Interpretation

An examination of the history of biblical interpretation in the Christian church does reveal the significant influence of philosophical and cultural factors on the process. This is seen clearly, for example, in the dominance of allegorical modes of interpretation in the early church.

Origen (*ca.* 185–254), the church's first great exegete, lived in Alexandria, an environment influenced by the literary work of Philo (*ca.* 25 B.C.—A.D. 40), the great Jewish interpreter who relied heavily on allegory. For example, Philo saw in the four rivers of Gen. 2:10–14 the four Platonic virtues of prudence, self-mastery, courage, and justice. "Eden" referred to the wisdom or Reason of God (*Legum Allegoria* I.63–73).

Origen speaks of the "flesh," "soul," and "spirit" of a text, terms intended for the three aspects of man, but generally limits himself to the "flesh" and the "soul" (*On First Principles* 14.1) The Samaritan woman's five husbands (John 4:18), for example, refer not merely to five literal husbands but also to the five senses, by which the soul is governed before it comes to faith in Christ.

Modern interpreters have shown little sympathy for the allegorical methods of the early church. It is true, of course, that fanciful meanings were imported into the text at the expense of the plain grammatical meaning. The Platonic and Neoplatonic philosophies exerted negative influences not only upon the doctrine of the Christian life, but also upon biblical interpretation. As Rushdoony has observed, when the material world is depreciated, allegorical interpretations will proliferate, since the "true" and "spiritual" meanings are only to be found through allegories and forced typologies.[2] The otherworldly orientation of allegory deflects attention away from the dominion mandate (Gen. 1:28) given the people of God to subdue this world of matter, space, and time to the glory of God.

At the same time, the critics have tended not to recognize the positive aspects of the early church's allegorical methods and the historical conditions that called them forth. Allegory was an accepted literary convention in second century Alexandria among Greek philosophers, who had long been accustomed to interpreting the Greek poets along allegorical lines in order to purge them of the more crude and often embarrassing characteristics attributed to the gods. The use of allegory by Origen and others helped to meet the criticism of Celsus and other pagans that the Christians were obscurantists and irrationalists. As Robert M. Grant has observed, the allegorical method, at a critical moment in Christian history, "made it possible to uphold the rationality of Christian faith."[3] And Hanson has pointed out that by the early decades of the third century it was no longer adequate for a Christian theologian speaking to an educated Greek-speaking public to rely on an "invocation of a long list of proof texts by way of expounding Christian doctrine."[4] In their own way and in their own historical situation these allegorists were attempting to *contextualize* the message for their particular audience in a new missionary environment. These attempts were not altogether successful, but nevertheless the particularities of each situation and its needs should not be overlooked.

2. R. J. Rushdoony, *Infallibility: An Inescapable Concept*, p. 56.
3. Robert M. Grant, *A Short History of the Interpretation of the Bible*, p. 88.
4. R. P. C. Hanson, "Biblical Exegesis in the Early Church," p. 449.

It should also be noted that the New Testament was first subjected to allegorizing not by the orthodox church but by the Gnostics and other groups at the fringes of apostolic Christianity.
According to Tertullian, the Gnostics interpreted the parable of the
foolish virgins (Matt. 25:1—13) to refer to the five deceptive senses
(De anima 18.4). The orthodox adopted allegorical interpretations
of the New Testament somewhat in self-defense, in order to extract
meanings from the text believed to be more in accordance with
the apostolic traditions.[5]

The allegorical exegesis of Alexandria was opposed by the more
literal methods of the school of Antioch in Syria. Diodorus (d. 394),
Theodore of Mopsuestia (d. 428), and Theodoret of Cyrrhus (d. 460)
were representatives of this school. Their work was popularized
by John Chrysostom (d. 407), the patriarch of Constantinople and
greatest preacher of the Greek church.

According to Photius, Theodore of Mopsuestia "did his utmost
to avoid allegories; he made his interpretation according to the
historia"—i.e., the literal sense.[6] While the school of Antioch had
little use for allegory, they did not, like some modern interpreters,
entirely reject typological meanings in scripture. And even Theodore of Mopsuestia, who was perhaps the most insistent on the
literal, historical sense, allowed that Psalms 2, 8, 45, and 110 were
messianic.

The Antiochene emphasis is a significant one in the history of
interpretation, but it did not exert any considerable influence on
the hermeneutical practices of the Middle Ages. By and large, both
the Greek and Latin churches continued to favor allegorical methods which presupposed multiple levels of meaning in the text.

About the year 425 John Cassian formulated for his monks at
Marseilles a fourfold theory of meaning that was to have great
influence in the church for centuries thereafter. According to Cassian, the literal meaning dealt with the historical events; the allegorical with doctrine, especially Christology and ecclesiology;
the tropological with morals (from τρόπος, "moral character"), and
the anagogical with individual eschatology and the heavenly life.
Thus Jerusalem was simultaneously a reference to a literal city,
the catholic church, catholic morals, and the heavenly city.

5. Ibid., p. 416
6. K. Grobel, "Interpretation, History and Principles of," p. 720.

The theory of the fourfold sense was expressed by the popular rhyme: *Littera gesta docet, quid credas allegoria, moralis quid agas, quo tendas anagogia.* That is, the "letter teaches the events, allegory what you are to believe, the moral sense what you are to do, anagogue whither you are to strive."[7]

It was also a common practice during the medieval period to posit a correlation between the three nonliteral senses and the three cardinal theological virtues. The allegorical sense (doctrine) was associated with the virtue of faith, the tropological (morals) with love, and the anagogical (eschatology) with hope. The concept of the three cardinal theological virtues was derived from Paul's statement in 1 Cor. 13:13.

While the fourfold theory of meaning was the dominant one during the medieval period, there were some significant influences in the direction of a more literal and historical approach. During the latter part of the eleventh century in France the influential Jewish biblical and talmudic scholar Rabbi Solomon ben Isaac ("Rashi") held to the primacy of the literal sense. Commenting on Exod. 6:2–9, he wrote, "Therefore I say let Scripture be expounded according to its simple meaning, each word in its proper context—and let the midrash-interpretation be only a hint."[8] The school of Rashi influenced the Christian church through the school of St. Victor, founded at Paris in 1110, and also through Nicholas of Lyra (d. *ca.* 1349), a Franciscan professor at the University of Paris and author of the first biblical commentary ever printed, *Postillae Perpetuae* (Rome, 1471–72). According to Nicholas, "All [senses] presuppose the literal as a foundation."

This concern for the primacy of the literal sense is reflected in the work of Thomas Aquinas, the greatest of the medieval theologians. According to Aquinas, "In holy scripture ... all the senses are founded on one—the literal—from which alone any argument can be drawn. ... Nothing necessary to faith is contained under the spiritual sense which is not elsewhere put forward by the scripture in its literal sense" (*Summa Theologica* 1.1.10). This significant statement does not repudiate nonliteral senses but insists on the primacy of the literal meaning in all matters of Christian faith. Robert M. Grant would not appear to be overstating the case

7. Ibid., p. 721.
8. Ibid.

when he says that this position of Aquinas "marks theology's declaration of independence from the allegorical method."[9] The distance between Aquinas and Luther and Calvin at this point is not very great. By the thirteenth century, when Aquinas worked, the influence of Platonism, which had been the dominant philosophy for the early church fathers, was beginning to wane and was being supplanted by the philosophy and epistemology of Aristotle. The Aristotelian epistemology, with its emphasis on the physical senses as the primary avenues of knowledge, pushed biblical interpretation back toward a greater respect for the this-worldly and historical dimensions of scripture.

Martin Luther broke not only with the medieval church's doctrines of salvation but also with its traditional methods of biblical interpretation. Recalling his earlier training and practice, Luther stated that "when I was a monk, I was an expert in allegories. I allegorized everything" (*Table Talk*, I.136). "Since that time," he wrote, "when I began to embrace the historical meaning I have always abhorred allegories and have not used them unless either the text itself exhibited them or [allegorical] interpretations could be cited from the New Testament."[10] Luther reasserted in no uncertain terms the primacy of the literal-historical sense but did not exclude all allegorical or typological references. Allegorical meanings might be used for homiletical embellishment or illustration. In such cases, "if ever you wish to use allegory," Luther stated, "do so observing the analogy of faith; that is, accommodate it to Christ, the Church, faith, and the ministry of the Word."[11] And unlike some modern interpreters, Luther knew that the literal-historical sense considered in itself did not guarantee spiritual benefits. The witness of the Holy Spirit to the biblical text was essential. "Experience is necessary for the understanding of the Word. It is not merely to be repeated or known, but to be lived and felt. God must say to you in your heart, This is God's Word."[12]

Like Luther, John Calvin insisted on the primacy of the literal-historical sense. In his *Commentary on Galatians* he stated that "the true meaning of Scripture is the natural and obvious meaning;

9. Grant, *Short History*, p. 125.
10. Grobel, "Interpretation," p. 723.
11. James D. Wood, *The Interpretation of the Bible*, p. 90.
12. Grant, *Short History*, p. 132.

and let us embrace and abide by it resolutely."[13] The Reformer's emphasis on the principles of *sola scriptura* and the perspicuity of scripture implied scripture's freedom from a tangle of allegorical meanings. The central saving message of the Bible was accessible to all.

Calvin also insisted on the work of the Spirit in producing a true conviction of the Bible's saving message and divine authority. "The Scripture . . . owes the full conviction with which we ought to receive it to the testimony of the Spirit" (*Inst.* I.7,5).

The spreading influence of the historical-critical approach to scripture in the German universities during the post-Reformation period led to a minimizing of the role of the Holy Spirit in illuminating the text for the believer. These rationalistic trends led to a reaction in the form of German pietism. Johann Jacob Rambach (1693 – 1735), a professor in Giessen and a follower of August Hermann Francke, in his *Institutiones hermeneuticae sacrae* (1724), reflected the concerns and insights of the pietist movement. The exegete should love Christ and God's Word in order to rightly interpret it; in some cases there may be spiritual senses beyond the purely grammatical ones.

The pietists' protest against the reduction of all biblical texts to a single meaning was not, however, to carry the day. Not only on the continent, but also in England, the historical-critical method established itself as the reigning hermeneutical orthodoxy. Benjamin Jowett, then Regius Professor of Greek at Oxford, in a famous essay, "On the Interpretation of Scripture," in *Essays and Reviews* (1859), expressed the dominant opinion. "Interpret the Scripture like any other book," said Jewett. "Scripture has one meaning— the meaning which it had in the mind of the Prophet or Evangelist who first uttered or wrote, to the hearers or readers who first received it."[14]

Almost a hundred years earlier the Leipzig scholar Johann August Ernesti, in his *Instituto Interpretis Novi Testamenti ad usus lectionuum* (1761), had expressed very similar views. All books, human or divine, were to be interpreted in the same manner. In their reaction to the excesses of medieval allegorizing, the historical-critical scholars had taken a position which alienated

13. Wood, *Interpretation*, pp. 92−93.
14. David C. Steinmetz, "The Superiority of Pre-Critical Exegesis," p. 27.

their hermeneutics from that of the New Testament writers themselves. During the twentieth century biblical scholars began cautiously to recover a sense of the proper validity of typological and other forms of nonliteral meaning (See pp. 260–263).

## Presuppositions and Principles of Evangelical Hermeneutics

Any system of interpretation reflects basic theological and philosophical commitments, and evangelical hermeneutics is no exception. The basic concern in this section will be to explore some of the implications of evangelical convictions concerning the nature of God and biblical inspiration for the proper interpretation of the Bible. The concern here is to give a theological overview of certain important hermeneutical issues, rather than to discuss specific approaches to the various biblical literary genres such as gospels, prophecy, epistles, poetry, apocalyptic, and so on. For discussion of such particulars the reader is referred to such standard conservative works as Bernard Ramm, *Protestant Biblical Interpretation;* Berkeley Mickelsen, *Interpreting the Bible;* Louis Berkhof, *Principles of Biblical Interpretation;* and Milton Terry, *Biblical Hermeneutics.*

### Presuppositions

The first basic presupposition of evangelical hermeneutics is that there is only one, all-wise, and self-consistent God who is the ultimate author of all scripture. The biblical doctrine of the unity, wisdom, and self-consistency of God may seem obvious, but it has not always been so in the history of Western civilization. The truth of the unity of God was impressed upon Western civilization by the Christian church only after a long and arduous struggle with Greek, Roman, and barbarian polytheism. Any polytheistic religious outlook undermines the authority of divine revelation. As Carle C. Zimmerman has pointed out with respect to ancient Greek religion, during the Homeric period "the gods were always quarreling among themselves; at least one god was sure to be on either side of any issue."[15]

The doctrine of the unity and self-consistency of the one God—biblical monotheism—is of fundamental importance for evangel-

15. Carle C. Zimmerman, *Family and Civilization,* p. 465.

ical hermeneutics. The Bible is not an assortment of diverse messages from many diverse gods; behind all scripture stands the one God and Father of our Lord Jesus Christ, the same God who made the heavens and the earth. Unlike the gods of pagan Greece and Rome the God of scripture is not subject to limitations of either power, wisdom, or moral integrity. The Bible reflects the basic unity and coherence of the God who inspired it.

A second presupposition important for evangelical interpretation is the conviction that the omnipotent and sovereign God of the Bible cannot ultimately be frustrated by human sin—either the sin of individuals or the sin of cultures. God, in his desire to communicate a saving revelation to mankind, has both the desire and the ability to do so successfully, in spite of the recalcitrance and immaturity of sinful human instruments. "I am God, and also henceforth I am He. . . . I work and who can hinder it?" (Isa. 43:13). If God wishes to communicate with man, he can do so: "So shall my word be that goes forth from my mouth; it shall not return to me empty, but it shall accomplish that which I purpose, and prosper in the thing for which I sent it" (Isa. 55:11). The sovereign power of God is not limited by the sinful dimensions of human culture. This biblical conviction of the sovereignty and omnipotence of God is basic to any assurance that the Bible is in fact an authoritative divine revelation rather than merely a distorted human record of religious experiences. Without a clear understanding of the sovereignty of God over human culture it is difficult, if not impossible, to achieve clarity with respect to questions of cultural conditioning and biblical interpretation (pp. 276–279).

These two presuppositions, together with the fact of plenary inspiration (2 Tim. 3:16, πᾶσα γραφὴ θεόπνευστος), establish a fundamental harmony in the teachings of scripture. All scripture is of divine origin; all scripture reflects the wisdom of the one God whose intention to communicate clearly and savingly to mankind has not been defeated by human sin. Consequently, the evangelical interpreter presupposes a basic harmony among the various parts of the canon and within the various works of a single writer. These three presuppositions are the theological basis for the principle of the *analogy of scripture*—that is, scripture is to be interpreted by scripture. This principle falls to the ground if in fact there is no basic coherence in the biblical message as a whole.

It is unfortunately necessary to emphasize some assumptions

which may appear obvious and elementary to the average conservative reader of the Bible precisely because they have been emphatically denied by practitioners of the historical-critical method. The German New Testament scholar Ernst Käsemann, a former student of Bultmann, has declared that it is an "incomprehensible superstition" to suppose that "in the canon only genuine faith manifests itself everywhere." According to Käsemann, "The canon as such . . . legitimates more or less all sects and false doctrines."[16] Such a belief in the doctrinal incoherence of the biblical canon destroys the Reformation principle of *sola scriptura* and the supreme authority of scripture for Christian theology.

A fourth presupposition of evangelical hermeneutics is that *all* scripture is profitable for the edification of the Christian church (2 Tim. 3:16; 1 Cor. 10:11; Rom. 15:4). This is so because of plenary inspiration; because of the basic constancy of human needs across time and culture; and because we, like the New Testament writers themselves, live in the new age between the resurrection of Jesus Christ and his parousia. This fourth presupposition should, in practice, mean that the evangelical minister will teach and preach the whole counsel of God, from the Old Testament as well as the New. Some conservative preachers, unfortunately, seem to concentrate on the Gospels and Pauline epistles, to the neglect of the other parts of canonical scripture which God has given to the church.

### Some guidelines

The foregoing presuppositions can be specified in a number of guidelines that may be helpful in the actual process of exegesis and interpretation. As noted earlier, the concern here is a theological overview, not a detailed discussion of the various literary genres of scripture.

First of all, it should be said that a biblical text is not to be interpreted in a sense that contradicts the clear meaning of another text. This could be called the "coherence postulate." It is an alternate way of expressing the principle of the analogy of faith. For example, rather than concluding that James 2:21 teaches justification by works and thus contradicts Rom. 3:28, which teaches justification by faith apart from works of the law, one should seek

---

16. In Gerhard Maier, *The End of the Historical-Critical Method*, pp. 37–38.

contextual factors that could resolve the apparent conflict. James is stressing the fact that true faith is no mere verbal profession (2:19) but a life-transforming relationship to God—a point certainly affirmed by Paul (Gal. 5:6, faith *working* through love). Paul, on the other hand, in the context of a controversy with the Judaizers is concerned to show that works prior to conversion can have no *meritorious* significance in reconciling us to God. "Works" and "faith" have different connotations for James and Paul because of the different ecclesiastical situations they are addressing, but both agree that true saving faith is manifested in works of love and charity (cf. Eph. 2:10). The different emphases represent not contradictions, but different ways of contextualizing truth for specific needs in ministry.

Second, the grammatical-historical ("literal") sense is the basic sense. This was a point made strongly by the Reformers in relation to the excesses of medieval allegorizing. It should be noted that the "literal" sense in some cases may be poetic or symbolic. When the psalmist writes, "Let the floods clap their hands; let the hills sing for joy together before the Lord" (Ps. 98:8), the language should be understood in its natural sense,—i.e., a poetic invitation for the creation to join God's people in the praise of God. The literal sense is not necessarily a *literalistic* sense; rather, the literal meaning is the sense intended in the original context. The questions of typological meanings in scripture will be discussed in a subsequent section.

Third, the text should not be interpreted in a sense that excludes the possibility or reality of the supernatural. In the context of a debate with the Sadducees on the resurrection Christ rebuked them, saying, "You are wrong, because you know neither the scriptures nor the power of God" (Matt. 22:29). Significantly, the proper understanding of a biblical doctrine is here linked with a proper concept of the power of God. In the modern era rationalistic theologians and exegetes are guilty of the same error, having a deistic understanding of God's relationship to the created order. Bultmann's mistaken philosophy of science implied a closed system of mechanical laws, a universe in which God could perform no miracles. Other biblical scholars deny the reality of predictive prophecy, thereby denying the omniscience of God and God's transcendence over time. Others deny the reality of angels, spirits, and demons. Some biblical scholars bring a metaphysical skepticism to their use of form and redaction criticism, denying the historicity of various sayings of Jesus in the Gospels on the basis of an over-emphasis on his humanity at the expense of his deity. The evangelical interpreter will treat the Bible for what it truly is, namely, a supernatural revelation of a supernatural redemption. Any hermeneutic that suppresses or denies the reality of the supernatural cannot do justice to the text.

Fourth, the New Testament is the key to the proper interpretation of the Old. The New Testament is the definitive revelation of Jesus Christ, and he is the true meaning of the Old Testament. "You search the scriptures. . . . It is they that bear witness to me" (John 5:39). "And beginning with Moses and all the prophets, he interpreted to them in all the scriptures the things concerning himself" (Luke 24:27). Jesus came not to abolish the law and the prophets but to fulfill them (Matt. 5:17). Consequently, the messianic prophecies of the Old Testament (e.g., Isa. 53:4—6, the suffering servant) find their true interpretation in the New (cf. 1 Peter 2:24—25). On ethical matters such as divorce, laws of the old covenant (e.g., Deut. 24:1—4) must be interpreted in the light of the teachings of Christ (Matt. 19:3—9).

It has been customary to distinguish between the ceremonial, civil, and moral laws of the Old Testament. The predominant position in the history of the church has been that, in the light of the New Testament, the moral laws of the Old Testament are still binding on the Christian church, while the ceremonial and civil laws are not.[17] With respect to the ceremonial laws, the New Testament teaches that the old sacrificial system has been fulfilled and superseded by the priestly work of Jesus Christ on the cross (Heb. 10:1—10). The dietary laws are superseded, because Christ has declared all foods clean (Mark 7:19; cf. Acts 10:9—16). Circumcision is no longer required for full status among God's covenant people (Gal. 5:2—6). With respect to the civil laws of the Old Testament, the New Testament assumes that the Christian lives under

17. At least in their original form and application. In a real sense, however, the *principles* of Old Testament ceremonial and civil law are still valid and instructive: the sacrificial system teaches the necessity of atonement for sin through a divinely appointed substitute; the civil laws teach God's demands for a just and humane social order. Consequently, no section of the Old Testament should be ignored in the church's teaching ministry. The particular question of the continuing validity of Old Testament penal law will be discussed in relation to the question of theonomy (see pp. 266—270).

the authority of various civil orders (Rom. 13:1–7) rather than within a specially covenanted theocratic order, as was the case with Israel. The moral law, however, is of perpetual validity. In the New Testament, Christian love is the fulfilling of the moral law of the Old Testament (cf. Rom. 13:8–10).

Fifth, passages which, in the original context, were addressed to an individual should be interpreted in the light of passages on the same subject which are addressed to the entire church. For example, on the matter of the Christian's relationship to wealth and possessions, Luke 18:22 ("Sell all that you have and distribute to the poor") is certainly relevant. At the same time, the more broadly general instruction of 1 Tim. 6:8 should be taken into account: "If we have food and clothing, with these we shall be content." The Luke 18 passage addresses a specific individual whose love of wealth was a prime obstacle to his obedience to the demands of the kingdom. 1 Tim. 6:8 speaks to Christians in all conditions, reminding them to be content with the simple necessities of life rather than being driven and preoccupied by desires for an ever higher standard of living.

Sixth, the descriptive passages of scripture are to be interpreted in light of the didactic passages. That is, not everything described in scripture is thereby endorsed as an ethical ideal or norm for conduct. In the old covenant God clearly tolerated polygamy; great men of God such as Abraham and David had more than one wife. Nevertheless, it is not these Old Testament practices but rather New Testament precepts (e.g., Matt. 19:5, recalling Gen. 2:24) that are to be the Christian's ethical guides. The Bible very honestly describes the less-than-perfect lives of the people of God in a fallen world, but such examples are instructive as patterns to be avoided rather than imitated.

Seventh, incidental references to a given practice or doctrine are to be interpreted in light of the more systematic passages. For example, the Mormon practice of proxy baptism appeals to 1 Cor. 15:29–30 ("what do people mean by being baptized on behalf of the dead?"). But such practices are clearly inconsistent with the understanding of baptism presupposed by such texts as Acts 2:38 and Rom. 6:1–11, which treat the issue in more than a passing fashion. Christian faith and practice are to be based on the clear texts which consciously address the issue in question.

As another example one might consider the appeal to 1 Peter

3:19 (Christ preaching to the spirits in prison) in support of a belief in a "second chance" for those who might have died in unbelief during this life. Such a deduction from the admittedly difficult text is dubious in light of clear texts such as Luke 16:26 ("between us and you a great chasm has been fixed") and Heb. 9:27 ("it is appointed for men to die once, and after that comes judgment"). The general thrust of the New Testament emphasizes the decisive importance of response to God and Jesus Christ in *this* life—not a future one.[18]

This seventh guideline is simply another way of stating the principle that the more obscure texts of scripture are to be interpreted in light of the clear. As such, it is an example of the principle of the analogy of scripture and an application of the presupposition of the basic coherence of scripture.

## Issues in Old Testament–New Testament Relationships

As we have already seen (pp. 257–258, fourth guideline), the crucial link between the testaments is Jesus Christ himself, who is the fulfillment of all the promises of the old covenant. Richard Longenecker has properly observed that at the heart of the New Testament writers' use of the Old Testament is a Christology and a Christological perspective.[19] And as G. Schrenk has observed, in the last analysis the apostle Paul is claiming no less than that "the Old Testament scripture finally belongs to the Christian community rather than to the Jewish."[20] "Whatever was written in former days was written for our instruction" (Rom. 15:4).

While the general Christological orientation of the New Testament hermeneutic is quite clear, three particular issues connected with the relationship between the covenants need further discussion,—namely, typology, dispensationalism, and theonomy. The first has been an enduring interest of the church at large over the centuries, while the latter two represent more recent concerns in conservative Protestant circles.

18. For a helpful discussion of the 1 Peter 3:19 passage, together with 4:6, see E. G. Selwyn, *The First Epistle of St. Peter*, pp. 313–62.

19. Richard Longenecker, *Biblical Exegesis in the Apostolic Period*, p. 207.

20. G. Schrenk, "γραφή," I, 759.

## Typology

According to the New Testament scholar W. G. Kümmel, typological interpretation represents the "basic attitude of primitive Christianity toward the Old Testament."[21] As we have already had occasion to note, the theme of fulfillment dominates the New Testament writers' perspectives on the scriptures of the old covenant. The persons, places, and events in the older dispensation point beyond themselves to the new reality introduced by Jesus Christ, who is their true meaning.

While allegory seeks for hidden meanings in language, typology seeks correspondences between persons and events, and discerns the recurrence of significant redemptive patterns in history. The New Testament writers see correspondences between Adam and Christ (Rom. 5:12—21; 1 Cor. 15:21—22), between Melchizedek and Jesus (Heb. 7:1—17), between the flood and Christian baptism (1 Peter 3:21), and between the baptism of Israel under Moses and that of the church under Jesus (1 Cor. 10:1—13). These are only a few examples from the New Testament writings. The most extensive application of a typological approach to the Old Testament is found in the Book of Hebrews, where the Levitical priesthood and service of the tabernacle is seen to foreshadow the priestly ministry of Jesus Christ.

The popularity of nonliteral methods of interpretation in the early church at times led to contrived and far-fetched results. One notable example of this problem can be found in the Epistle of Barnabas, where the 318 servants of Abraham (Gen. 14:14) are supposed to contain a mystical reference to Jesus, since in Greek the characters T I H make up the cross plus the first two letters of Jesus' name.[22]

Such abuses of allegorical and typological methods tended to discredit these approaches entirely in the eyes of postmedieval scholars. According to the English deist Anthony Collins, in *A Discourse of the Grounds and Reasons of the Christian Religion* (1724), even the New Testament writers themselves were guilty in this regard, using faulty rabbinic methods of interpretation in their approach to the Old Testament. According to Collins, the messianic interpretation of Isa. 7:14 in Matt. 1:22—23 was illegitimate

21. In Earle Ellis, *Prophecy and Hermeneutic in Early Christianity*, p.165.
22. Grant, *Short History*, p. 60.

Collins' opinion has become a fairly common one in modern biblical scholarship.

It has become quite evident that modern practitioners of the historical-critical method feel somewhat embarrassed about the New Testament writers' methods of interpretation. James Barr has observed, "One of the embarrassments of theology today is the considerable alienation of exegetical science from the earlier exegetical tradition of the Church. The steady repudiation of allegory is part of the reason for this alienation."[23]

Even such a conservative New Testament scholar as Richard Longenecker has hesitations in this regard. Since we are not the recipients of direct revelation, we cannot duplicate the pesher, midrash, or allegorical methods of the New Testament writers, though we accept the inspired results. According to Longenecker, all this "is strictly part of the cultural context through which the transcultural and eternal gospel was expressed."[24] There is some question, of course, whether such a sharp separation between methods and results can be maintained. If divine inspiration endorses the results, can the methods be entirely illegitimate?

Other conservative writers have drawn different conclusions. According to Louis Berkhof, the necessity of "recognizing the mystical sense is quite evident from the way in which the New Testament interprets the Old."[25] The presupposition here is that, under the guidance of divine inspiration, the New Testament authors have in fact discovered valid meanings in scripture beyond the literal ones.

This point of view has been stated more forcibly by David Steinmetz in an intriguing article which appeared in *Theology Today*, "The Superiority of Pre-Critical Exegesis." The idea that "scripture has only one meaning is a fantastic idea and is certainly not advocated by the biblical writers themselves," he states.[26] The single-meaning theory defended by historical-critical orthodoxy neither is consistent with apostolic practice nor does it well serve the religious needs of the Christian church.

Even E. D. Hirsch, a leading advocate of the primacy of authorial intent as a norm of valid meaning, has acknowledged the possi-

---

23. James Barr, *Old and New in Interpretation*, p. 132.
24. Longenecker, *Biblical Exegesis*, p. 218.
25. Louis Berkhof, *Principles of Biblical Interpretation*, p. 140.
26. Steinmetz, "Pre-Critical Exegesis," p. 32.

bility of further meanings: "The human author's willed meaning can always go beyond what he consciously intended so long as it remains within his willed type."[27] By "willed type" Hirsch means the author's conscious intent plus meanings logically implicit in that intent. If, for example, a legislature passes a law requiring all "wheeled vehicles" to stop at intersections, would a newly invented vehicle riding on a stream of compressed air be covered by the law? A judge ruling on the question at some later date could legitimately find such a vehicle to be included, since the real intent of the law was concerned with all forms of transportation using the highways, and not merely those happening to be in existence at the time the statute was originally drafted.

It goes without saying that the situation with respect to scripture is more complicated than that pertaining to human law, since the process of inspiration of scripture involves both a human and a divine author. Consequently, two levels of intentionality and two possible meanings must be considered in biblical interpretation.

When, for example, the angel Gabriel tells Mary that her son will one day sit upon the "throne of his father David" (Luke 1:32), the meaning of the phrase "throne of David" cannot be limited to the conception of David's kingship Mary might have had at the time. In the mind of God, reigning upon the throne of David had a much wider meaning that became apparent only after the resurrection, Pentecost, and the ascension of Christ to the right hand of the Father (Acts 2:29–36). The Old Testament prophets did not fully understand the messianic prophecies they delivered under inspiration (1 Peter 1:10–11). Their full meaning became apparent only in light of the Christ-events themselves.

At this point proponents of the single-meaning theory are likely to object, "But doesn't this leave the whole enterprise of biblical interpretation floating in a sea of subjectivism?" One can easily go astray by seeking nonliteral meanings, but the problem is not quite so simple. The single-meaning theory has its own dangers: forcing the text into the procrustean bed of its own hermeneutical theory and casting aspersion upon the inspired practice of the apostolic authors. Can we really claim to understand the Old Testament scriptures more profoundly than they did?

The boundaries of nonliteral meanings are placed by the canon

27. E. D. Hirsch, Jr., *Validity in Interpretation*, p. 126, n.37.

itself, which has given the church a "universe of meaning" centered on the saving events of the life, death, and resurrection of Jesus Christ. The common sense of the church can distinguish between the fanciful attempts of the Epistle of Barnabas and the type of practice exemplified in the book of Hebrews.

The modern preacher however, would, be prudent to limit the use of typology to points of embellishment and illustration. The main points of the message should depend upon the grammatical-historical sense. The responsible homiletician will not build an entire message on a doubtful interpretation.

During recent years Old Testament scholars have been showing a renewed appreciation for typology—e.g., R. V. G. Tasker, *The Old Testament in the New Testament* (1954); H. E. W. Turner, *The Pattern of Christian Truth* (1954); C. Westermann, *Essays on Old Testament Hermeneutics* (1963) and *The Old Testament and Jesus Christ* (1970). Such scholarship is a welcome corrective to the rather one-sided emphases of an earlier day.

### Dispensational hermeneutics

Dispensationalism is a system of biblical interpretation that exerts a broad influence in American evangelicalism today. Since its appearance in 1967, the *New Scofield Reference Bible* has sold over a million copies. The notes in this Bible, like those in its predecessor, are written from a dispensational perspective. The older *Scofield Reference Bible* sold over two million copies between the years 1915 and 1945, and constituted a major instrument of dispensational teaching. At the more popular level Hal Lindsey's *Late Great Planet Earth*, concerned with prophecy and the end times and written from a dispensational perspective, has sold more than thirteen million copies since 1970 and continues to sell at a brisk rate.

The dispensational system of interpretation was first developed in the nineteenth century by the Englishman John Nelson Darby, one of the chief founders of the Plymouth Brethren. The views of Darby and his followers were popularized during the nineteenth century through many Bible classes and conferences, as well as through the writings of Darby himself.[28] During the modernist-

28. For the historical background of the dispensational movement, see C. Bass, *Backgrounds to Dispensationalism*.

fundamentalist controversies of the earlier part of the twentieth century many prominent conservative leaders held to this system of interpretation. In recent years its most scholarly exponents have included Louis Speery Chafer, Charles Ryrie, and John Walvoord, all associated with Dallas Theological Seminary. Other conservative schools disposed toward a dispensational point of view include Grace Theological Seminary, Talbot, Moody Bible Institute, and Western Conservative Baptist Seminary.

According to the *New Scofield Reference Bible*, a dispensation is a "period of time during which man is tested in respect to his obedience to some specific revelation of the will of God."[29] Traditionally, the church has read the Bible in terms of two dispensations, corresponding to the old and new covenants. According to dispensational interpretation, seven separate dispensations can be distinguished in scripture: Innocence (Gen. 1:28); Conscience (Gen. 3:7); Human Government (Gen. 8:15); Promise (Gen. 12:1); Law (Exod. 19:1); Church (Acts 2:1); Kingdom (Rev. 20:4, the millennium). Some dispensationalists, however, do not insist on the sevenfold division as essential to the system. According to the Dallas Seminary statement of faith (1952), the three essential dispensations are the Mosaic, the Church (Grace), and the Kingdom.

It is not the purpose of this section to discuss the dispensational system as a whole (including particular doctrines such as the pretribulational rapture), but rather to focus on matters which bear directly on scripture as a whole, especially the relationship between the testaments. Here two issues are especially significant; namely, the question of the literal fulfillment of Old Testament prophecy and the relationship of Israel and the church.

Dispensationalism insists on a literal approach to the interpretation of Old Testament prophecies which are yet to be fulfilled. God's covenant with Abraham (Gen. 12:1–4; 15:18–21; 17:7–8), which included promises of land for his posterity, still has significance, it is held, for postbiblical Israel. Those who favor the dispensational approach tend to be sympathetic to the claims of the present State of Israel in Middle Eastern politics, seeing Israel's recent history as a fulfillment of Old Testament prophecy.

Likewise, the covenant made with David (2 Sam. 7:8–17), promising the perpetuity of the Davidic dynasty, is held to imply the

29. *New Scofield Reference Bible* (New York: Oxford University Press, 1967), p. 3.

restoration of a literal Davidic monarchy during the millennial period when Christ reigns with the saints (cf. Rev. 20:4–6). The dispensational approach would see in Ezekiel 40–44, Ezekiel's vision of the ideal temple, predictions of the future rebuilding of a physical temple and the restoration of animal sacrifices—not to supplement in any way the sacrifice of Christ on the cross, but to commemorate it. In support of such a literal approach it is argued that since details of Old Testament prophecies concerning Christ's first advent (e.g., his place of birth, mode of death) were fulfilled in a very literal fashion, it is reasonable to suppose that this will likewise be the case in regard to the events associated with his second advent.[30]

Dispensational hermeneutics is also characterized by a sharp distinction between Israel and the church. It is said that Israel was promised a national and earthly kingdom, whereas the church in the New Testament is an international and heavenly kingdom (cf. 2 Cor. 5:1; Eph. 2:6; Phil. 3:20; Col. 1:5). These distinctions between earthly and heavenly kingdoms apply during both time and eternity; Israel and the church have quite distinct roles to play in the drama of redemption.

Interpreters such as Oswald T. Allis, representing the Reformed or covenant theology point of view, argue that the dispensational system breaks up the organic unity of scripture and the one plan of salvation presented throughout scripture. According to covenant theologians, Old Testament prophecy concerning Israel is fulfilled in the one church of Jesus Christ, encompassing both Jew and Gentile (cf. Acts 2:16–21/Joel 2:28–32; Acts 15:14–18/Amos 9:11–12; Gal. 6:16, the "Israel of God"). Christ did not come to offer the Jews an earthly kingdom; he in fact rejected earthly conceptions of messiahship (John 6:15; 18:36; cf. Acts 1:6). Jesus himself interpreted some Old Testament prophecy nonliterally—e.g., Mal. 4:5 ("Elijah"), seeing its fulfillment in the ministry of John the Baptist (Matt. 11:14). Restoration of animal sacrifice is not to be expected in light of the once-for-all sacrifice of Christ on the cross (Heb. 10:12, 18). Christ's death is to be commemorated through the Lord's Supper, and not by other means.

Rather than sharply distinguishing between Israel and the church, covenant theology stresses their organic unity in God's

30. Charles C. Ryrie, *Dispensationalism Today*, p. 88.

plan of redemption (Rom. 11:17–24, image of root and branches). The covenant with Abraham is the foundation of God's offer of salvation to the Gentiles (Gal. 3:8–9, 14). The Christian church of both Jew and Gentile is the true "Israel of God" (Gal. 6:16).

More recently Daniel Fuller—in *Gospel and Law*, a comparison of the hermeneutics of dispensationalism and covenant theology—has proposed a corrective to the older covenant approaches. Traditionally covenant theology has posited a distinction between a covenant of works, based on obedience (citing Gen. 2:7; cf. Lev. 18:5), and a covenant of grace, based on faith (Gen. 15:6; Gal. 3:9). Rather, argues Fuller, the key to both Mosaic and New Testament covenants is the concept of the obedience of faith (cf. Rom. 9:31–32). "The only difference between the old and new covenants . . . was that the new covenant brought in a new inclination of heart to obey the commands that were already stated in the old covenant [the Mosaic law]."[31] This stress on the obedience of faith does have the merit of seeing a unified and consistent relationship between grace and obedience throughout the biblical plan of redemption.

### Theonomy

In American Reformed circles the question of the relationship between the testaments has been raised quite sharply in recent years by the "theonomy" movement. This perspective on the applicability of Old Testament law to modern life is most prominently associated with the work of R. J. Rushdoony (*Institutes of Biblical Law*), and Greg L. Bahnsen (*Theonomy in Christian Ethics*). In the area of economics this point of view is espoused by the conservative Reformed economist Gary North.

The hermeneutical arguments for the theonomic position have been set forth in greatest detail by Bahnsen, whose stated purpose is "to demonstrate from Scripture that we have an ethical obligation to keep all of God's law."[32] According to Bahnsen, "the officials of the state are responsible today, just as in ancient Israel, to enforce God's law." Since the penal laws of the Old Testament are neither arbitrary nor temporary, and reflect the justice of God for social relations, the civil magistrate has an obligation to enforce

31. Daniel P. Fuller, *Gospel and Law*, p. ix.
32. Greg L. Bahnsen, *Theonomy in Christian Ethics*, p. xiii.

those sanctions today. "The magistrate is under moral obligation, then, to apply death to those who transgress God's law at places where God requires the life of the criminal."[33] Evidently the theonomic thesis implies that the civil magistrate should execute homosexuals, sorcerers, and children who maliciously strike their parents Lev. 18:22; Exod. 21:15; 22:18).

Not surprisingly, the theonomy movement has generated a good deal of discussion and controversy. Some of the initial criticism appears to be based on a misreading of the true intent of the position. Walter Chantry, for example, has identified the movement with the heresy of legalism. "A new legalism is binding the Christian conscience," he writes. "It is dictating to Christians that it is their duty to labor to impose Old Testament regulations in exhaustive detail upon their nations and societies."[34] The charge of "legalism" is somewhat misleading, insofar as the theonomists are not arguing *justification* by works of the law but rather, as they understand it, a more consistent use of the law in *sanctification* and societal reformation.

Chantry claims that with respect to the Mosaic economy, its "usefulness passed away with the coming of Jesus Christ."[35] This criticism does not appear to be sufficiently nuanced. While it is generally agreed that the moral provisions of Old Testament law are still binding, and that the ceremonial provisions have been superseded by the priestly work of Christ, the continued relevance of the civil legislation is a bit more perplexing. Even those who reject the theonomic thesis must admit, in the light of 2 Tim. 3:16, that Old Testament civil law is still in some sense instructive for the church. The precise manner in which it is to be instructive is, of course, the issue under debate.

Before taking up additional criticisms of the theonomic position, it would be well to consider some of the positive contributions of the movement. Theonomy certainly represents a significant attempt in the contemporary scene to apply a comprehensive biblical world view. God, the authority of scripture, and the reign of the resurrected and enthroned Christ are seen to have vast implications not only for the institutional church but for the world and its major institutions. Theonomy represents a comprehensive

33. Ibid., p. 470.
34. Walter J. Chantry, *God's Righteous Kingdom*, p. 100.
35. Ibid., p. 106.

challenge to secular humanism in American life today, on all fronts, on the basis of biblical theism and biblical authority.

The theonomic movement also represents a call to the church to demonstrate principled, God-centered action in the midst of a decadent and permissive society. Not pietistic retreat but, a confident and aggressive attempt to extend the kingdom of Christ in the world is the proper response to the social crises of the day. The theonomists have correctly seen that the humanistic faith at the foundation of Enlightenment culture is now in the process of crumbling, and must be replaced with biblical foundations. Even those who disagree with the details or even the central thesis of the theonomists can agree that our major institutions need to be reconstructed along more biblical lines.[36]

At the same time it would seem doubtful that the theonomists have made a convincing argument for their full position. Israel was a "fully covenanted" nation; the people of Israel voluntarily gave virtually unanimous consent to the Mosaic covenant and placed themselves under its stipulations (Exod. 24:7; Josh. 24:19–22). This is not the case in the United States today—or, for that matter, in any modern nation.

Paul Fowler has pointed out that Bahnsen's exegesis of Matt. 5:17, the text upon which the case of *Theonomy in Christian Ethics* is based, suffers from a number of methodological flaws. In attempting to render πληρῶσαι as "to confirm" rather than "to fulfill," Bahnsen does not give adequate attention to the actual usage of the term in Matthew, and makes too much use of English dictionaries, synonyms, and antonyms to explicate a Greek term.[37] The real focus of Matt. 5:17 is not on the law itself but on Jesus and his mission as the true fulfillment of the meaning of the Old Testament dispensation.[38]

There is also real question as to whether the theonomic position has done adequate justice to the particular historical conditions surrounding the Mosaic covenant and to the reality of development within the redemptive plan of God over time. The stern discipline of the old covenant may be likened to a "battlefield

36. For example, in the light of the degradation of American criminal justice, the Old Testament concept of requiring the criminal to make restitution to the victim may be an idea whose time has come.

37. Paul Fowler, *God's Law Free from Legalism*, p. 68.

38. Ibid., pp. 172–73.

discipline." During the Mosaic period the plan of redemption was focused on one small ethnic group, quite immature spiritually and ethically, threatened by a world of alien culture, without the resources of the full canon, the fullness of the Holy Spirit, and the power of the crucified, resurrected, and ascended Christ. Defections which threatened the very existence of the redemptive community had to be punished with the severest measures. A similar situation seems to have applied in the embryonic church in the Book of Acts, where infractions were visited with capital punishment divinely inflicted (Acts 5, Ananias and Sapphira).

Today the situation is significantly different. The church has the resources of the full canon, the historic creeds, and the power of the Holy Spirit and the ascended Christ to preserve the community's redemptive witness in the world. The church is not limited to a small ethnic group, but has established a firm beachhead around the world.

The church now bears a different relation to Old Testament law than did Israel prior to the coming of Christ. The law was a schoolmaster (παιδαγωγός) to lead us to Christ (Gal. 3:24). This language clearly implies development within the redemptive plan of God with respect to the law; it would be inappropriate to simply re-pristinate the Mosaic order *en toto*. The strategy of mission in the New Testament era is significantly different from that under the old economy. Kingdom conquest is not by the power of the sword, but through the preaching of the gospel and the converting power of the Holy Spirit. Kingdom principles are effectively spread not by a "Constantinian" imposition from the top downward, but through a gradual process of leavening (Matt. 13:33). The disciples of Christ are not to call down fire on the heads of opponents (Luke 9:54), but to rely on the powerful converting influence of the Holy Spirit. Persuasion, not coercion, is the New Testament *modus operandi*.

Nevertheless, all this does not mean that believers are not to attempt to reform civil law along more biblical lines. The matter of appropriate criminal penalties must be considered on a case-by-case basis in light of the circumstances of the time.

On this matter of the abiding significance of Old Testament law, the words of the Rev. Timothy Cutler, in a sermon in 1717, seem much to the point: "The moral [laws] stand in full force and obligation on us to observe them. The political [civil] deserve the greatest reverence as the result of perfect wisdom and rectitude; and are most reasonable to be observed by us where our circumstances run parallel with theirs."[39] The entire Old Testament, as the inspired and inerrant Word of God, is perpetually instructive for the church (2 Tim. 3:16). Christian attempts to reform civil law will take into account both the Mosaic precedents and practical considerations, such as the enforceability of a given statute. A law which, though ethically ideal, is simply unenforceable, does not increase respect either for legal justice or for Christian social action. The primary, though not exclusive, thrust of Christian social mission must be a reliance not on legislation but on the gospel and the Holy Spirit.

## Modern Philosophical Hermeneutics

### Hermeneutics and the modern mind

For the last several centuries much of Protestant theology has been preoccupied with an attempt to accommodate the Christian faith to the so-called modern mind. Since the time of the Enlightenment the rise of the historical-critical method, which weakened belief in verbal inspiration and propositional revelation, the spread of the scientific world view, and the impact of Kant's critical philosophy all contributed to a belief that new ways of interpreting the Bible were necessary in order for it to be meaningful to modern man. As Hans Frei has observed, by the latter half of the eighteenth century "all across the theological spectrum the great reversal had taken place; interpretation was a matter of fitting the biblical story into another world with another story rather than incorporating that world into the biblical story."[40]

Many of the post-Enlightenment hermeneutical projects have been infected with anti-supernaturalistic presuppositions, and thus wrestle with problems that are not problems at all for evangelical theology—e.g., How can the miraculous elements of the Bible be made meaningful for those who reject the possibility of the miraculous?

Nevertheless, it would be a mistake to conclude that evangelical theology has nothing to learn from the post-Enlightenment her-

39. Alice M. Baldwin, *The New England Clergy and the American Revolution*, p. 16, n.4.
40. Hans Frei, *The Eclipse of Biblical Narrative*, p. 130.

meneutical developments. While the evangelical tradition strongly affirms the supernatural dimension of the Christian faith, its own understanding of the relation of the Bible to scientific questions has been refined and modified in the light of new scientific discoveries. While rejecting the naturalistic presuppositions often associated with the historical-critical method, evangelical theology's own understanding of inspiration and inerrancy has been refined in light of continuing study of the historical context and detailed phenomena of the biblical text. The question of communicating to the modern mind while most urgently pressed by theological liberals, is merely one example of the broader missionary task of contextualizing the biblical message in terms of the diverse cultural groups to whom it must be addressed. Evangelicals will disagree with many of the presuppositions and results of modern hermeneutical discussions, but at the same time evangelicals would not be wise to simply ignore them.

### Schleiermacher, Dilthey, Heidegger, Gadamer, Hirsch

Since Germany was the birthplace of Kantian critical philosophy and a leader in the development of the historical-critical method, it is not surprising to find that leading figures in modern hermeneutical developments have been German. Schleiermacher, Dilthey, Heidegger, and Gadamer are the prominent figures in these discussions. Their contributions, together with the criticisms of E. D. Hirsch, an American literary scholar, will be surveyed in this section.

Friedrich Schleiermacher (1768–1834), the "father of liberal theology" who based Christian theology on religious experience rather than propositional revelation, also devoted much attention to the practice and theory of biblical interpretation. Schleiermacher was concerned to develop a theory of "global" as opposed to "local" hermeneutics. Prior to this time there had been specific hermeneutical traditions that focused on biblical, legal, or literary texts; Schleiermacher wished to develop a general theory of human understanding which would be applicable to the interpretation of all written texts.

His interests reflected the philosophical currents of the time, especially those of Kantianism and the romantic movement. From Kant came the interest in the architectonic and universal aspects of the human mind and its operations. From the romantic movement came an appreciation for the role of imagination, empathy, and intuition in textual interpretation. The words of the text could be properly understood only in light of an empathetic understanding of the author's interests and spirit.

Schleiermacher merely summarized the work of many previous workers in his hermeneutical rule: "Everything in a given text which requires fuller interpretation must be explained and determined exclusively from the linguistic domain common to the author and his original public." In this view valid interpretation must be truly historical and contextual interpretation.

Schleiermacher also stressed the importance of properly understanding the particular literary genre represented by a text— whether biblical, legal, or literary. This, of course, was not an original discovery, but Schleiermacher did give the principle new prominence. The individuality of both the text and the author must be appreciated if the document is to be properly understood.

Schleiermacher's interest in a general theory of human understanding was continued in the work of Wilhelm Dilthey (1833–1911), a philosopher who succeeded to Hegel's chair at the University of Berlin. Dilthey was concerned to distinguish the proper goals and methodologies of the natural sciences (*Naturwissenschaften*) and human sciences (*Geisteswissenschaften*). He stressed that the human sciences, unlike the natural sciences, must take account of human goals and purposes, self-consciousness, and cultural conventions and traditions.

According to Dilthey, hermeneutics was not merely concerned with texts but, more basically, with human life and activity, as concretized in the artifacts of human culture. "Understanding and interpretation are always active in life itself." Particular texts are understood only in the context of the broader stream of human history; universal history is the most general "text" for human understanding.

Martin Heidegger (1889–1976), one of the more influential philosophers of this century, has had a significant impact on recent hermeneutical theorizing through both Rudolf Bultmann and the practitioners of the "new hermeneutic."[41] His existentialist ap-

41. For a discussion of the new hermeneutic, a school associated with James M. Robinson, Robert W. Funk, Gerhard Ebeling, and Ernst Fuchs, see Robinson and Cobb, eds., *The New Hermeneutic*.

The value of Heidegger's theories should be evaluated in the light of the events of his

proach to the understanding of man was developed most notably in *Being and Time* (1927). Heidegger's writings have been characterized by a sustained polemic against traditional metaphysics and "objectifying," subject-object types of thinking.[42]

Heidegger insisted on the "hermeneutical circle" as a paradigm for human understanding: the object of knowledge is not separable from the whole context of human experience, which is always historically conditioned. As Hirsch has pointed out, Heidegger's exaggerated concept of man's "historicity" leads to historical skepticism: the meaning of an ancient text can never be precisely reduplicated, since man's *being* is presumably so historically conditioned that it cannot be identical from age to a age.[43]

Heidegger's later writings were characterized by a fascination with language as the self-expression of Being. Language is the "house of Being"; "it is language itself that speaks." According to Heidegger, "man acts as though *he* were the keeper and master of language, while in fact *language* remains the master of man."[44]

Language, especially in its poetic expression, is the key to understanding Being in its primordial reality, at a deeper level than that represented by normal conceptual analysis. James M. Robinson, a follower of Heidegger, has noted that the master's "later thinking is non-conceptual in that it does not think of language as composed of or seeking after clearly defined and rationally fixed concepts, whose static and compartmentalized nature would insure their clarity."[45]

The obscurity of Heidegger's thought is thus no accident of style or translation; it is intrinsic to his concepts of language and Being. It is doubtful, however, that in this case obscurity can be equated with profundity. Heidegger's new mythology of language and Being seems to be a secularized version of biblical theism: "Being" is

own life. For discussions of Heidegger's dubious connections with Nazism, see Ivan Strenski, "Heidegger Is No Hero," *Christian Century*, May 19, 1982, pp. 598–601, and Helmut Kuhn, "German Philosophy and National Socialism," *Encyclopedia of Philosophy*, III, 315 – 16. In a 1933 address delivered as the rector of the University of Freiburg, Heidegger hailed the Hitler state as the political actualization of true philosophy.

42. Thiselton has noticed the affinities of Heidegger's thought to Zen Buddhism at this point: both are characterized by a suspicion of logical, conceptual thinking (*The Two Horizons*, p. 342).

43. E. D. Hirsch, Jr., *The Aims of Interpretation*, p. 81.

44. Martin Heidegger, *Basic Writings*, ed. David F. Krell, p. 324.

45. James M. Robinson and John B. Cobb, Jr., *The Later Heidegger and Theology*, p. 23.

substituted for God and "language" for revelation. But there is a transformation both of content and form: the biblical content and its clarity are transformed into mystagogy and the vagaries of poetic metaphor. Heidegger's followers who have attempted to apply his later thought in the new hermeneutic have been characterized by a similar obscurity of thought and expression.

Heidegger's most influential student in recent hermeneutical discussions has been the German philosopher Hans-George Gadamer, author of *Wahrheit und Methode* (1960; ET, *Truth and Method*). Gadamer continues Heidegger's stress on the historicity of man and the process of understanding. According to Gadamer, the meaning of any text is codetermined by the horizons of the author and the interpreter. Understanding a text involves a "fusion of horizons" (*Horizontverschmelzung*) between past and present. He believes it is impossible to simply reduplicate the original author's view, because our contemporary perspective is always fused with the text in any act of interpretation. This means that in Gadamer's hermeneutics authorial intent is not decisive for determining the meaning of the text. Drawing upon Heidegger's speculations on the nature of language, Gadamer argues for textual autonomy; the subject matter (*Sache*) of the text itself, rather than authorial intent, is decisive for meaning.

Gadamer's views have been sharply criticized by E. D. Hirsch, Jr., professor of English at the University of Virginia. Hirsch argues that Gadamer's rejection of authorial intent as a norm of textual meaning leads to "cognitive relativism": the text really has no determinate meaning at all, only an endless stream of meanings as perceived by successive interpreters. If the norm of authorial intent is abandoned, there is no practical way of adjudicating between conflicting interpretations. Meaning, after all, "is an affair of consciousness and not of physical signs or things."[46] The language mysticism of both Heidegger and Gadamer treats language as though it had an independent life and mind of its own; Hirsch's more realistic view sees actual texts and speech-acts as the expressions of real individual *persons*. Consequently, meaning cannot be separated from the intentions of actual persons, whether of humans or of God.

46. Hirsch, *Validity in Interpretation*, p. 23.

Hirsch also argues that Gadamer exaggerates the influence of the interpreter's context on the perception of meaning. Gadamer "exaggerates a difficulty into an impossibility." It may be difficult to "bracket" my own cultural categories in rendering an ancient text, but the labors of countless biblical and literary scholars, Bible translators, anthropologists, and archaeologists demonstrate that it is possible to imaginatively transcend one's own categories with some degree of success and identify sympathetically with the categories of a different culture. An observer can identify a given physical object or person in any number of given contexts; similarly, a text has a determinate meaning (the original author's) for various interpreters, irrespective of the various perspectives from which they may be viewing it.

Hirsch points out that Gadamer has confused *meaning* and *significance*. The meaning of a text is that intended by the author, and is thus a determinate entity. Significance, on the other hand, which involves the value or impact of a text in relation to the interpreter, will vary from context to context. Paul's concept of justification by faith meant exactly what Paul intended for it to mean, no more and no less. The contemporary significance of that concept for, say, psychology or the health professions may well transcend what Paul consciously intended. New contexts lead to new significance for an original meaning. The same point could be made by saying that an original, determinate *meaning* may have various *applications* in different cultural contexts.

In a comparison of the contrasting hermeneutical theories of Gadamer and Hirsch it would appear that Hirsch has the better side of the debate. His insistence on the normative role of authorial intent saves the process of interpretation from the quagmire of cognitive relativism. Yet Gadamer's concept of "fusion of horizons" is helpful for evangelical theology and hermeneutics, especially when modified by Hirsch's key distinction between meaning and significance. The method of contextualization (pp. 60–72) in evangelical theology seeks a fusion between the horizons of the biblical writers and those of the culture in which evangelism and missions are undertaken—with the biblical horizon as the norm for the translation process. The *meaning* of the biblical text is to be the source of new significance in the diverse cultures where the gospel is to be preached.

## Hermeneutics and Cultural Conditioning

### The problem stated

During the last several centuries, due to the work of both evangelical missionaries and secular anthropologists, the church has become acutely aware of an issue known as the "cultural conditioning of the Bible." Missionaries and anthropologists have been impressed with the diversity of cultural patterns and categories found in nonwestern cultures. The categories of a culture influence that culture's perception of reality. To what extent is the message of the Bible conditioned—or even distorted—by the ancient cultural forms through which it was transmitted? How can the modern interpreter distinguish between those teachings that are truly universal and transcultural, and those which may be limited in applicability to a particular time or culture? Does, for example, Paul's directive in 1 Tim. 3:2 that the elder be the husband of one wife automatically disqualify a converted African tribal chieftan, who may have several wives, from a position of church leadership? Should some of the wives be divorced? Or can one appeal to the Old Testament precedents of Abraham and David as spiritual leaders who had multiple wives? Is 1 Tim. 3:2 intended to be a transcultural statement, or does it merely presuppose the monogamy of first century Jewish culture? This is only one example of the practical and perplexing questions of interpretation that arise with respect to revelation and its cultural context.

Earlier research in anthropology tended to suggest the relativism of cultures and morals, at least in the popular mind. This point of view was epitomized in the aphorism from William Graham Sumner's *Folkways* (1907): "The mores can make anything right." Franz Boas, in his classic, *The Mind of Primitive Man* (1911), issued a call to appreciate other cultures on their own terms, rather than seeing them as inferior versions of our own.

The field research of the anthropologists does indeed show that the issue of cross-cultural communication is not an artificial one. A Pacific islander, who has never seen an airplane may be familiar, in another context, with each of the terms in the statement, "The man flies," and yet not understand the meaning intended by the speaker. In Chinese "fruit" and "nuts" are a single concept. A Bible translator working with an isolated African tribe may not find it easy to decide whether or not the tribal word for "God" is a suitable equivalent of the biblical term. In such cases the issue of the cross-cultural equivalency of meaning is hardly an academic one.

### Anthropological constants

The exaggerated impression of an almost limitless cultural relativism created by some anthropological studies in the nineteenth century has been corrected by later research. There are in fact consistent bases upon which cross-cultural comparisons can be made. Biologically, all humans are of the same species; socially, human beings are governed by certain universal functional needs (e.g., role assignments, reproduction, socialization of new members, control of disruptive behavior); and ecologically, humans must adapt to a limited range of geographic and environmental conditions.[47] The accumulated field evidence appears to show rather clearly that all cultures have some form of religion, have used tools, cultivated plants, created pottery, woven cloth, domesticated animals, developed systems of writing, established forms of government, created works of art and music, and disposed of the dead.

Clearly there are perceptual and intellectual constants across cultures as well. An analysis of basic color terms in ninety-eight languages disclosed a pattern in which the sequence of terms accorded with the general social complexity of the culture. There was a universal pattern of development of the color terms which reflected a transcultural human pattern of color perception.[48]

Human patterns of reasoning are similar across cultures. Aristotelian canons of logic cannot be dismissed as merely "Western" cultural conventions.

### Theological principles

The functional, perceptual, and intellectual constants discussed in anthropological research are not surprising in light of the biblical doctrine of man's creation in the image of God (Gen. 1:26–27). All human beings, whether believers or unbelievers, are in fact bearers of the image of God, created with a common humanity. "He made from one [blood] every nation of man to live on all the

---

47. Walter L. Jonner, "The Search for Psychological Universals," p. 146.
48. Ben-Ami Scharfstein, "Cultures, Contexts, and Comparisons," p. 34.

face of the earth" (Acts 17:26). A state of unbelief in an individual's mind does not alter the metaphysical *fact* of the creation of all men by the same sovereign God.

As we have noted earlier (pp. 253—255) the biblical doctrine of divine providence is crucial for discussions of revelation and culture. The same God who sovereignly guides all events of history toward their appointed ends (Eph. 1:11), and apart from whose will not even a sparrow falls to the ground (Matt. 10:29), also controls all the developments of human culture. His sovereign will to communicate clearly and savingly to mankind is not frustrated by human culture; his word does not return to him void (Isa. 55:11).

It has been said that since "God wanted to inspire the Pauline epistles, he created a Paul to write them." The Jewish and Hellenistic cultural forms of the Bible become, under the sovereign, providential control of God, adequate media for the message divinely intended.

The questions of properly distinguishing transcultural principles in scripture from the specific cultural forms containing them is admittedly a complex one. Nevertheless, it seems that several criteria in this regard would be widely recognized within the evangelical community.

If a biblical teaching is explicitly tied to the order of creation this is a clear indication of a transcultural principle. The basic distinction between male and female (Gen. 1:27) derives from God's original creative plan. Monogamous, enduring marriage is likewise the creational norm (cf. Matt. 19:8). Consequently such practices as homosexuality, polygamy, and divorce represent a disordering by sin of God's original creative will.

If a biblical teaching is found throughout the canon, this is again a clear indication of a transcultural principle. The Bible is itself a cross-cultural document, reflecting not only some two thousand years of Hebraic culture but also, in the New Testament, the interaction of divine revelation with Greco-Roman culture. Throughout the canon the practice of homosexuality is forbidden (Lev. 20:13; Rom. 1:27), indicating that the Old Testament prohibitions were not merely temporary reactions to Canaanite religious practices. On the other hand, the matter of foods appropriate for the people of God has been a variable one in canonical history. Under the terms of the Noachic covenant the eating of pork was permitted (Gen. 9:3); it was forbidden under the Mosaic covenant

(Lev. 11:7); it is again permissible for the New Testament believer (Mark 7:19). Food in itself is good, being created by God (Gen. 1:31; 1 Tim. 4:4), but the believer's relationship to it can vary, depending upon the developments in the plan and purpose of God and circumstances in the church (Rom. 14:13—23).

The two foregoing principles are quite general and hardly exhaust the matter, but they would appear to be broadly valid. Whether the specific question of revelation and culture arises in Bible translation, evangelism, or cross-cultural missions, the objective is to reproduce the original meaning of the biblical text in an appropriate form in the receptor culture.[49] The praise of God in music, for example, is a universal norm; the particular instruments used may vary from culture to culture. The ancient Hebrews used timbrels and pipes (Ps. 150:4); in other cultural settings guitars or African tribal instruments could be appropriate. The point is to *contextualize* the message of the Bible for all cultures in fulfillment of the Great Commission, in order that at the close of the age a numberless host from *every* tribe and tongue and nation (Rev. 7:9) will gather before the throne of the God who has eternally redeemed them.


## Bibliography

Allis, Oswald T. *Prophecy and the Church.* Phillipsburg, N.J.: Presbyterian and Reformed, 1947.

Bahnsen, Greg L. *Theonomy in Christian Ethics.* Nutley, N.J.: Craig Press, 1977.

Baldwin, Alice M. *The New England Clergy and the American Revolution.* 1928; rpt. New York: Frederick Ungar, 1958.

Barr, James. *Old and New in Interpretation.* London: SCM, 1966.

Barrett, C. K. "The Interpretation of the Old Testament in the New," in P. R. Ackroyd and C. F. Evans, eds., *The Cambridge History of the Bible.* Cambridge: Cambridge University Press, 1970. I, 377—411.

49. In arguing the case for "dynamic-equivalence theologizing" in *Christianity in Culture*, Charles Kraft writes that this involves the reproduction in "contemporary cultural contexts of the theologizing process that Paul and the other scriptural authors exemplify" (p. 291). The key issue here for evangelicals is to reproduce the biblical *content* and *meaning*; process is secondary. Kraft's work, though characterized by some weaknesses in the area of epistemology, is a valuable contribution to the entire discussion of revelation and culture.

Bass, Clarence. *Backgrounds to Dispensationalism*. Grand Rapids: Baker, 1977.

Berkhof, Louis. *Principles of Biblical Interpretation*. Grand Rapids: Baker, 1950.

Bultmann, Rudolf. *Existence and Faith*, tr. S. Ogden. London: Collins, 1964.

Carson, D. A. "Hermeneutics : A Brief Assessment of Some Recent Trends," *Themelios* 5 (1980):12 − 20.

Chantry, Walter J. *God's Righteous Kingdom*. Edinburgh: Banner of Truth, 1980.

Clouse, Robert G., ed. *The Meaning of the Millennium*. Downers Grove, Ill,: Inter-Varsity, 1977.

Daor, Dan. "Modes of Arguments," in Scharfstein, *et al., Philosophy East/Philosophy West*. New York: Oxford University Press, 1978.

Dilthey, Wilhelm. "The Development of Hermeneutics," in *Selected Writings*, ed. H. P. Rickman. Cambridge: Cambridge University Press, 1976.

Dreyfus, Hubert L. "Holism and Hermeneutics," *Review of Metaphysics* 34 (1980):3−23.

Ellis, E. Earle. *Prophecy and Hermeneutic in Early Christianity*. Grand Rapids: Eerdmans, 1978.

Ermath, Michael. "The Transformation of Hermeneutics," *Monist* 64 (1981):175 − 94.

Fairbairn, Patrick. *The Typology of Scripture*. Philadelphia: Smith and English, 1854.

Fowler, Paul B. *God's Law Free from Legalism: Critique of "Theonomy in Christian Ethics."* N.p., n.d.

Frei, Hans. *The Eclipse of Biblical Narrative*. New Haven: Yale University Press, 1974.

Fuller, Daniel P. *Gospel and Law*. Grand Rapids: Eerdmans, 1980.

Gadamer, Hans-Georg. *Truth and Method*. New York: Seabury, 1975.

Grant, Robert M. *A Short History of the Interpretation of the Bible*. New York: Macmillan, 1948.

Grobel, K. "Interpretation, History and Principles of," *The Interpreter's Dictionary of the Bible*. Nashville: Abingdon, 1962.

Hanson, R. P. C. "Biblical Exegesis in the Early Church," in P. R. Ackroyd and C. F. Evans, eds., *The Cambridge History of the Bible*. Cambridge: Cambridge University Press, 1970. I, 412−53.

Harvey, Van A. "D. F. Strauss' *Life of Jesus* Revisited," *Church History* 30 (1961):191−211.

Hazard, Paul. *European Thought in the Eighteenth Century*. New Haven: Yale University Press, 1954.

Heidegger, Martin. *Basic Writings*, ed. David F. Krell. New York: Harper, 1977.

Hirsch, E. D., Jr. *The Aims of Interpretation*. Chicago: University of Chicago Press, 1976.

—————. *Validity in Interpretation*. New Haven: Yale University Press, 1967.

Jonner, Walter L. "The Search for Psychological Universals," in Harry C. Triandis and William W. Lambert, eds., *Handbook of Cross-Cultural Psychology*. Boston: Allyn and Bacon, 1980. I, 143 – 204.

Kluckhohn, Clyde. "Universal Categories of Culture," in A. L. Kroeber, ed., *Anthropology Today*. Chicago: University of Chicago Press, 1953.

Kraft, Charles H. *Christianity in Culture*. Maryknoll, N.Y.: Orbis, 1979.

Kuhn, Helmut. "German Philosophy and National Socialism," *Encyclopedia of Philosophy*. New York: Macmillan, 1967.

Longenecker, Richard N. *Biblical Exegesis in the Apostolic Period*. Grand Rapids: Eerdmans, 1974.

Maier, Gerhard. *The End of the Historical-Critical Method*. St. Louis: Concordia, 1977.

Martin, L. John. "The Contradiction of Cross-Cultural Communication," in H. D. Fischer and John C. Merrill, eds., *International and Intercultural Communication*. New York: Hastings House, 1970.

Meiland, Jack W. "Interpretation as a Cognitive Discipline," *Philosophy and Literature* 2 (1978):23 – 45.

Mickelsen, Berkeley. *Interpreting the Bible*. Grand Rapids: Eerdmans, 1963.

Muhammed, 'Abduh. *The Theology of Unity*, tr. I. Musa'ad and K. Cragg. London: Allen and Unwin, 1966.

Muller, H. "Type, Pattern," *New International Dictionary of New Testament Theology*. Grand Rapids: Zondervan, 1978.

Palmer, Richard E. *Hermeneutics*. Evanston: Northwestern University Press, 1969.

Polanyi, Michael. *Personal Knowledge*. Chicago: University of Chicago Press, 1958.

—————. *The Tacit Dimension*. Garden City, N.Y.: Doubleday, 1966.

Polanyi, Michael, and Prosch, Harry. *Meaning*. Chicago: University of Chicago Press, 1975.

Preus, James S. *From Shadow to Promise: Old Testament Interpretation from Augustine to the Young Luther*. Cambridge: Harvard University Press, 1969.

Ramm, Bernard. *Protestant Biblical Interpretation*. Boston: W. A. Wilde, 1956.

Ricoeur, Paul. "The Task of Hermeneutics," in Michael Murrey, ed., *Heidegger and Modern Philosophy*. New Haven: Yale University Press, 1978.

Robinson, James M. "Hermeneutic Since Barth," in Robinson and Cobb, eds., *The New Hermeneutic*. New York: Harper, 1964.

Robinson, James M., and Cobb, John B., Jr., eds. *The Later Heidegger and Theology*. New York: Harper, 1963.

Rushdoony, R. J. *Infallibility: An Inescapable Concept*. Vallecito, Calif.: Ross House, 1978.

————. *Institutes of Biblical Law.* Nutley, N.J.: Craig Press, 1973.

Ryrie, Charles C. *Dispensationalism Today.* Chicago: Moody, 1973.

Scharfstein, Ben-Ami. "Cultures, Contexts, and Comparisons," in Scharfstein, *et al., Philosophy East/Philosophy West.* New York: Oxford University Press, 1978.

Schrenk, G. "γραφή," *Theological Dictionary of the New Testament.* Grand Rapids: Eerdmans, 1964. I:744 – 61.

Selwyn, Edward Gordon. *The First Epistle of St. Peter.* London: MacMillan, 1958.

Smalley, Beryl. *The Study of the Bible in the Middle Ages.* New York: Philosophical Library, 1952.

Steinmetz, David C. "The Superiority of Pre-Critical Exegesis," *Theology Today* 37 (1980):27 – 38.

Stendahl, Krister. "Biblical Theology, Contemporary," *Interpreter's Dictionary of the Bible.* Nashville: Abingdon, 1962.

Strenski, Ivan. "Heidegger Is No Hero," *Christian Century,* May 19, 1982, pp. 598 – 601.

Terry, Milton S. *Biblical Hermeneutics.* Grand Rapids: Zondervan, 1974.

Thiselton, Anthony C. *The Two Horizons.* Grand Rapids: Eerdmans, 1980.

Wallace, Ronald S. *Calvin's Doctrine of the Word and Sacrament.* Grand Rapids: Eerdmans, 1957.

Weingreen, J., *et al.* "Interpretation, History of," *Interpreter's Dictionary of the Bible Supplementary Volume.* Nashville: Abingdon, 1976.

Wood, James D. *The Interpretation of the Bible.* London: Duckworth, 1958.

Zimmerman, Carle C. *Family and Civilization.* New York: Harper, 1947.